B. L, SUNRISE

From Sunrise to Sunset

B. L, SUNRISE

From Sunrise to Sunset

ISBN/EAN: 9783741190100

Manufactured in Europe, USA, Canada, Australia, Japa

Cover: Foto ©Andreas Hilbeck / pixelio.de

Manufactured and distributed by brebook publishing software (www.brebook.com)

B. L, SUNRISE

From Sunrise to Sunset

FROM SUNRISE TO SUNSET.

CHAPTER I.

IT was June and it was sunrise! Do not the words themselves give you a feeling of light, air, and freshness? Look at the fiery orb of day as he rises from his bed of woods, of hills, of rushing sea or waving corn! the rose-tinted atmosphere of early morn that dims the face of the quivering earth; the flowers as they shake off their night-tears and drop their tender petals to gaze with brighter eyes upon the awakening day. Tell me, are they not perfect? The birds whirring a fleet passage through the air, are singing hastily their matin-song, and the old rook with his deep caw awakens his more sleepy brethren. The butterflies and bees spread out their dainty wings, that a stray sunbeam may become enamoured of their beauty; the wee lambs frolicking amongst the buttercups, are full of young life after their early meal, and their mother close at hand bleats lowly now and then to keep them within her call. The cows coming out of the shed whisk their long tails, delighted to be able once more to chew the grass lying so fresh and green around them; the rabbit, knowing his captors never hunt so early, leaves fearlessly his buried home and nibbles gleefully on the flowering clover, looking so pert and pretty in the glorious sunlight, fitted truly for a Landseer's ideal.

Perhaps nowhere would the sun cast his first glance upon a prettier picture than that presented to his view on the terrace of Halston Hall: The grand old building faced the east, and the pale yellow beams glorified in their radiance its grey ivy-decked walls. On the terrace, where many fair and rare flowers bloomed, a child of some nine summers stood, herself their equal in youthful freshness; by her side was a large tawny-coloured dog, whose black muzzle and liver-coloured jaws gave ample evidence of his breed.

They formed a pretty picture, those two strange friends, with the ancient gothic mansion for their background and the first fruits of summer's advent round them. The soft south wind blew gently the child's long curls, and tinted her cheeks a deeper rose-hue.

"Rollo! Rollo! you bad fellow, give me my hat!" she demanded of her canine companion, who had seized the article in question, and was steadily walking away with it between his teeth, turning now and then to see if his movements were watched by his young playfellow.

Rollo took no notice of the command, and then the romp commenced. In and out, round and about the happy pair ran, down the broad white steps to the grass plot below; or close to the edge of the fountain wherein gold-fish glittered.

"Florry! Breakfast!" startled the chasing pair, and Florence hastened to the hall-door, where Leonard, her guardian's son, awaited her.

"I am coming, Leo, now; but just look at my hat!"

By this time she had managed to capture her somewhat tattered headgear, and with it in her hand advanced towards Leonard. Arriving at his side, she demanded his examination of the article in question. He took it from her, and laughingly placing it upon her head carried her into the breakfast-room, where Mr. and Mrs. Thornton were seated.

"Well, mater! how are you this morning?" Leonard questioned, as he bestowed his usual morning salute.

"Quite well, my boy; and how is my pet?" she answered, encircling Florence with her arm.

"Oh, aunty! look at my hat! Rollo did it."

"Never mind your hat, love, but come and eat your breakfast before it gets cold. We can examine your hat afterwards," and drawing a chair near to her own, Mrs. Thornton placed Florence in it.

Whilst they are at breakfast let me give you, dear reader, a short account of who and what Mr. and Mrs. Thornton were—not pages upon pages of past events—for I think nothing so wearisome as having to read a long unnecessary introduction to a tale.

Mr. and Mrs. Thornton were married young, the latter a girl of sixteen when the wedding-ring was placed upon her finger; an emblem of the golden fetters she must wear through life. She had been early left an orphan, and possessed but one friend in the world, Lizzie Warden by name. Having a small income of her own, she arranged to make the Wardens' house her home until her marriage, which event took place about four years after she had first entered her friend's family.

Some six years passed before she had the pleasure of assisting at Miss Warden's marriage; and it was a sad day in her life, the one on which Lizzie, now Judge Hardman's wife, left England to accompany her husband to India.

Ten years soon slipped away, when one bright morning Mrs. Thornton received the sad intelligence of her friend's death; in two more the husband followed his wife to the grave, and left his baby-heiress to the guardianship of Mr. Thornton. The latter, a man of some property, gladly welcomed the little lady to his daughterless home, and tender and true was the love lavished upon her from all.

Leonard Thornton was an only son, and had decided to follow the medical profession, and was at present preparing for his preliminary examinations, being at the time my story opens a youth of nineteen.

Now we will return to the breakfast party who, during our glimpse of past events, have finished their meal and are ready to follow their inclinations to try and pass pleasantly the long summer day.

Mr. Thornton, as was his wont, mounted his sturdy cob, and rode off on his usual tour of inspection round the farms. Mrs. Thornton hastened to arrange her household matters, leaving Florence and Leonard to procure amusement for themselves.

"Well, little woman, what shall we do?" Leonard questioned.

"I should like to go down to the brook with you, Leo, and there you might read me that pretty tale you promised me if I was good."

"But, dear, you will be tired in an hour by the brook, and it is too far for you to go for a short time."

"Oh no! indeed I will not be tired. Leo, please take me."

"Very well then—first go to Annie, and ask her to give you another hat and put your little cape on, for I am afraid you might feel the damp."

Florence hastened to obey, and Leonard took

up the *Times* to glance at the leading articles; he had scarcely had time to notice the headings when one of the farm-labourers presented himself at the open window.

"Please, Master Leonard, Jem sent me to tell you a mad dog has been seen in the neighbourhood, and to ask you if we had not better take tools, and go in search of him."

"Where was he last seen, Thomas?"

"By the brook, sir; and he seemed making for the village then."

"Well, I will just tell my mother, take my gun, and go round the grounds. Don't you delay in having the cattle well looked to, and send some one to warn my father—he has already started on his rounds."

Thomas disappeared from before the window, and Leonard went in search of his mother, forgetting in his anxiety his promise to Florence. Having cautioned Mrs. Thornton of the danger, he procured his rifle and went in quest of the doomed animal.

It was almost mid-day before his search was over, and returning through the orchard he lingered to notice the heavy fruit-laden trees, and wonder how long the damsons would remain on their branches. A rustling at his feet startled him, and looking down he saw in advance the mad dog he was in search of; his horror was tenfold when right in the path he perceived Florence and Rollo at play. He watched them a second, then steadily levelled his rifle and fired. In that brief glance he had time to note the strange instinct of brave Rollo, who, almost before the report of the gun was heard, threw himself upon his little mistress, thus protecting her from harm. The rabid animal was not killed, but approached the pair with quick strides; a second volley, however, arrested his steps, and with a fearful howl the brute fell dead, the foam all thick on his parched lips and his once intelligent eyes glassy and set.

Rollo shook his tawny body as he raised himself from off the prostrate form of his little mistress. Florence, angry at the seeming violence of her playfellow, beat him passionately with her tiny hands.

"Florence, I am ashamed of you!" startled her in the midst of her fury.

"He pushed me on the ground, rude doggie, Leo."

"My pet, Rollo did his best to save you from harm. O my little one! I cannot bear to think of what might have been;" and taking her in his arms, Leonard kissed, again and again, the upturned face.

"Was that dog going to bite me, Leo?" the little woman urged, pointing to the dead beast.

"Yes, yes, dearest, but it cannot harm you now; let us go home."

"O Leo! I am so glad you shot him—and I love Rollo, too;" and loosening herself from Leonard's embrace, she ran towards Rollo, kissing his long hair and calling him by a thousand endearing titles. At last she considered she had won his pardon for her abuse a few moments ago, and with a happy laugh raced with him to the house, leaving Leonard to follow more slowly.

In the evening, whilst smoking his usual after-dinner cigar on the terrace, Leonard was struck with the quiet beauty of the scenery around.

At his feet the small village of Denham lay; with its one quaint street and tall cathedral towers, its ancient grammar school, where, as a boy, he had known his hours of joy and sorrow. How vividly the remembrance of those days came back to him. The road, too, how well he knew every inch; the path across those low-lying meadows and over the little wooden bridge—how often he had stopped in the centre to watch the jack-sharps at play—and those stunted willows, with their bushy heads, standing like a line of sentinels along the flowering banks; then in the winter months, when the high winds arose, the little stream became ambitious, and, bursting its bounds, buried in its troubled waters all the grass-hidden fairies and pale blue forget-me-nots. He noted the tall chestnuts, wherein the hornets made their nests, and far away in the ploughed field the hedge where the thrush and linnet chatted in their homes, the yellow corn was bending gracefully to the breeze, and the bright poppy-heads caught on their flushed cheeks the last beams of sunset. He loved it all, that verdant English landscape, so full of earthly beauty, so perfect from the Maker's hand; it was his home, his native love, and he blessed it for its fairness.

The gradual darkening of the atmosphere warned him to enter; doing so he found his mother awaiting his presence, patiently as was her wont, only the glad look in her eyes telling how she had counted the flown moments.

"Mater, you do not look well," he remarked, seating himself in a low chair by her side.

"I feel quite well, my boy; only a little upset with the occurrence of this morning."

Leonard drew his chair a little nearer, and resting his head on her knees, followed her gaze down the dim long avenue, where the chestnuts were casting their pink and white blossoms to the earth.

"I cannot think you are really my little Leo, who was so tiny and fair; have you measured yourself by your favourite tree lately?"

"I have, mother mine, but cannot drag myself up to the desired six feet, I am half an inch short of it still."

"I am afraid then, dear, you will have to content yourself; after twenty, they say, people seldom grow."

"You must put me under the rolling pin, like cook does the pastry, and see if that will not answer."

"I am afraid there is not much material to roll out, Leonard."

Mr. Thornton entered and put a stop to their conversation; lights were brought and the usual game of whist commenced.

CHAPTER II.

It was a fortnight after the events recorded, that the postman trudged his way up to the Hall. Florence was awaiting his arrival in the open doorway, and carried off with delight the packet of letters he intrusted to her care.

Hastening into the breakfast-room, where Mr. and Mrs. Thornton and Leonard were doing ample justice to ham, chickens, patties, etc., she distributed her treasures, and soon all were engrossed in the perusal of their epistles.

"Governor, may I ask him down?" Leonard remarked, pushing an opened letter to his father's side.

Mr. Thornton read the few words scrawled over a large business-looking sheet of paper, then answered:

"Certainly, Leonard. I am always pleased to see your friends, and Collingwood is an especial favourite of mine. What day must we expect him?"

"He mentions Thursday, and to-day being Monday, we have just time to prepare for him."

"Well, you can take the drag down and ask Thomas to put Rock in the shafts for you. You will appreciate a nice turn-out when you go to meet Collingwood, who is, if I remember rightly, something of a judge in horse-flesh."

"Thanks, sir; you have, as usual, hit the mark in my affections, and I will be careful with your favourite," and, rising, Leonard left the room. As he was crossing the hall he heard a low voice calling him, and, turning, he perceived Florence hastening to his side:

"Well, what is it, small maiden?"

"Leo, please take me with you to the station. I will learn all my lessons every word for Miss Walton if you only will."

"I am afraid I cannot, Florry; the drag will not hold us all, and Collingwood will have some luggage."

"But, Leo, I will be so good," and she nestled her head against his hand.

"Well, well, we will see about it, there is time before Thursday; and now, little one, I must be off," and, stooping, he kissed and left her.

Thursday came, bright, warm and sunny. At four the drag was in waiting, but Florence was not one of its inmates; she was far better pleased by being allowed to ride to the station on her Shetland pony, and Leonard, to satisfy her, consented to ride too.

"Oh, look! Leo, there comes the train," exclaimed the small Amazon, watching the fiery horse come panting and puffing into the quiet country station.

"Stay by the rails here, Florry, whilst I go and meet the old fellow," Leonard commanded in quick tones, and throwing his bridle to Thomas disappeared through the ticket-office. In a few moments he returned, accompanied by Collingwood.

"Well! is this Miss Florence?" questioned a deep mellow voice.

"I am Miss Hardman, sir," she answered for herself, vexed at a stranger presuming to call her by her christian name.

"Oh! Miss Hardman, are you? You make a pretty pair, you and your pony," and, approaching nearer to them, Collingwood bent to kiss her.

"You sha'n't!" she exclaimed, roused into a childish fury, and taking her riding-whip she struck his dark face.

Leonard, who hitherto had been attending to the luggage, came up just in time to witness the hasty action.

"Florence, is this the way you welcome my friend? Beg Collingwood's pardon immediately," he exclaimed, looking sternly into the child's flushed face.

Florence remained silent, with her eyes cast down.

"Leave the babe alone, Leonard; I vexed it, I suppose, with my rough ways," Collingwood interrupted, unwilling to commence his visit with an unpleasant scene; and turned to approach the drag.

"Stay, Coll; unless Florence apologises to you she must ride home with Thomas."

The child's face grew very long at these words, for she enjoyed nothing so much as a ride alone with Leonard.

"You will do what I ask you, dear," he urged, placing his hand upon her shoulder, softened by the look on her face.

Two big tears trembled on the long dark lashes, but the childish lips remained closed.

"Thomas, I will drive; you escort Miss Florence home," Leonard called out, joining Collingwood.

"Thornton, you are hard upon the wee one," said the latter when they were seated in the drag.

"My dear fellow, that small lady is not too wee to have a temper of her own, and the mater spoils her, so I am obliged to use the rod of correction sometimes." Then they conversed upon other matters and soon found themselves in front of the Hall door.

Mr. and Mrs. Thornton were waiting to welcome them, and Collingwood was as usual delighted with the fine old building and kindly greeting.

"Florence, I want you," called Leonard, as

they stood on the lawn admiring the peaceful scene.

Florence obeyed the summons, looking very crestfallen and stumbling many times over her habit.

"Florence, you will go and speak to my friend now, won't you, dear?"

She still hesitated, and looked up pleadingly into Leonard's face; but seeing no relentance there, with unwilling feet made her way to her enemy's side.

"I am sorry for being rude," was all she would say.

"Why, my little lady, you only gave me what I deserved for insulting such a proper small person by offering her a kiss. Suppose you give me one of those red roses to make friends," he continued, pointing to a splendid standard by his side.

"I cannot reach them," she answered, without however trying.

"Well, never mind, I will be the donor," and he plucked a fair blossom just bursting from its green prison. Florence took the flower without comment; then, seeing Leonard, she hastened to his side.

"Well, are you friends now?" he questioned.

"Oh yes, capital ones," replied Collingwood, and related the history of the rose.

"Run in, Florence, and change your dress;

I see Lallah looking out for you. And, Coll, come and have a squint round the old place; I have some few extra treasures to show you," and linking arms they strolled off together.

Mr. Thornton, who was watching them through his study window, remarked to his wife who stood near:

"What a tall fellow that Collingwood is: I am sure he is above six feet."

Mr. Thornton was right in his calculation; Collingwood, to use a common phrase, stood six feet one in his stockings. Many considered him a handsome man: his broad white forehead and deep grey eyes gave him a claim to be considered such; but the thick eyebrows and heavy moustache lent a somewhat fierce expression to his face. He appeared much older than he really was, looking thirty when his life only numbered twenty-two years.

The long summer days passed quickly to the two friends; and Collingwood began to hint it was time for him to take his departure.

"Oh, Coll, you must come down and try a rod by the stream before you go; suppose we disappear down there this morning," Leonard proposed as they sat lazy over their breakfast.

"Certainly, Leonard, if you wish it; but I fear we shall not catch anything—the day is rather bright."

"Well, never mind if we don't; I will provide us with books and a rug, and I dare say, so fortified, we shall manage to kill time and amuse ourselves. Mother will send Thomas with our lunch, and Florence will, I know, be delighted to accompany him when her lessons are over."

"Rollo, Rollo! come, dear old fellow, come!" Florence urged, pulling Rollo's coat as he lay basking in the sun, and seeming very reluctant to avail himself of the invitation.

"Rollo, you must," she commanded, and gave his ears a very energetic tug. Finding himself forced to obey his little mistress, Rollo shook off his slumbering propensities and followed her out through the open doorway, down the long avenue to the lodge where Thomas with her pony and provisions awaited them.

"Miss, shall I lift you on?" Thomas asked when he saw her.

"No, thank you, Thomas, I mean to walk with Rollo; it is not very hot to-day."

The butterflies, however, soon tempted her from her sedate pace, and away she ran, with her hat in the air, in vain pursuit of the pretty bright-winged creatures. Rollo, with his deep bark, helped in the chase; forgetting all about Thomas or the pony, the happy pair were soon out of sight.

"Well, this is a nice job," Thomas muttered on finding himself deserted; having waited a few minutes to see if the truants returned, he decided to proceed upon his way.

Leonard and Collingwood he found stretched upon the grass under the shade of some wide-spreading oak-trees, the sunbeams glancing down upon them here and there through the little windows left by the leaves; the chattering brook at their feet sparkling over its stony bed.

"Well, Thomas, where is Miss Florence?" Leonard questioned, missing the little lady.

"Please, sir, she and Rollo went after the butterflies, and I left them at it."

"Surely you never left them alone in the meadows."

"Please, sir, and sure I waited, but could not take the pony along with me, so I was obliged to come on."

"Well, leave Daisy here, and return in search of Miss Florence."

Thomas accordingly retreated in quest of the wanderers, but although he returned exactly the way he came and searched well the meadow wherein Florence had disappeared, he failed to discover any trace either of the child or dog. At the end of nearly an hour he retraced his steps to where Collingwood and Leonard lay; the latter, made uneasy, proposed their joining in the search. They parted accordingly, each choosing a different route. Collingwood decided to follow the stream, and strolled off with his usual long swinging strides. He congratulated himself on the beauty of the afternoon; not too hot, for the heat of the July sun was tempered by a westerly breeze, which swayed the yellow corn-heads backwards and forwards in its swift passage; a thousand songsters were twittering love-ditties to one another in the boughs overhead, and in amongst the grass the beetles, ants, and spiders chirped. For some time Collingwood's search seemed fruitless, but when on the point of turning his face homewards he was startled by Rollo's deep bark; hastening his steps he soon came up to where the dog stood. At his feet little Florence lay, quite white and motionless, with the sun glistening on her wet curls; with a fast-beating heart Collingwood knelt down by her prostrate figure, and pressing his hand against her heart felt it throb gently. Raising her in his arms and rolling his coat around her, he made his way back to the Hall.

There all was confusion and bustle, and he was the only one who maintained his presence of mind; for, carrying his tiny burden down to the wide old kitchen, he placed her before the glowing fire and rubbed and chafed the little stiff limbs until the blood flowed once again through her blue veins.

For several days Florence lay ill—a feverish cold, the doctor said; but when the small maiden was able to get about again she was nervous and shy, quite unlike the bright little fairy of a few days ago. Leonard laughed at her for being such a coward, but his eyes were wistful as they rested upon her pale sweet face.

A change of air was decided upon, and Mrs. Thornton agreed to go to some quiet sea-side place, hoping thereby to bring back the bloom to her darling's cheeks and the laughter to her eyes. Leonard unfortunately could not accompany them, for it was time for him to return to his studies; Collingwood therefore offered his services as escort, and persuaded Mrs. Thornton to fix upon the village of Heaton, situated on the Cheshire coast and facing the Welsh hills.

Florence wept passionately on Leonard's neck when the moment of departure came; all Collingwood's promised fairy-tales and Mrs. Thornton's tempting bonbons failed to console her, and with tear-stained cheeks the little maiden started on her journey.

The sun was just setting in crimson and gold when they arrived at their destination. The cottage they had engaged faced the sea, and nothing but hills of sand intervened between it and the wave-breasted ocean.

Having packed Florence off to bed, Mrs. Thornton proposed their making a visit of inspection through the village. It consisted of a few thatched cottages, one or two better built than the rest, amongst the latter the one they occupied; here and there a small shop denoted the principal wants of the inhabitants; lounging about the sandy road the fishermen in their great south-westers stood. To the east and north a hill topped with trees boarded their horizon, and to the south and west the blue sea lay. There was a feeling of strange rest and stillness in the air, as if sin or sorrow had not yet visited that one spot of earth.

"It is a sort of place one dreams of but very seldom sees; there is something hushed and calm in the very atmosphere—do you not think so?" Collingwood questioned as they turned their steps homewards.

"I was just pondering over the same thing. I think I should like to die in a place like this, it seems so easy to pass into eternity over those quiet waters," his companion rejoined, gazing at the far-stretching sea.

"And yet they are so cold, so cold, those laughing little waves. It is strange, Mrs. Thornton, but when I look upon the sea I feel as if I looked upon my grave. Do you believe in presentiments?"

"Hush, Owen! I must not let your fancy create such dismal pictures; I trust, dear, when the time comes that you will be laid in a grave, it may be near those you love, and where the flowers grow."

Collingwood remained silent, but his eyes looked

across the vast water world, and a stranger would have been struck with the sad puzzled expression that dwelt in them.

The following day being still one of summer's own choosing, the little party took a boat and went for a sail round a small island that lay out not far from the shore. Florence dipped her hands into the salt-tasting waters and laughed her own happy laughter as she watched the fishes glide here and there under the tiny waves. As Collingwood lifted her from the boat he bent his head and snatched a hasty kiss from her pouting lips, but this time she did not upbraid him, but clasped her arms about his neck, and nestling her head against his breast, said:

"I will kiss you now many kisses."

Several days passed, and the roses stole back into Florence's cheeks, and out of her eyes the tinge of sadness crept. By the hour together she and Collingwood would stroll through the fields watching the shy rabbits creep out of their holes or chasing the red-and-brown-winged butterflies; sometimes it was down amongst the rocks where the crabs and mussels formed seas for themselves in the pools of glittering water, and the transparent shrimp jumped with his tiny legs under the green sea-weed.

At last Collingwood was forced to bid his friends adieu. Mrs. Thornton thanked him heartily for his thought and kindness to her darling, and Florence gave him for keepsake a broken dolly, which was her dearest daughter. Collingwood felt a strange regret at leaving the quiet little village; the gentle matron and dark-eyed babe had gathered his heartstrings in their fingers, and he felt a strong reluctance to part from them. The years seemed so long since he had felt any kiss upon his lips. One night he remembered in the far-distant time and the winter frost a vision radiant with golden hair and glistening jewels bent over his baby-crib. Was it a dream, he wondered, that lay so vividly impressed upon his memory—was it in a dream he had heard words that told of a woman's anguish, deep sighs of unutterable grief, fevered breathings of a great despair? Were they tears he had felt drop one by one upon his baby-face? What had that young mother, whom his father never named, what inheritance of loneliness had she left him? In her quiet grave, over which the cypress wept, did she sleep in peace, and never long to clasp her first-born to her heart again? Surely these were only fancies, there could be no romance in his father's life, he was a man too cold, too proud, to be influenced by a woman's ways.

Arriving at Chester, Collingwood jumped into a smoking-carriage and drove away his sadness in the fumes of a cigar. With a jerk the train arrested its swift progress at Flint, and Collingwood, descending, found Adams, his groom, awaiting him. He gave a passing order about his luggage, and vaulting lightly into his saddle soon left the withered trees and solitary ruined castle far behind him.

Quickly he approached his wild Welsh home, which from afar he had seen standing out dark and gloomy against the sky, the fir-trees surrounding it and the tall mountains overshadowing it, jealously guarded it from the sun's bright glance. And yet it had a strange attraction of its own, that old Tudor house in which, in years gone by, a boy was born, who by his beauty and grace had won the heart of a queen.

The harvest days were shortening when Mrs. Thornton wrote proposing to visit Owen Lodge on her way home. Both Collingwood and his father were delighted to welcome her, so one peaceful evening, just after the sun had died down, the welcome guests made their appearance.

A few days after their arrival the harvest festival was held in the village near. Florence begged very hard to be allowed to accompany Collingwood on his visit to his rejoicing tenantry. Soon after their six o'clock dinner, therefore, the pair set out.

"Please, Mr. Collingwood, may we take Brutus with us?" petitioned Florence, alluding to a favourite setter of Collingwood's.

"Yes, dear, if you wish," and he whistled shrilly. The dog came shambling along to his master's knees, brushing his silky head against him to induce a caress from that beloved hand.

Arriving at the village a glad welcome awaited him from every homestead, for he was well loved by all, both young and old; everywhere his little companion was made much of, great and small seeming to vie with each other to honour the small maiden.

The moon was hanging high and luminous in the sky, the golden harvest moon that shows its face but once in the long glad year, when Collingwood and his baby friend turned their steps homeward. Slowly Florence's feet bore her past the sombre fir-trees that all in the shadow lay, with here and there a stray moonbeam penetrating their darkness; past the tall hedges where, beneath, the glow-worm was burning his short life out; up the steep hill where the beetles whirred through the air, or a rumbling corn-laden waggon broke the surrounding stillness. The end of her journey was nearly reached when the little feet refused their office, and Florence sank down quite weary just where a coy moonbeam caught her.

"Are you tired, dear?" questioned Collingwood, looking down into her face.

"Very, very," she murmured, and leant against a friendly trunk behind her.

"Come, little woman, let me carry you," kneeling by her side, he urged, noticing with pain the pallor of her cheeks.

"But I am very heavy."

"Heavy! you tiny mite, why I could carry a dozen your weight."

"You are sure then I shall not tire you?"

"Quite sure, little one;" and without more words he lifted her in his arms and proceeded on his way.

He had not gone very far when he felt the little head drop heavily on his arm, and looking down he saw Florence's eyes were closed in sleep.

He loved to feel her thus all his own, that little brown-eyed thing that had crept into his heart, and there made herself queen; whose baby ways and happy laughter had gladdened his lonely home; whose rosy lips had been the first for so many long years to press kisses upon his brow.

CHAPTER III.

Six years have passed since the events recorded in my last chapter. The bustle of the Grand Hotel was at its height. Number 217 pressed twice and again his white-buttoned bell, to arrest the attention of some stray valet de chambre, but without success. Clothes were scattered here, there, and everywhere, filling every corner of the small French room; order was certainly not a virtue possessed by Number 217.

"Hang the toads! I shall be late now," was a phrase often bestowed upon the unoffending portmanteau, rug, or hat-box. Soon the patience of Number 217 was exhausted, and seizing his hat, he hastened down the long stairs to the bureau, where he made an ample complaint on the want of attendance in the hotel, and engaged two seats for table d'hôte, then after scrawling over two sheets of paper, he bustled out of the hall, and arriving in the Boulevards, called a cab, ordered his coachie to drive with all speed to the Louvre, and as they rattled along, fumbled in his pocket for his gloves and purse, and before he had accomplished the feat of putting the former on, he found himself at his destination.

Walking quickly up the stairs he entered the picture gallery on his right and looked anxiously round for the friend whom he had come to meet; not seeing him, however, he bestowed his attention upon the various paintings that greeted him on every side: here a Watteau, with his gaily-decked shepherdess; there a rounded limbed woman from Rubens' pencil; anon a Tenniers, inimitable, in his mellow tints, or a faded beauty of the Vandyke school.

In front of a world-famed picture by David stood an old man. His eyes burned with feverish light as he scanned eagerly the painting he copied. The threadbare coat and scanty trousers gave evidence of his poverty; the bent shoulders and withered hands, the thinness of the body and hollowness of the cheeks, told of hunger often kept at bay.

Collingwood (for 217 was he) shuddered as he passed him by: then returned again and again as if drawn by some strange fascination to the old man's side. Three was on the stroke when he noticed the painter preparing for his departure, and as he left the room, Collingwood, without questioning his reason, followed him. Down the Rue de Rivoli, across the Place de la Concorde, over one of the handsome bridges that span the Seine, and along darker streets of the ancient Paris, they took their way. Here the lovely city had cast off her fair outward garments, and nothing but the rottenness and misery of her hollow grandeur was visible. The half-naked children played amongst the dust-heaps and gutters, their mothers stood watching them in the open doorways. Each face was marked with lines of a deadly hunger, and many a small hand was clenched in anger as a childish voice upbraided Heaven with its hard lot. One group in particular attracted Collingwood's attention: it consisted of three figures—a man of perhaps thirty years, with a dark, handsome face, wrinkled here and there, but not with age; by his side stood a brown-eyed girl looking the picture of tattered misery; a tall slender woman completed the group; her head was bent upon her breast, and her whole frame shook with unsuppressed sobs. Collingwood could not pass them by, his heart was touched by their silent misery. He arrested the painter's steps, and after a few words with him, approached the poverty-stricken family.

Theirs was the common oft-told story, of sickness, debt and poverty. An accent of truth ran through it all, and decided Collingwood in offering them his aid to procure them employment. He left his name and address with the man, and appointed to meet him at a named time in a certain café not far from the Grand Hotel, the following morning; then pressing a little money for their immediate wants into the woman's hand, he left them, and hastened to rejoin the painter. For some time longer they continued their course, then before one of the most miserable-looking houses the old man stopped and entered the doorway. Up some dark stairs they ascended, then along a gloomy corridor with light given from the top, for it ran directly under the roof. Arriving at the farthest extremity, Collingwood's companion came to a sudden halt, and pulling a key from his pocket, unlocked the door, and ushered them into the room. The sight that greeted them Collingwood never forgot. Through the skylight window the sun came pouring; its rays fell upon the figure of a little child who lay with all its fair limbs dazzling in the glorious light. A scarlet cloth half covered it, but the tiny arms and snowy neck were bare, and in the upturned face a sweet smile lingered, a mass of golden curls half sheltered its rare beauty, and the long dark lashes cast a deep shadow on the thin cheek. It was the form and face of a Raphael's angel, or a Cupid killed on the wing.

The old man knelt down by the reclining figure, and gently awoke the little slumberer. With a quick gesture of affection the child arose and stood still and silent, gazing timidly at the stranger; then, as if ashamed of its half-nude beauty, it nestled its head under the painter's coat, seeking a protection there.

"Is it your child, sir?" Collingwood questioned.

"My grandchild, sir."

"How old is the little one?"

"She is seven years old to-day, sir," gently answered the painter whilst caressing the hidden head.

"Well, let us arrange about my picture. I have brought you a portrait I should like you to copy, and as I shall not be remaining long in Paris, I would beg you to commence your work without delay."

"How long a time can you possibly give me, sir?" the other questioned whilst examining the imaged face of a dark babe with wondrous eyes that the case Collingwood had presented to him contained.

"Not more than three weeks, but you will let me have it before then if you can; fix your own price." And as he spoke he looked round the room.

Furniture it had none beyond an easel that stood under the small window; on a nearer view Collingwood was surprised to see the picture on it represent the little fair-haired child as he had first seen her lying in the sunlight with the scarlet cloth shielding her snowy limbs. The painter's voice aroused him from the reverie that the picture had thrown him into, and after a little discussion on art he took his leave.

Arriving at the hotel he found Leonard waiting for him, and it being late they hastened into table d'hôte. They found themselves seated opposite to three ladies—two somewhat elderly in appearance, and the third both youthful and good-looking; their vagaries amused highly our friends, and when their party was increased by the addition of a gentleman, their conduct became still more diverting.

"It is decidedly a case of how happy could I be with either if t'other charmer were away," Leonard remarked after watching them for some moments in silence.

"Hush, Leonard, they will hear you!" Collingwood remonstrated.

"Nonsense, Coll, they are a great deal too busy trying to hook their fish to mind me; what fools they are, though, not to see the man is bored to death with their pressing invitations to the goods of life; and by Jingo! I trust they have sufficient choice in the shape of wines."

This latter remark was called forth by the piteous look of the poor garçon, who was nearly run off his legs in complying with the numerous demands made by the ladies for the said luxury.

"Leonard, pray be careful; I saw the young lady looking this way; I am sure she must have heard what you said."

"They are Germans, so will not understand. I dare say she thinks I am raving about her beauty."

"Don't be too sure, Leonard; and besides your words, if she does hear them, are hardly polite."

"Now, Coll, do not turn Mentor, there's a dear fellow; I shall be quite overcome if you do."

"I have no such intention, for I am afraid I should find but a poor Telemachus in you." Then after a few moments' pause, he continued: "I have taken seats for us at the opera; do you care to go?"

"I must visit my patients at the hospital afterwards then, for I have one very bad, poor thing, and needing all my care."

The table d'hôte over, they strolled leisurely to the opera-house, admiring the brilliantly-lighted shops and gay boulevards on their way.

They found their box faced one occupied by their vis-à-vis at the table d'hôte, and Leonard used his opera-glass in that direction to some purpose, judging by the various comments he made during the performance.

"Coll, I declare the most ancient demoiselle seems determined to embrace her chevalier; by Jingo! her back hair looks in an uncertain state, at least she appears to be holding it on with her hand."

"Leonard, do cease," interrupted Collingwood, the chatter of his friend preventing his hearing every note of Meyerbeer's well-loved opera.

"I cannot say much for the singers; their voices are flat after Patti and Nilsson."

"I told you you would find it slow, Owen; for myself I never bother listening to their energetic howls, for generally I only come here to escort a friend."

"Leonard, I am sorry to hear you say so; how will your mother like you appearing in that character?"

"I must sow my wild oats, old fellow; I dare say yours are in flower by this."

"Ah! you see I have been in countries where luckily oats don't flourish, and I fear you will find the reaping of your grain anything but pleasant." Then turning his attention once more to the stage he stopped all further conversation.

Somehow to-night he found his mind would wander; for the scenes he had witnessed that day had impressed him strongly, and amidst the glitter of the luxurious opera-house the little fair-haired child with her shining limbs seemed flitting; if he looked up into the higher boxes he seemed to see her there in her miserable home and bare surroundings; if he turned his eyes upon the stage she still seemed there, pleading with her violet eyes for love and protection; she haunted him, that lovely little babe, and he could not shake off the feeling that she was waiting for him to come to her relief, and put his strong frame between her and misery.

The crash of the final chords aroused him from his reverie, and as Leonard was impatient to be off he rose and left the opera-house.

Linking arms the friends proceeded homewards. Leonard had had the gratification of returning a handkerchief he had seen dropped by the attractive damsel, and was considerably taken aback by being thanked in English for his attention.

"Will you come up and have some wine, Leonard?" Collingwood asked, arriving at the Grand Hotel.

"I cannot to-night, old fellow, for I must go round by Beaujon, I have a patient very bad there," and, saying a hasty good-night, Collingwood soon lost sight of him down the long boulevards.

It was striking one as Leonard passed under the hospital doors. Proceeding upstairs he entered the accident ward and approached the bed on which his patient lay. She was a woman of, perhaps, thirty-five years; sin and sorrow had disfigured a face which in years gone by had been good to look upon; there was left nothing now but her sex to plead for gentleness from any hand. Leonard's, however, was as tender in its touch as that of a loving mother, as he unbound the bandages from off the shattered arm and examined the fearful wound. Several groans escaped the closely pressed lips of the woman, and her face was convulsed with the agony she endured; seeing one of his fellow-students hastening by, Leonard stopped him to ask his assistance.

"Your patient looks worse, Thornton," his companion remarked, whilst he supported the suffering woman.

"Yes. I am afraid I must ask Dr. Lois to see her to-morrow; amputation I dread will be necessary."

They both looked down sadly on the wasted form lying unconscious before them. What lesson did it teach them?

"Had you not better tell the Sister to bestow a little extra attention on your patient to-night?"

"Yes; I will go to her now," and with a last glance at the still figure before him, Leonard walked softly down the ward.

Many of the occupants of the white beds were sleeping—one the sleep that knows no waking. A child's moan of suffering arrested his attention, and, going up to the little one, Leonard shook up her pillows and bathed her aching head. A sweet smile was his recompense, and bending down he imprinted a kiss upon the fair young face; he knew before many suns would rise in daily splendour, that pure soul would be called to its short reckoning, and the little one be numbered amongst the celestial hosts.

He found the Sister watching by an old man who was slowly dying. A Priest in his long black cassock was also there, and his words of hope and eternal love encouraged the wearied soul to take fearlessly its everlasting flight.

Leonard whispered his directions, then turned to leave them. The dying man feebly beckoned to him; going up to his bedside, Leonard bent his head until his lips almost rested on the aged and wrinkled forehead; it was difficult to hear the low uncertain words:

"God will bless you for your gentleness to the aged and poor," was the murmured phrase. A feeling of awe crept over Leonard as he heard it.

There was silence among the little group, then the sufferer closed his tired eyes, and Leonard with noiseless movements arose from his seat and made his way out of the hospital.

CHAPTER IV.

ALMOST before the sun was up the noise of the awakening city startled Collingwood from his dreamless sleep.

He arose and descended; the silence in the hotel forming a strange contrast to the bustle and confusion in the boulevards, for even at that early hour cabs and conveyances of every sort were being driven quickly up and down, and men and women hastening to their daily employments filled up the spaces between the stiff square-cut trees. Strolling along, Collingwood soon found himself at the Church of the Madeleine; he entered and watched with admiration the sunbeams steal slowly over the wings of the silent marble angels. Mary, on her cloud-built throne, was the last to be clothed in the radiant light, and on her lovely face it seemed to linger, as if loath to wander from so sweet a resting-place. Returning to the hotel, Collingwood found Leonard.

"Well, Coll, great news! The mater, governor,

and small fry, are all going to put in an appearance here to-morrow!"

" Ah!" answered Collingwood, somewhat taken aback by such a greeting.

" By Jove! that is not all; fates have ordained that we are all to be packed off to Ragatz, the old party considering that remote region will take a liking to his gout and relieve him from that pleasant companion. The mother suggests your being smothered in the parcel—what say you?"

" I will think about it."

" Don't think, Coll. I never come to any comfortable decision by thinking; pray decide without thought. Now let us toss up—heads you go, tails you stay at home;" and taking a ten-centime piece from his pocket, Leonard suited the action to the word. "Heads, by Jove! Go now you must; it is always dangerous to trifle with fate."

" Well, since you have decided for me, I suppose it must be; remember any evil results are to be laid at your door."

Leonard shivered, and looking towards his companion, rejoined:

" What makes a fellow shiver? I have heard old nurse say some one is walking over your grave. Blow it! graves are uncomfortable things to bother one's brains with on a sunny morning, so come out with me, Owen, for I cannot stay: I have an important case on hand at the hospital."

"I am sorry I cannot accompany you, Leonard, for I have a business engagement which detains me in this neighbourhood."

"*Au revoir, alors,*" answered Leonard, and left his friend to his meditations.

That evening, when they again met, Collingwood in the course of their conversation inquired news of Leonard's patient.

"She is dead, poor thing; died under the knife," Leonard answered, and a sad look swept for the moment the brightness from his face.

CHAPTER V.

It was several days before the friends again met —days of intense heat and parching dryness, when the Champs Élysées with its endless trees afforded but a scanty shelter from the burning July sun; the atmosphere seemed dazzling in its excessive brightness, and the tall white houses made your eyes ache as they threw back their glaring whiteness into the unstirred air. High up in many garrets the poor lay fever-stricken and dying.

It was the hottest hour of one hot day that Leonard presented himself at Collingwood's rooms.

"Well, old fellow, the governor has played us a pretty trick in never turning up yet, hasn't he?"

"Have you heard when we are really to expect them?" Collingwood replied.

"In a day or two at furthest; but I have come to-day, not to chatter about their movements but about your own. Now tell me particulars of the unhappy painter you seemed to have been overcome by last time we met. What about the portrait?"

"Can you come with me now to see it? if so, I will order a cab."

"All right, hunt up a vehicle; I am at your orders for the rest of the day."

Accordingly they started, being jogged over the stones and made deaf by the noise and thirsty by the dust, heat, and glare.

Arriving at the old painter's dwelling, Collingwood showed the way upstairs, dark even on this bright day. Knocking at the small door, he was surprised at receiving no summons to enter. Forcing the lock with his knife, he soon managed to let Leonard and himself in.

By the side of a straw mattress that served as a bed, the little child knelt, her golden curls buried in the folds of an old rug. Beneath this spare covering the painter lay. Neither moved at the entrance of the strangers, and it was only Collingwood's voice as he addressed them that roused them.

"You are ill, my friend," he said, speaking in French.

The child raised herself from her bent attitude, and answered in weeping accents:

"Oh, sir, he is so ill, so ill!"

"Hush, my little woman; my friend here will cure your grandfather; do not distress yourself;" and Collingwood stroked tenderly the tossed but radiant hair.

Leonard during this time had approached the bed, and was feeling the pulse of the sufferer. He shook his head as Collingwood turned to ask his opinion. "There is very little to be done; we had better remove him to the hospital." And after some further conversation on the best means of doing so, Collingwood decided to undertake the removal of the few articles in the garret, and Leonard charged himself with the invalid.

It was with some difficulty he persuaded the old man to consent to his plans, but on a promise being given him that his grandchild should be allowed to wait upon him, he at last consented; and wrapped in all the warm coverings that could be found, he descended the narrow stairs, and before long found himself in a white, clean bed, in a private room of the great hospital.

Collingwood being left alone in the bare, cheerless, and now deserted home, looked round with a strange interest. On the easel he found a finished portrait of his dark-haired baby-love; and near it, but on the floor, was the picture that had arrested his attention on his first visit. Again did it draw from him an exclamation of admiration — the beauty of the fair-faced child, the sweet languor of the shining, rounded limbs, the vivid colouring of the tattered scarlet petticoat, the brilliancy of the noonday's glorious light—it was truly an artist's fingers that had put such living life into that stiff canvas; more than an artist's eye that shaded every curve in those soft childish limbs. Turning from his contemplation of the picture, Collingwood collected the few articles worth removing, then hailed a cab and returned to the hotel.

A few days passed, and gradually the old painter faded; slow and painless were his lingering hours, and when told to prepare for his last journey, the calm of a great peace rested upon his face. His pilgrimage had been long and weary; he was thankful now to find his rest; all his loved ones had gone one by one before him, and it was only the golden threads of a child's rippling curls that bound him still to earth. When he looked upon that little face his strength for a moment failed him; with a firmer pressure he held the tiny hands, and a few tears stole one by one down his withered cheeks; the words of consolation he longed to utter refused to pass his lips, and only through the pleading eyes did the voice of affection speak. It seemed cruel to part these two—protecting age and reliant childhood—but the decree was passed through the heavenly courts, and the angel of death with his sombre wings was already on his downward journey.

It was midnight, and all in the little room was hushed with the hush of a dying hour; the heavy long-drawn breaths of the invalid bespoke the presence of the mighty conqueror. With a last effort the old painter spoke; it was Collingwood who raised the aged head upon his breast.

"My child, my darling! who will care for you?" were the low words, and the anguish in every tone made your heart stand still.

"Fear not, my friend; your darling shall never want a friend whilst I am here to help her."

"Hush! I must speak a few words before my time is spent. Long years ago, when a husband of but a few years' standing, I rescued from death a fair and lonely woman. I knew not her name or station, nor did I ever ask it; a baby boy she carried at her breast. We took her in, my wife and I; her boy married our Jeannette—this is their little one; but these papers will tell you more, only death must part them from me."

The old man was exhausted, he fumbled for something beneath his pillow, then having with great difficulty extracted some papers he placed them in Collingwood's hand, and, falling back, in a few moments he had found his eternal rest.

An awful silence reigned, nothing but the ticking of the small clock broke it; the Sister of Charity stood with bent head praying softly for the soul in its heavenward flight. The child lay unconscious, clasped still in the stiffening arms of death, and Collingwood, awed, gazed down upon the empty clay with the yellow papers in his hand.

Leonard's entrance aroused them, and he having

pressed his ear for a moment upon his patient's heart and closed the sightless eyes, lifted the child from her cold resting-place, put her into Collingwood's arms and motioned the latter to leave the room.

The night was calm and cloudless, with only the pale moon casting silver beams athwart the darkened streets; the long line of trees appeared like black sentinels, and their shadows were motionless in the dim light.

Collingwood pressed the child warmly to his great generous heart, and once, under a gas-light, stayed to gaze for a moment on the pure upturned face, where great tears, like dewdrops, rested on the transparent cheeks. Into the empty garden of his lonely life he gathered this stray blossom, and vowed to cherish and love it as long as its young life lasted.

The bright-winged angels looked down, and the recorders took out their golden-plumed pens to write the act on their books of life; the choirs tuned their celestial harps to sing a *Te Deum* chorus, and wafted through the sin-laden air of the peerless city, a stray echo of their music reached the one soul for whom they chanted, and into it a strange joy entered.

The lamp was burning dimly in Leonard's apartment as Collingwood entered it with his light burden. Gently he placed the sleeping little figure upon the bed, and covered it warmly with a handsome rug at hand; he pulled the wooden sabots from off the tiny feet, and pushed the golden curls away from the flushed cheeks. Then moving the lamp into the adjoining sitting-room, he took the yellow papers from his pocket and settled himself to peruse them.

As he read his face grew white and whiter, and his hands shook until they seemed too feeble to hold those thin ink-stained papers, his eyes flashed and grew moist, and now a sob or a curse parted his closely-pressed lips. Those papers, what tale did they tell him? what pages of a closed book did they re-open? It was his mother's fingers that had traced those uneven characters, *his* mother's son that had married a poor painter's daughter! How he cursed the sister who had been the cause of that mother's grief! How he hated the man who had forced that sister into deceit and others into misery! Again and again did he read every word of the closely-written pages. He knew it all now—all —all the history of the bitter past—how his mother, to win a sister's love, had lost a husband's confidence; how, in a moment of passionate anger, she had fled from her wild Welsh home, carrying with her her baby boy—and his brother—his little golden-headed brother, he had died in the battle fray, winning glory for a foreign land! Over and over again he spelt out the clear-writ signature.

No, there could be no mistake; Eleanor Collingwood—that was his mother's name—there was but one Owen Lodge in Flintshire. Alas! alas! it was all too true.

The lamp burned dead, and through the curtained window the day-beams crept. Collingwood aroused himself, and, taking his hat, hurried out into the lonely streets, where, as yet, no sound of the awakening city rose.

On and on he wandered until the barriers were passed and the still and hushed summer-clothed wood was gained. The gens-d'armes, just entered on their daily duty, gazed wonderingly at the tall sad-faced man, but let him pass without comment, being one of the extraordinary Anglais.

Utterly wearied at last, Collingwood threw himself face downwards on the grass, where all around the trees were swaying, all above the birds were waking, far below the city was sleeping, in the lake the fish swam blinking, through the air the breeze blew sighing, in the sky the clouds were flying, and the earth was bathed in sunrise. A little bright-winged bird perched himself close to the prostrate form and, raising his tiny head heavenwards, burst his throat with a sweet matin song, then, seeing no movement in the dark figure, pecked gently one outstretched hand.

Collingwood raised his face, and the sun looked into it; an angel of love saw it too, and flying down covered with his wings its white cold misery; the sight of that great heart bleeding, touched even the celestial messenger, and with one look upwards he pleaded for comfort for his earthly brother.

Oh for the past to come back again, those two suffering ones to find shelter in his great love! if he could but have them near him for a few short moments to tell them of his sorrow for their sufferings. But they were dead! dead! he could never look upon their faces, and through the morning's freshness the weary words were ringing. They were gone; he might wander through the world and never meet them. Alas! alas! that endless regret—must he live his life through with that cruel pain gnawing at his heart? Have we not all some hidden pain, some bleeding wound? Do we not cover it carefully with smiles and laughter, so that none may see the blood-red drops of anguish that flow from its hidden source?

The carol of the birds became louder, the wings of day spread themselves over the vast vault of heaven, the hum of the aroused city broke the still air before Collingwood arose from amongst the crushed grass-blades and took his way back to Leonard's apartment.

It seemed like years since he had traversed the white-walled street, the tree-bound boulevards; the rush of the carriages over the stone pavement almost deafened him; in amongst the crowd he started ever and anon, as his gaze fell upon the figure of a lonely woman or a fair-haired youth—the ghost of his dead mother, with her bent head of grief, haunted him.

As the sun flashed on a soldier's gay trappings the words of the yellow-paged letter came surging into his brain; for thus attired had not his brother marched out of the peerless city to meet his death-shot! How quickly he had learned to love them, those two dear dead ones, whose fate he had mourned in the wood where the birds were singing, and the far-off chime of some grand cathedral dome echoed through the air their death-knell.

In one summer day the light of his life was dimmed, and never could he look back upon the past without a feeling of pain.

It was past midday when Collingwood reached Leonard's apartments, and on entering he was surprised at the stillness that reigned.

On the bed the child still slept, her little limbs lying motionless in wearied slumbers. Collingwood paused a moment to wonder at the perfect loveliness of the childish face; then, stooping, he opened the blue-veined lids with a kiss. The great violet eyes looked out, and with a glad low cry the wee one nestled closer to her protector, little knowing how doubly dear she had become to that lonely man, who in pity had vowed to cherish her, and was so soon rewarded for his charity.

"Collingwood, you are wanted," in Leonard's voice, startled them; and, turning, Collingwood faced his friend who had entered the room unheard.

"I think it is the labourer whom I have engaged to work in my place at Flint; I fancy to-day was the one fixed upon for his departure. Will you look after the small maiden whilst I go and settle with my man?" and he disappeared into the inner room, leaving Leonard to soothe the newly-awakened grief of the child.

After a time Collingwood returned to them, and taking the little girl upon his knee remarked:

"I have engaged a nurse for my little ward; I mean to consider this small maiden in that light for the future. Her name is Lilly; we will christen her Lilly Collingwood," and he kissed her softly upon her golden curls; then they all sat down to breakfast.

CHAPTER VI.

"WELL! Florence, don't you remember Collingwood?"

"Of course, I don't remember him," answered a saucy voice.

"My memory is better than yours, then, Miss Hardman, for I have not forgotten our first meeting."

Collingwood, extending his hand, replied, with difficulty keeping near his companions in the bustle of the terminus of the "Gare du Nord."

"Now, Florence, you must not be shy, but keep your eye on Owen whilst I go and help the old parties. I see the governor in a nice fix down there. The doors will soon be opened, and you must show Collingwood your boxes, and he will find a vehicle," saying which Leonard elbowed his way through the crowd to where Mr. and Mrs. Thornton stood.

Boxes found, the party collected; a vehicle something in the shape of a small omnibus discovered, our heroes and family soon arrived at the Grand Hotel, where tea being ordered in a private sitting-room, they collected round the inviting repast and *fell to* with some vigour.

After the meal was over Collingwood requested Mrs. Thornton's permission to introduce his young ward to her; a willing consent being given, Miss Lilly was brought in by her nurse.

Florence was the first to hasten to her side, but the golden-haired little maiden looked anxiously to where Collingwood sat; then, disengaging herself from her new friend, hurried to his side and nestled herself in his arms.

Florence stood for a moment in the centre of the room gazing at the two figures so strangely united; then, with a smothered sigh, turned to address Leonard who was sitting near.

"What a lovely little thing she is; come, Leo, you must tell me all about her, and how Mr. Collingwood comes to be her guardian."

"You must ask him yourself, Florence. I can only tell you an old painter died and left her to him as a legacy."

"You are very stupid, Leo; I am sure you could tell me all about it if you would, but I see you mean to be disagreeable."

"Disagreeable! I think you are severe; have you ever found me anything but agreeable to do your wishes?"

"Don't catch up every word, Leo; it is so horrid."

And to avoid any further conversation Florence

rose and seated herself near Collingwood, where she soon made friends with baby Lilly.

Everybody seeming very tired, the party soon broke up, and Collingwood offered to escort Leonard to his apartments.

"Do you think Florence much changed, Owen?" was Leonard's first question as they hastened along the boulevards.

"Yes; I am afraid I should not have recognised my baby-love again."

"That's fortunate, for you must not fall in love with her now; I consider her my property."

"Indeed, are you engaged then? You never told me so."

"We are not engaged, but it was a promise made by our mutual mammas that if it were possible their children should marry when a suitable age."

"Those sort of promises are a mistake, Leonard; try and win your bride, not have her won for you."

"Wise advice, as yours always is, Owen; but then you see I prefer to have my little wifie all ready made for me, then I have no bother of imagining what she will be like, etc., etc."

"Chacun à son goût," answered Collingwood, between the puffs of his cigar, and almost in silence the friends proceeded on their way.

"I am going to ship Lilly off to-morrow with her nurse; will you come to bid my maiden farewell?" were Collingwood's parting words.

"Of course, of course," was the reply.

The following morning therefore witnessed a scene of partings. Florence, who had offered to accompany them to the station, was surprised to see the evident affection that existed between the self-appointed guardian and his little ward; deep in her heart there was just a tiny feeling of jealousy that another child had crept into the life where before she had reigned as baby-queen.

The last good-byes said, the last kisses given, then Lilly and her nurse had left them; and Florence Collingwood and Leonard re-entered the cab and ordered their coachie to drive back to the hotel; arriving there they found a messenger had been in search of Leonard, whose presence was wanted at Beaujon. Mr. and Mrs. Thornton were also out, so Collingwood offered to escort Florence to the Bois de Boulogne if she cared to go.

As they descended at the gates from their cab, his memory went back to the last time he had wandered all heart-sick through the summer-bent wood; a shiver of pain shook him as they passed the spot where his sorrow had conquered him. His companion noted the wearied sad expression, and said impulsively:

"What makes you look so miserable, Mr. Collingwood?"

He started as he heard her words, and hesitated before answering them.

"Nay, do not tell me if you would rather not; it was a foolish remark of mine."

"I will tell you some day perhaps, but not now; you are too young to hear tales of sorrow."

"I am not too young to sympathise; and you used to love me when I was little, you would have told me then."

She had hardly finished her sentence before she regretted her words; it was like asking for his love and confidence.

"Well, you ought to have remained little. I cannot feel at home with a grown-up young lady."

And turning the conversation into a more lively vein, they walked slowly onwards.

Arriving at the borders of the lake, Collingwood proposed their taking a boat, and having selected one, they seated themselves in it, and he taking the oars rowed away from the side.

Florence began to feel strangely bright and happy as she listened to her companion's tales of his American travels; and the vivid pictures he drew of the wild beauties of that western world charmed and pleased her. She was quite surprised when she noticed the sun sinking behind the tree tops, and thus giving her a gentle warning of the lapse of time.

"They will think we are lost," she said, as Collingwood helped her out of the boat.

"I am afraid the island is hardly large enough for us to enact Robinson Crusoe on, is it?"

"Well, even if it was, where is man Friday?"

"Why, you would have to be Friday, to be sure."

"Indeed I would not; do you think me like a black?"

"Oh yes, very," answered he, looking into her eyes with an expression in his own she did not understand.

During their drive homewards she noticed again that strange look on his face, and wondered what brought it there.

A general exclamation of surprise greeted them on their arrival at the hotel, and Florence blushed rosy red as she made her lame excuse for being late.

"I shall not leave you in Owen's care again, young lady; you will bolt altogether next time," said Leonard whilst they hurried down to table d'hôte.

It was a gay bright scene—the long tables with their shining silver and blooming flowers, the well-dressed guests and splendid gas-lights, the murmur of many voices, the sparkling of bright eyes; Florence enjoyed it thoroughly, and was never tired of expressing her admiration to her companions.

Table d'hôte over, Mrs. Thornton was anxious they should all retire early on account of their starting for Ragatz the following day; but notwith_ standing her earnest entreaties that they should do so, it was after eleven before the young people separated.

"Now, mater, we are certain to miss the train unless you hurry up," exclaimed Leonard on entering his mother's room about half-past six the following evening.

"I am ready now, Leo; carry these rugs down, and I will follow you."

He took the wraps and disappeared, and shortly afterwards the two cabs, very full, started for the station.

It was a bright sunny morning with a fresh wind blowing when they arrived at Belfort, a great deal too fresh Florence thought as she jumped down in anything but a tidy state from the carriage; Leonard and Collingwood were both waiting to help her, and they could not restrain their laughter on seeing her disordered dress and untidy hair.

"It is very mean of you two to laugh; I wish you had been half-smothered in rugs, then we should see how you would turn out."

"If you said you had been in a bag, dear, I should not have disbelieved you," Leonard answered, hurrying along to the buffet, where they found some excellent coffee and bread and butter waiting for them.

On starting anew, Collingwood and Leonard joined the rest of their party in the carriage.

Florence chose the seat by the window, and

Collingwood took the one opposite. Her eyes were fixed upon the changing scenes that passed like an endless panorama before her; his, upon her face, that in the bright light looked pale and weary.

The beauty of their drive increased with every mile: here the lofty mountains shaded a smiling valley from the sun's scorching rays, and through its centre a rippling streamlet ran; there the bare rocks rose high and snow-crowned beyond the borders of a placid lake, in whose bosom the blue face of heaven lay reflected; anon, a mighty forest, with tall trees bending in the breeze, re-echoed through its depths their fiery horses' footsteps; now, up high was perched a pretty village with graceful little châlets, all vine-wreathed, and a pointed church tower shining in the sun; then a noisy river, with thousands of rushes wetting their feet in its flowing waters, and the toad and water-hen singing their vesper hymn among the stiff reeds. Sometimes a hazy cloud enveloped them in its misty wings, or a dark tunnel shrouded them amongst its earth-worms; quickly they crashed through a heavy thunderstorm, whilst the war of the elements blasted the music of earth's children; slowly they hissed into a peaceful white-housed town, where a summer fair was held, and the people, with bright happy faces, were hastening to and fro.

The day wore on.

The hour when the earth blushed came: when the mountains with their perpetual glaciers, the lakes with their unruffled stillness, the corn with its poppy-headed nosegays, the meadows with their flecked-backed cattle—when the whole of the vast lovely scene was steeped in a rose-tinted atmosphere, the hour of sunset came.

It was a Doré picture with a last touch given by a Divine hand; beauty that pencil can never equal, that words never paint, whose loveliness is never realised except in a heavenly land.

The daylight had all faded before they steamed into Ragatz.

Collingwood had been watching Florence's face in the twilight, and had noted "tired eyelids creep over tired eyes." He felt loath to wake her, but Leonard's exclamation: "Here we are at last!" did the office for him, and then they bustled themselves as best they could out of the "waggon."

Many minutes had not passed before they found themselves settled in the omnibus belonging to the Tamina Hotel, and before they had ceased their comments upon their journey they arrived at their destination.

It was all so strange to Florence that she was still in a state of bewilderment when tea was announced, and as she entered their little sitting-room Mrs. Thornton remarked her puzzled face.

"No wonder I look puzzled, aunty, for I seem to have dropped into a strange place all in a minute. I must really be given half an hour's grace to collect my ideas." Florence always called Mrs. Thornton aunty, by way of endearment, and it pleased the old lady.

"Well, Flory, how do you like your new abode?" Leonard questioned, as he entered the room.

"I have hardly had time to look around me yet, Leonard, but the small black-whiskered man with the gold band on his hat, who acted as guard for our omnibus, amused me immensely; he seemed in such a fluster."

"They say the hotel is very full, so I dare say we shall meet some nice people."

Then old Mr. Thornton and Collingwood dropped in, and they commenced tea.

Early the next morning Florence was wakened by the tinkling of the goat-bells, and being anxious to inspect her new quarters, she dressed quickly and found her way out of the hotel. Leonard met her at the door, and gazing wistfully in her face, said:

"How do you feel after your long journey? You looked very tired last night."

"I am all right this morning, and quite ready for my breakfast."

"You must not think of breakfast yet: the governor has only just swallowed his first glass of water, and I believe he means to dispose of some half-a-dozen more, so calculate when we shall be able to relieve the inner man."

"But I really must have something to eat, Leo."

"Well, I thought that would be your cry, so you see I have provided against famine;" and he pulled from his pocket some fine peaches, which Florence was not slow in tasting.

"Let us go to the gardens, Florry; I believe there is some music to be heard there at the Kursaal, and we shall see the people."

"You have soon learned the rules of the place, Leonard."

"Yes, I caught hold of a fellow last night, and made him tell me all the amusements there were to be had."

They sauntered slowly along towards the bridge that spans the Tamina, and arresting their steps in its centre, admired the lovely cascade formed by the torrent a little higher up, and the pretty iron bridge that stands guard over it. Then they moved on under the shadow of the trees and past the old Hof Ragatz, and the sheltered promenade with its graceful pillars, enticing shops, and dripping fountains.

Leonard amused his companion by the severe

criticisms he passed on the various couples they encountered.

First it was a dashing widow that nestled up to the fountain and filled scrupulously her daintily-cut glass; then a stout papa, who looked gouty, followed by a tiny regiment of hopefuls; next a smart dandy came lounging along, and ha! ha!'d himself into the widow's good graces; then a last season's belle, all powder and paint, brought her charms to be doubled by the youth-giving waters; then an ancient soldier, all pains and aches, came grumbling along with his military pace; slowly a wise politician made his way towards them, quite unheeding two blushing damsels who gazed awe-stricken into his face; lastly, an invalid with sad and weary eyes was drawn in his bath-chair to the sparkling water's side; meekly he drank the beverage, then, with a sigh, turned his face away from the happy bustling crowd around.

Florence's eyes rested pityingly upon the paralysed form of the blue-eyed sufferer, and turning towards Leonard she was surprised to see his gaze fastened upon the same object.

"How sad to be so stricken, Leo, is it not?"

"It is, it is indeed, my darling. How could one bear to see a loved one so?" and taking her hand, he moved hurriedly away. He did not turn homewards, but hastened through the gardens to an orchard beyond, where, finding a secluded seat, he sat down, and, wondering, Florence did likewise.

"What is it, Leo?" she asked, astonished at his behaviour, and startled by the look of horror that rested on his face.

He did not answer her at once, but held her hand so firmly in his own that the pressure hurt her.

"Florence," at length he said, and his voice sounded hollow, "I had a horrible dream last night. I know it is foolish to believe in dreams, but the sight of that boy brought mine so vividly back to my memory that I felt shocked—for I saw him in my dream just as we saw him then, paralysed. Gradually, however, as I gazed, his face and form changed, and in his place in that very chair you lay. I awoke with a cry of horror, and Owen, who heard me, came up to my bed thinking I was ill. I was ashamed to tell him my dream, and indeed it would have passed out of my memory if we had not seen that boy."

"It was only a dream, Leo," answered Florence, but her face had gone white to the lips.

"Oh! my darling, I have not alarmed you, have I? Harm shall not come to you when I am near."

"Hush! hush!" she interrupted, and rose to leave the seat.

On their way back to the hotel they met Collingwood, who gave them particulars of a plunge he had had in the swimming bath.

After table d'hôte they refreshed themselves with coffee and cigars, partaking of them in the little garden behind the hotel, the chief ornament of which consisted of a jackdaw, who managed to entertain the company in general with his pranks. When the noonday heat was passed, Leonard proposed their visiting Friudenburg, a ruined castle situated on a rocky hill-top, and about half an hour's walk from the hotel.

There was a soft wind blowing against their faces as they sauntered under the tree-arched pathway, and on up the sloping hill-side. Here and there a little brooklet came tumbling down to their feet, or some meek-eyed cattle rubbed their white noses against a dead tree-stump. One or two cottages they passed where brown-cheeked children were playing with pussy on the steps. Now and then the sound of the woodman's axe re-echoed through the warm still air, or a tourist's voice startled them with its laughter.

Arriving at the summit of the hill, they passed through the wooden gates and admitted themselves in amongst the ruins of the old castle's towers.

The view before them was a sufficient reward for their walk.

To the west and east the fair valley lay, bordered in all its length by lofty mountain heights—some grey and moss-grown, with great rents in their sides like wounds given by a Jupiter's hand; others covered with green bending trees with boughs wherein the birds were whispering; below the meadows sloped patches of Indian corn raising a thousand feathery heads to the sun's bright rays; and far down, half buried in its stony bed, the noisy Rhine flowed; away in the distance was a pine forest, half inclosing in its shade a white-towered village.

Over all the radiance of the summer air glowed, and as the day lengthened the rosy hue of sunset came creeping in from the western shores, leaping from peak to peak, from mountain to valley, from tree-top to tower, and away, away to the snow-crowned Alps, until the whole lovely scene was steeped in a crimson dye.

Then the beauty of the last hour of the day's bright life, the gradual fading of the brilliant light, the gradual hush of the humming insect voices, the droop of the flowers, the sigh of the breeze, the death of the songsters, the low bend of the trees; then it was the soul felt what a paradise the earth might be if sin and sorrow, and poverty and death, could find no home upon its surface.

Collingwood and Leonard sat upon the broken wall gazing down on the perfect picture. Florence stood near with a bunch of scarlet berries in her hand, and a dreamy expression buried in the depths of her fathomless eyes.

The presence of some other visitors aroused

them all, and Leonard, looking at his watch, declared it time to return. Florence refused compliance with his wishes, and wandered away to show her independence of their company.

Collingwood followed her, and together they mounted the stony path that leads to the front of one old tower, and settled themselves on a little wooden bench perched there.

"Where did you find your flowers?" he, noting her sprig of berries, questioned.

"Do you think them pretty?" she replied, pulling nervously the little pointed leaves.

"Yes, very; but do not destroy their beauty," he continued, stooping to pick up one or two bits of foliage that had already been torn from the slender stem.

"Well, you two know how to make yourselves comfortable," exclaimed Leonard, making his appearance.

"I suppose you have been taking a nearer inspection of the German lady with the fair hair; you cast several sly glances at her from afar," retorted Florence, making room for him by her side.

"Are you jealous?" looking earnestly at her, he replied.

"Jealous! why should I be? You are surely at liberty to admire or love any one you see."

"Not exactly, Florence; neither are you," he answered seriously.

The crimson blood rushed up to Florence's face and dyed her cheeks and neck; she raised her eyes and they encountered Collingwood's; she felt angry, vexed with Leonard, and jumping up from her seat showed the way down the steep narrow pathway.

During the evening, as Florence stood in the balcony of their little sitting-room Collingwood came out to her, and after a moment's pause begged the branch of berries she had fastened in her hair.

"Let me unfasten them for you?" he requested, seeing how her fingers trembled as she endeavoured to unloose them from amongst her curls.

"Well, do not pull my curls off."

And she turned her head towards him, the darkness hiding her flushed cheeks as she felt how gently he undid her ornament.

"Do you think I would rob you of a hair, my little maiden! for you were mine six years ago. I cannot spare you to Leonard yet."

How sad, but oh! how sweet his voice sounded! thought Florence, and something stuck in her throat.

"Do you remember your visit to Owen Lodge, Florence? or have you forgotten quite all of those bygone days?"

"I have not forgotten anything," in a low voice she replied; and a strange tight feeling about her heart made her wonder again what influence was at work within her that made her feel so strange to-night.

They re-entered the sitting-room and found it empty; seating herself on the couch out of the line of candle-light, Florence waited for her companion to continue the conversation.

Collingwood went back towards the open window and stood there some moments in silence; then he took off the large gold locket that hung at his watch-chain, and going over to the girl's side, said quietly:

"Do you know who this small woman is?"

She started and took the locket, bending her face low to study its contents.

Two big tears forced themselves into her eyes. What was the matter? How she hated herself for being so weak. The door opened, and Leonard entered the room. She felt so thankful that some one had come to relieve her from her embarrassment. Then settling herself once more in her corner she listened to her companion's talk, but took very little interest in it.

CHAPTER VII.

It was the first day of September, a bright, glorious sunny day; Florence awoke with the sound of the band playing a gay waltz in the baths near.

"Why it is my birthday," she whispered to herself, and jumping up performed a hasty toilette and made her way to the chapel, anxious to beg her Maker's blessing on the year she was entering that day.

On leaving the church she was surprised to encounter Collingwood standing on the stone steps outside the iron gateway.

"Let me be the first to wish you many many happy returns of the day," were his greeting words, and a happy eager look beamed over his dark face.

"Thank you for your kind wishes, Mr. Collingwood; I hope they will come true."

As they passed the fountain, he spoke again:

"Will you come a little way on the Rhine banks with me? I have something I want to show you; it is early yet."

She assenting, they turned their backs to the village street and walked quietly towards the station, then along under the stone bridge to the wooden one that spans the noisy river, then away to the green fields where the birds in the heavens were singing.

Florence began to wonder for what reason her companion had brought her such a ramble, when Collingwood broke the silence.

"Will you accept this little present from me?" and he put into her hand a jewel-case. She opened it, and started back with surprise on seeing a handsome *porte-bonheur*, all brilliant with diamond stars.

"Indeed, Mr. Collingwood, I cannot accept such a splendid present; it is far too beautiful for me," and she held the case towards him. He seized her hands firmly.

"You will pain me so much if you refuse my offering. Nay, let me clasp it on your arm," and pushing up her sleeve he slipped the costly toy upon her wrist; then, taking a small golden key from inside the case, he said in eager tones:

"To-day I hold the key to the door of your happiness in my hands, Florence; I wish I dare hope you would never have any other jailer."

She blushed a rosy red at his words; then turned to retrace her steps homewards. As they re-crossed the railway bridge she plucked up her courage sufficiently to ask:

"You will give me the key to my bracelet; I might want to take it off."

"Oh no! I mean to keep the key, so when you want to be happy you must ask me to open the doors for you."

The words hurt her; made a strange fear of him and her enter into her heart. She was sixteen years old to-day. Did he consider her still a child? Neither were sorry when the hotel was reached. Florence ran upstairs and entered their sitting-room breathless. There a shower of glad greetings awaited her; and Leonard insisted upon having a kiss in return for the handsome gold locket he presented her with.

Amid much chatting and laughter they finished their breakfast; then a great consultation was held as to the best means of spending the memorable day.

"I propose our going to Valens and passing by Pheaffers on the road. Perhaps we can induce the governor to accompany us that far, and Florry shall have her famous steed to help her up the mountains. The mater has one blue ticket left, I believe. Have you not, mother mine?"

"Yes, dear," and, opening her purse, Mrs. Thornton produced the desired article.

"I am off then," said Leonard, with a nod to the company and a quick kiss for his mother.

Soon all were ready, and with light hearts they

started, taking their road through the village street, and passed the various small shops on to the curving white Pheaffers highway; the noisy torrent Tamina on their left was casting a thousand diamonds into the sun-lit air, and the grey towering rocks beyond told no tales of its false fairness; on their right a wooded mountain raised its green head, and here and there a bench invited them to rest if weary, or stop to admire one of the many lovely valleys through which their roadway led. Sometimes the sun, disappearing behind a mighty wall of rock, left them in a dim shadow; sometimes a triple cascade, formed by the rushing waters, arrested their attention; now they gazed upon a natural archway that spanned their path; anon it was a giant's cave that forced a word of admiration from them.

After about an hour and a half's walk they arrived at the Etablissement de Bains de Pheaffers, an ancient monastery, whose white walls rise in solemn majesty from amongst the vast mountains and green foliage around.

They entered by the front door, a small one, and found themselves in a low-roofed corridor, into which the doors of several sitting-rooms opened.

Table d'hôte was just commenced, and Mr. Thornton proposed their assisting at it; all agreed, and Leonard having made the necessary arrangements, they were ushered into the refectory.

Florence felt uncomfortable at the many curious

glances that were fixed upon her, but when seated she regained her self-possession, and was soon listening with an amused smile to Leonard's remarks on his various neighbours.

After taking their coffee and resting, they procured a guide to show them over the establishment.

With various feelings they inspected the sombre old building, with its hot baths buried in the bowels of the earth, and its quaint dark passages, where the ghosts of the dead monks seemed to whisper their low Latin prayers through the stillness.

Florence's imagination was busy picturing the tall dark forms flitting to and fro, and the fight of human passions that the damp stone walls had witnessed: how many hearts, once brave and true, had wrecked their eternal happiness in that strange dwellinghouse? how many last gasps of despair had that close air been rent with? and, in the farthest bygone days, how many a pure soul had been willingly rendered to its Creator, how many a weary pilgrim here found his rest?

It had its history, its memories, its glory, that aged monastery buried in the shadow of the verdure-covered hills; but its beauty was now all faded, and its honour laid low.

They ended their inspection in a large lofty hall supported by grey stone pillars. Florence, leaving the rest of her party, approached one of the fountains to taste of its waters; as she raised the glass to her lips, her sleeve fell back and disclosed to Leonard's view the bracelet Collingwood had that morning given her.

He seized her arm and arrested it in its upward posture, startling her by his angry exclamation of:

"Florence, who gave you this?" and he dropped her arm hastily.

She tried to look indifferent as she replied:

"I thought I told you Mr. Collingwood gave it to me this morning."

"Thought you told me! don't think but speak another time when any one gives you a handsome present."

"Why should I speak, Leonard? it is nothing to you what presents I get." There were crimson blushes dying her cheeks and a flash of anger lighting up her dark eyes.

"Florence! Florence! do you forget my affection for you? All that concerns you concerns me, at least I would have it so."

"Never mind discussing the subject now, Leonard; we will talk about it another time;" and she turned to join the others.

They were soon following the guide across the wooden bridge that spans the Tamina, and along the giant corridor formed by the bare rock sides; a wooden footway had been formed by planks right under the overhanging ledge of rock; below them the waters flowed in a wild mad torrent, casting into the air a warm steamy vapour; no sun-ray penetrated into the corridor, except in one spot, where, through a rent in the rock, a pale beam crept; during a greater part of the way they were obliged to open their umbrellas to protect themselves from the spray showers, which were pouring down here and there.

After a few minutes' walk in the midst of this unique freak of nature, they came upon an open space where the atmosphere was dimmed by a hot steam. Two large iron doors in the side of the mountain on their left showed them the entrance to the springs they had come to visit; the guide ordered them to remove their cloaks, and otherwise prepare themselves for a few moments of intense heat; a small candle was given to each, and Florence, taking hers, turned to Leonard with a shade of fear in her eyes—she wanted his encouragement; but he turned away as if he had not seen her pleading look, and taking up his light, disappeared into the cave.

Collingwood, who had watched them, came towards her, and gently placing her hand within his own, preceded her into the misty darkness. The rush of heat and steam that greeted them blinded Florence for a moment, and almost unconsciously she arrested her footsteps, and grasped tighter her companion's hand. Its reassuring pressure comforted her, and without further hesitation she proceeded onwards, arriving in a few seconds' time at the iron barrier which protects the springs.

The guide offered them a glass of the hot waters. They each tasted it, and Florence, casting a last glance into the dim depths where nothing but the boiling steam was visible, turned to leave the cave; becoming nervous, she dropped her candle, extinguishing the light. A low, smothered cry arrested Collingwood's attention as he listened to the guide's oft-told tales. In a moment he missed Florence from his side, and hastening through the mist with his candle, he soon found her pale and trembling in the darkness. Putting his arm around her, he half carried her out into the open air.

Leonard quickly followed them. As his glance fell upon Florence's face, an anxious expression crossed his own. Taking a flask from his pocket, he insisted upon her swallowing part of the contents ; and just then Mr. and Mrs. Thornton joined them, and they all started back to the establishment, Florence quite recovering her spirits on the way.

After a few words of adieu, the younger members left Mr. Thornton and his wife, and proceeded on their way to Valens—Florence mounted on her four-footed friend.

They took the lower road, stopping a few moments to admire the natural bridge formed by rock that joins the two mountains, and spans the

Tamina. The water beneath its arched dome looked like a silver line of light buried among the roots of lovely green-headed shrubs. Overhead a canopy of leaves hid the sky from sight, and no sounds but the murmur of their voices broke the surrounding stillness.

Along the narrow, flower-strewn pathway then they wandered, sometimes amusing themselves by a song, at another a wild tale of adventure made the moments fly quickly.

At length the green curving valley of Valens burst upon their sight; they stood still to take in every shade of the beautiful silent picture. Below, hidden in a cleft of the rocks, the Tamina was flowing, singing its endless song, beyond it a long white road encircled the side of the opposite mountain; on its summit the village of Pheaffers with its white-towered church, stood out against the azure sky; dotted amongst the verdure, picturesque châlets, with their overhanging roofs, were sprinkled. Right from their path, stretching away to the heavens another verdant monarch rose, with here and there a wooden farm-house resting on its sides of green. Through the air the hay scent was wafted, and far above, an eagle, with outspread wings, was sailing to his home.

The day was declining as they reached Valens, and they hastened their steps to visit the church before the brilliant light had gone; the little graveyard with its simple wooden-cross head-stones pleased them; the mighty naked Alps with their snow-crowned peaks seemed watching carefully over those buried ones. Florence stood like one in a dream, hushed and soothed by the wondrous beauty around. She little knew what a sweet picture she herself made, with the old grey church for her background, and the yellow-headed flowers and tall wild grass-blades kissing her feet, and the rose-light of sunset encircling her like a garment. There were two hearts that loved her in that hour.

"Come, it is time to make a move; we will call on Frau public, and see what she can do for us, to help on our homeward journey," broke in Leonard, recalling Florence to time and place.

They made their way up the hill again, and finding the hotel (a work of some difficulty when you cannot speak much German), they ordered refreshments and sat down in the clean comfortable sitting-room to await them.

Amongst various curiosities the room contained an excellent library, and the numerous works of Goethe were all to be found there; the Frau told them of the village scholar whose collection it was, and they saw him shortly afterwards walking down the street; a little old man with snow-white hair and wrinkled forehead.

Twilight with its pale radiance was winging through the atmosphere before they started on their return journey; they decided to traverse the higher road, although the Frau had cautioned them of its stoney steepness and dark dreary glens.

The hush and dimness of the coming night overtook them before half their way was passed, and Collingwood offered to sing to help their tired footsteps.

He chose Schubert's pathetic "Adieu." As the last words so full of exquisite sadness thrilled through the air, a bat flew against his face and blinded him for a moment; Florence gave a little scream, and was only laughed out of her fears by Leonard, who declared it was a black ghost come to visit the donkey.

They were all glad when the bright lights of the hotel gleamed in sight, and Florence declared she never felt more ready for bed.

CHAPTER VIII.

MORE than a week passed before Florence and her cavaliers were again able to venture upon an excursion; the rain came down in drenching showers, and the thunder crashed through the air, like the warning calls for a judgment day.

At last the weather changed, and taking advantage of a sunny afternoon the friends started to visit Wartenstein, an old ruin overlooking Ragatz.

Amid much laughter and fun they arrived at the summit, and were of course charmed by the lovely view of the fair green valley.

Descending, Collingwood slipped and severely injured his ankle; with Leonard's help, however, he made his way to the road and fortunately procured a cab, in which they all drove back to the hotel.

That evening Collingwood found himself an invalid for the first time in his life; he did not object to the position, for it procured him Florence for a nurse and waiting-maid.

"Mater, I think it is very jolly being a sick man; would you object to another patient in the hospital?" said Leonard, as they were all assembled in the sitting-room.

"It will be your turn next, my boy."

"No, indeed, aunty, it must be mine," interrupted Florence, who was assisting Collingwood to tea, and standing by his side with the cup in her hand.

"Well, Florry, I'll make a bargain; you shall be the invalid on condition you break your nose to become it."

"Indeed, Leonard, I should prefer to break my heart."

"Gracious! you must have a precious soft one to break it by one fall. Now you see, a nose broken can be mended; in fact, I'll engage to mend it for you—but a heart, Florry, I can hardly dare to venture to try and mend that."

"I should say a broken heart could never be mended," spoke Collingwood, and looked into Florence's eyes as he said it.

"I had a dream last night."

"Don't tell us any more of your dreams, Leonard; I have not forgotten that dreadful one you told me the other morning," interrupted Florence, whilst a shiver shook her slight limbs.

"I am sorry I told you of it, Florry; you must not think of it again, dear," urged Leonard, startled by her evident dislike of the subject.

The days passed slowly by, excessive heat had set in, and although Florence plunged into the warm swimming-bath, she failed to keep herself cool. One morning after coming in from her bath, she went as usual into their sitting-room, thinking Collingwood asleep; for the shutters were to, and he lay back motionless on the sofa. She, feeling tired, sank into a low easy-chair, and was just dozing, when her companion's voice aroused her.

"Florence, will you tell me the subject of Leonard's dream? I am anxious to hear all about it."

"Why?" she questioned.

"Did it concern you?"

"Yes, but I would prefer not to tell you anything about it; you know you profess not to believe in dreams, so it would be foolish of me to make myself a heroine of one."

"I do not mean to believe in this one, but I want to know what it was about all the same."

"I would rather not tell you."

"I am so anxious to know, dear; think how stupid it is for me lying here all day." His dark eyes pleaded for him, and Florence, unable to withstand their wistfulness, related the story of the strange dream.

"You must forget it, Florence; there is never any meaning in dreams, in fact they always say things occur just opposite to what you expect them; so no doubt you will have a long active life."

It was a vain effort to try and speak cheerfully on

the subject, and Collingwood, after he had spoken, fell into a musing fit. Presently he aroused himself, and taking up a volume of Longfellow's poems that was on the table near, he opened it at the " Golden Legend," and commenced reading aloud.

The little clock chimed the quarter, then the half hour, and still Collingwood read on; read of the pure young soul who by her willing sacrifice redeemed a victim from Pluto's region; of the strength of a child-woman's love; of the strange long pilgrimage; of a convent resting-home. How sweet were the words of the Nun's confidence:

> " As thou sitteth in the moonlight there,
> Its glory flooding thy golden hair,
> And the only darkness that which lies
> In the haunted chamber of thine eyes!
> I feel my soul drawn unto thine,
> Strangely and strongly, and more and more
> As to one I have known and loved before."

He paused, and repeated half to himself, " I feel my soul drawn unto thine." He felt it, knew it, that his heart, his whole being, was drawn from him, was overpowered by the intense love he felt for the sweet-faced girl who in the noontide sat before him, and amongst whose curls the stray sunbeams crept and lingered on the water-drops. Oh! could he have kept her always thus, always surrounded by the radiance of the sunlight; his babe, that in the years gone by he had carried in his arms and pressed to his bosom; that had gladdened by her happy laughter his wild Welsh home, whose kisses had been the only ones but his mother's to be pressed upon his cheek; his brown-eyed darling, his one ewe-lamb; was he always to be separated from her? all his lifetime?

* * * * *

It was broad still moonlight, and Collingwood, too weary to sleep, sat smoking by his open window, watching the fair queen of night sail slowly, so slowly, over the dark mountain heads, and the pale stars burned their night-lamps dim.

He was thinking of the future.

Dare he still hope? Could he prove himself traitor to a lifelong friendship? Must he resign his dream of bliss, that he had dreamed of for six long years? Should he never more feel the pressure of those coral lips upon his cheek? never smooth down tenderly the waving soft brown curls? The questions came surging into his brain, almost maddening him by their unanswered blankness. How must he act? how live? how wait for the day when his honour would force him to tear from his heart the strings of love that were bound round it?

In the misty light of that summer night he suffered alone in his agony, alone as he had ever done, deeply as when, months ago, the grass-blades had been his confidants, and the pipe of awakening birds his consolers; for the second time in his manhood he gave way to a sorrow that unmanned him.

Daylight was stealing through the atmosphere and lifting the veil of night from off earth's fair face before he aroused himself from his reveries; shiveringly he closed the window, then utterly tired out sought his pillow.

The morning sun greeted his awakening eyes; the glorious brilliant day-god, under whose glance all things become radiant and beautiful. Collingwood thought the brightness mocked him, for his heart felt cold and dead in the midst of the joyous light. Our mother earth, how cruel she is to us in our sorrow, how hard and pitiless under her mantle of green does she appear in the gold-winged summer hours.

It is only the happy who must turn to her for sympathy then, for she smiles even when her bosom is covered red with her children's life-blood.

Collingwood was at last himself again, and Leonard proposed their walking to Saragans, a small village about two miles from Ragatz. Mrs. Thornton agreed to join the party, her husband being busy entertaining a friend, who had come from Coire to visit him.

Down the poplar-bordered road they accordingly bent their footsteps, past the little church and quiet hospital, and along under the shade of the rose-decked hedge, then turning into a grass-grown pathway, they soon found themselves amidst the hay-cut meadows. The air was deliciously fresh and pure, and the atmosphere of that peculiar brightness seldom seen except in countries where much rain falls.

Collingwood forgot his trouble, forgot the dark future which a few nights since had caused him such anguish. Could he help being happy whilst watching the speaking countenance of his girl-love, and listening to the full chorus of the merry birds? Nature was smiling all around him, and by his side the darling of his heart was wandering, looking into his face every now and then, the sun dancing gaily on the scarlet poppies in her hand, and the soft wind kissing the rose-hue into her cheeks. Oftentimes as she turned to beg his help to tear from its hiding-place a timid graceful fern, or reach from on high a rare bunch of mountain berries, he longed to clasp her in his arms, to kiss her laughing lips or eyes, to press her lithesome form to his fond heart; but his honour forbade him. He must wander in the sunlight with his heart's secret untold, let slip from his grasp this one chance of happiness.

Arriving at a little brook formed by a sparkling cascade that tumbles down the side of a mountain hard by, the ladies expressed a slight unwillingness to venture across it. Leonard persuaded his mother to intrust herself into Collingwood's strong arms; but Florence objected to that mode of conveyance, and remained obstinately stationed on the opposite side of the stream.

Leonard, seeing her determination, sprang back to her side, leaving Collingwood to escort Mrs. Thornton.

The hour of sunset was drawing in, and the crimson dye spreading its radiance along the valley rested on the two forms walking side by side away down the grass-grown meadows.

Collingwood stood a moment, watching them, wondering if in the future their paths of life would ever thus be united. Would the crimson radiance of nuptial love surround them ever thus? Would the glory of their dying day be perfect in its beauty as this summer one just fading? and together would they face the night of lasting eternity? Together would they join their happy voices in the celestial chorus? Sighing, he turned his face away and rejoined his companion.

Leonard strolled on by Florence's side, feeling, as he expressed it, "Very jolly."

"Do you remember, Florry, when you were little how anxious you used to be to go to bed before the sun, and you used to ride to Lallah on my back?"

"I remember how good you always were, and what a troublesome brat I was."

"Don't let Collingwood hear you defile your pretty lips with slang, or else—"

And he whistled long and shrill, to prove thereby his friend's horrified amazement.

Florence laughed, and chatting gaily, they walked along. Again Leonard alluded to her childhood.

"Do you remember promising to be my little wife when you grew big, Florry?"

She blushed and then turned pale again, but gave no answer to his question.

"You are old enough to understand my pleadings, Florence, and I want so much, dearest, to call you mine. Tell me—will you fulfil your promise of long ago?"

But still she remained silent. He took her hands within his own and forced her to face him; she looked up, and he started as he met her gaze.

"Florry, you do not love me!" were his half-choked words; then he continued with passionate energy: "My own darling, you are young; do not answer me yet; oh! do not take all my hopes away, my love! My dearest love! try and remember all my care and affection for you, how since the day you first brightened Halston Hall by your sweet face, I have been your slave; my mother and father wish it so much, and it was your own young mother's dying prayer——" He saw her lips move; but the cold misery of her face frightened him, and he continued, in hurried quick tones: "Darling, you will think of it? Only promise me not to cast me quite out of your heart, and I will still hope on."

Florence did not answer one word; a hunted, startled look dwelt in her dark eyes, and the laughter was all gone from around her rosy lips.

Releasing her hands he walked quietly on—all the brightness of the day seemed gone, and the trees, bending to the breeze, seemed to weep out slowly the sad, weary words: "Too late, too late!" A shadow had come between him and his sun.

In a few moments they met Mrs. Thornton and Collingwood. The latter glanced but once into the girl's averted face, but that one look was sufficient to make his heart beat joyfully, and the wind seemed to whisper to him: "She is mine, she is mine."

CHAPTER IX.

"WELL! old fellow, you will be ready for us before Christmas?"

"Long before then, Leonard, so don't tire out my patience."

"No fear; Florence is preparing a trousseau for Miss Lilly's doll, so we shall turn up when all is ready," said Leonard, as he and Collingwood were waiting for the train in the Ragatz station.

The day following their walk to Saragans, Collingwood had received letters which he said obliged his immediate return to Wales; there was a general outcry against his decision, but he persisted in his determination, and was now about to commence his journey.

"I hear the whistle at Mayenfeld, so will go and make my adieux to your mother and Florence," he said, leaving Leonard in charge of his baggage, and approaching the two ladies who were standing out of the way of the crowd.

"I need hardly say how sorry I am to leave you, Mrs. Thornton; I never enjoyed a holiday so much, and feel grateful to you for allowing me to join your party."

"The pleasure of your company has added greatly to ours, Mr. Collingwood; and I feel very much inclined to blow you up for running away so soon."

The train's near approach warned Collingwood to hasten his parting words; holding out his hand, he grasped Florence's half-extended one, noticing her pale cheeks and downcast eyes, the nervous tremble of her voice as she offered him her best wishes for a pleasant journey. Bending over her, he said in an undertone:

"You will keep the *porte-bonheur* for my sake, and give me your Alpine flowers as a souvenir?"

The bell rang, the bustle of the little station became confusing, but Collingwood seemed in no hurry to move. Florence unfastened the pink blossoms from her dress and placed them in his hand; their eyes met, a look of radiant joy swept across his face, and the next moment he was gone.

"Mother, suppose you and Florence take a walk to Mayenfeld; it is a lovely day, and you both look grumpy," said Leonard, when the train had disappeared down the curving valley.

"My boy does not waste flattery on his old mother, but I think your plan a good one, so we will wish your lordship adieu."

Saying which, Mrs. Thornton and Florence

passed out of the station, and slowly wended their way under the arched stone bridge, and over the railway one. The girl's thoughts went back to her birthday morning, when she had crossed that bridge with such strange feelings. What made her feel so lonely now, and the sunlight so dim?

Mrs. Thornton, who dearly loved Florence, and was in Leonard's confidence, thought she guessed the reason of her pale cheeks and depressed spirits. She talked to her about the various places they intended visiting, about the people whom they had met; and by the time they had passed through the fields and arrived at the far-stretching pine forest, all her subjects were exhausted, and feeling somewhat tired, she found a seat for herself on the root of a grand old monarch, and made Florence take one by her side.

"Florence, dear, I want you to tell me what is it that is troubling you? What has taken all the colour from your cheeks and chased away all your happy laughter? I do not like to see you suffering alone, my child; come, tell me what all this misery is about?"

She unloosed Florence's hat, and smoothed down tenderly her long curls. The girl buried her face in her hands and burst into passionate weeping.

Mrs. Thornton looked pained; it was all so different to what she had hoped. Her anticipations of Florence's willingness to become Leonard's bride were gradually fading, and a faint suspicion of what the truth might be vexed her not a little.

"Florence, do you care for any one else, or are you only unhappy because you do not wish to think of marriage yet? I married when I was sixteen, and have never regretted it, dear. But if you wish it, the matter shall not be mentioned to you for a year to come, then you will be better able to know your own mind."

Between her sobs Florence managed to persuade Mrs. Thornton that her sorrow was caused by the suddenness of Leonard's proposal, and that since she might have a year to think about it, she would fret no more.

The conversation then turned on other matters, and after a time Florence rose from her seat and moved away through the thickly-planted wood. She longed to be alone—alone to think of the future spreading out before her, to question her own heart in the summer solitude, and see what secret lay hidden there; but as she stood leaning against the trunk of a stately pine she forgot to think, and only listened—listened dreamily to the whisper of the breeze as it swept over the tall tree-tops; to the carol of the lark, who with outspread wings fluttered down from his early visit to the sky; to the answering song of the thrushes in the neighbouring hedge; to the whirr of the great green grasshoppers dancing among the daisies, to the buzz of the bees on their homeward journey, to the rustle of the lizard amongst the dried leaves, to the far-off tinkle of the cattle-bells in the meadows all around.

Children's laughter awakened her ears to other sounds than those of nature's chorus. She watched the young sunburned cowherd and his black-eyed sister fetch the cattle in; merrily they performed their simple duty, flitting here and there in the sunlight like two big brown butterflies. They were stupid little things, no doubt, with only the sunshine in their hearts to cheer them; in winter they were frozen, in summer half burned up; at night a toss of dry grass and prickly thistles was their bed; in the day coarse garments only half covered their nut-brown limbs. They had no beauty in them, those little bare-legged things, and yet Florence envied them, longed for their liberty, their joyous hearts, their wild untamed life, their unfelt burden of sinless poverty. But truer thoughts soon followed these envious ones; those little souls were but half awake to the wondrous beauty of this wondrous world; their brute instincts their only guides in the paths of life; their animal passions the only ones to relieve their days from endless monotony. What joys, what sorrows, was not their life exempt from? what feasts of the mind and eye were they not blind to?

The little forms in the sunlight became subjects of pity to her as she pondered on all these things, and glancing up into the wide blue sky, she thanked God humbly "that she was not like unto one of them."

"A penny for your thoughts!" said a voice behind her, and turning, she faced Leonard.

"Have you seen aunty?" was her answer, wishing to divert his attention from herself.

"No; I came a new way, so I suppose I missed her."

"We had better go to her now, then; for she will wonder what keeps me away so long."

"You seem afraid of my company, Florence."

"Afraid!" she interrupted, her dark eyes flashing and her lips slightly curled with scorn.

"Nay, do not be angry at my using the word; but tell me, why do you always avoid me of late?"

"I am not aware of appearing to avoid you, Leonard; why should I?"

They came upon Mrs. Thornton suddenly, for she had left her seat, and was wandering in and out of the trees in search of her girl-companion.

"I was just wondering where you had got to, Florence. And how came you here, Leonard? I thought you were going to Coire with your German friends?"

"I made up my mind it would benefit my health more to come and hunt you up."

"I think it is time for us to return, so you will not have too much of our company, Leo," rejoined his mother, and showed the way homewards.

After table d'hôte they took a carriage and drove to Weissenthal, a small village situated in a valley, beautiful as a fairy's home we dream of, watered by a cascade and rippling streamlet; shaded by a deep thick wood, wherein the violet, primrose, and cowslip reared graceful nodding heads; guarded by tall mountains capped with snow—a true elf glen, a real earthly paradise.

Mr. and Mrs. Thornton decided to remain near the hotel, a small building with a wooden outhouse, where you drank beer out of long narrow glasses and watched other visitors do the same. Leonard and Florence were anxious to inspect the nooks and corners of the valley, and wandered away; passed the meek-eyed cattle, who raised their long-horned heads to gaze at the unwelcome strangers, tinkle, tinkle went their bells, giving warning to their comrades on high; passed the turbulent rivulet, which, tossing itself over a giant piece of rock, formed a brilliant cascade. Florence stretched her hands out to catch the spray showers, and, like diamonds, the drops rested on her eye-lashes and amongst the brown curls of her long hair.

Leonard sprang to her side, and forgetting her recent coldness, clasped her in his arms, calling her by every endearing name. Florence drew herself angrily from his embrace, and springing from stone to stone, reached the meadow height and fled into the vast wood beyond.

The boughs sighed as they bent over her head, the thrush stopped in his half-warbled song, the wood-pigeon hushed his cooing: did they not know a young heart had fled with its first wound to seek comfort from the deep echoes of their roofless home.

Leonard slowly followed her, grief and pain written upon every feature of his frank face; when in the shade of the forest he called her loudly by name, only the sigh of the breeze answered him. Twilight was drawing in, and over the tops of the surrounding monarchs the last crimson hue of sunset was resting in the sky; the far-off glaciers and snow-decked Alps glistened in the radiant light, but the quiet valley was hidden from the weary glance of the dying king.

Louder and louder did Leonard call his beloved's name, becoming anxious and fearful in his quest; the darkness gathered under the thick roofage of the full-leaved trees; the tangled fern-heads, red-brown blackberries, stinging nettles and prickly thistles clung about his feet, but, unheeding them, he wandered on, vexed with himself for not having more quickly followed her.

He found her at last, with her head buried in a bed of white-rock blossoms, and her curls hiding the violets from the sun's last love-glance. He knelt by her side and, touching her gently, said:

"Florry! Florry! forgive me if I have vexed you."

She regained her feet and met his questioning gaze:

"I do not love you, Leonard, and never shall."

Her words were cruel and abrupt. His face whitened as he heard them, and an angry expression was about to pass his lips when his eyes fell upon her; could he upbraid her? as she stood so calmly, so fair in young maidenhood, with the dim light making strange shadows around her?

"Why do you not love me now, Florence? You used to do some months ago; what has changed you?"

She clasped her hands, killing the pale blossoms she held in them.

"What changes us all at times, Leonard? I love you as a brother; cannot you be content with that?"

"Is a man content when he asks for bread and you give him stone? is a woman content when she asks for diamonds and you give her a square of glass? I will never be content with a sisterly love from you, Florence; give me all or nothing."

He spoke passionately, hurriedly, eagerly, his words piercing sharply the clear hushed air.

"I have told you, Leonard, I can never give you a wife's love; surely it is enough."

"Enough! enough! Yes, that is your woman's way; you drag us to your feet with every art with which Venus kissed you into birth, then when you have unmanned us you ask if it is enough! by Jove! a thousand times too much. Child, tell me, have you given your heart away?"

He drew nearer to her side, and his strong-knit frame quivered as he bent his head to read in her eyes the answer to his question; but the long lashes drooped and hid from his gaze those tell-tale windows of her heart.

The twilight had gathered in, under the tree-tops darkness was falling; he could not see her face, but her voice trembled as she answered him:

"You are cruel, Leonard; leave me in peace for a little while, have patience with me!"

"It is nearly dark, let us return," he replied, his voice hoarse and low. They walked in silence through the sweet-smelling meadows; what was the silent beauty of the earth to them? all blurred and dim by the shadow in their hearts.

Mr. and Mrs. Thornton were awaiting them, and the carriage being ready they delayed no longer, and started at once on their homeward journey. Once past Saragans the moon rose; the lovely scene was rendered wondrously beautiful by the silvery uncertain beams; the stars burned dim, and the rush of the river broke the still air with its wild strange music.

Leonard sat silent, turning now and then a weary glance into the half-shaded face of his lost love. He would win her yet, he vowed, maddened by the beauty of her moonlit face.

Arriving at the Tamina, each retired to their own room.

Extinguishing her light and opening wide her window, Florence sat before it thinking. The diamonds in her *porte-bonheur* flashed in the glimmering light; tenderly she kissed them one by one, murmuring to each some secret of her love.

She recked not of the wound she was inflicting on a heart, true and brave as ever beat under a Bayard or a De Guesclin armour; she had no gratitude for the man who had loved her since her babyhood; she was selfish as we all are in our first love: the deceits, the shallowness, the falseness of the world had not yet touched her; she knew not the value of one noble heart, but like a happy butterfly drank of the sweet love-honey from every rose's bosom, and questioned not the safety of her hiding-place; the winter frosts would come soon enough, and wither with their cold breath the tender leaves, leaving her sad and desolate outside her home of honey and love.

Too often, alas! is this celestial gift abused; few receive it, fewer value it; the numbers use as a curse the greatest blessing God can bestow upon man, debasing from its high pedestal that heavenly image, which a Divine Love created in our hearts; the purest, most perfect of human feelings is soiled and degraded until hell itself is but a fit receptacle for the victims of that unchaste passion.

I have wandered from my subject, wandered from the girl who sat in the moonlight, spelling out slowly the golden-lettered word. She saw but its glittering surface, understood not its hidden iron. Years afterwards she felt the sharp cruel edge with which each letter was pointed; her lesson was known when she stretched out her hands in her death-agony, and bridged over the gulf of woe by the aid of that four-lettered word; when through the thick folds of the life-mower's veil she gazed her last upon the one dear face the green world held; and smiled her parting words, remembering the everlasting home of love she was about to enter.

The date for their departure from Ragatz arrived, and neither Leonard nor Florence were grieved that their summer holiday was almost over. The last few weeks had been eventful ones in their lives, and both were anxious to think over the future and prepare to face it bravely.

Leaving Ragatz, they proceeded to Coire, intending to remain a few days in that neighbourhood. It was evening when they arrived, and taking up their quarters at the Restaurant de la Poste, amused themselves watching the various carriages come and go.

Next day was devoted to visiting the various

points of interest in the little sloping town, wandering through the cool cathedral naves, and puzzling their brains over its various ancient documents; sometimes they paused before a treasured Rubens, surprised to find it there, or a Holbein in the shaded light arrested their attention. Then they walked slowly through the grave-yard, where one white monument raised its spotless head to catch a glance from the noonday sun upon its angel's face, or bring for a moment a smile upon the cold lips of its marble hero : they were buried away from their own fair land, amidst the wild beauties of a stranger country, those brave true men who had spilt their life-blood to place a laurel crown on the brow of a second Alexander; and this was their reward—a white cold tomb, young wives left desolate, with babes just born! old mothers, sightless, with hunger gnawing ! first loves forsaken, old loves forgot! earth's happiness buried, eternity's perhaps lost! Ah, Bellona ! red goddess of strife and death, how many of thy crimson footprints disfigure the earth's fair face ! from how many a happy fireside does your war-cry entice the treasure !

Towards evening our party decided to visit the Rosenhügel; it was one of the principal attractions of Coire to watch the sun set from the heights of the sweet garden of roses. They strolled along the broad white roadway, and mounted slowly the garden's hilly path. Arriving at the seat near the fountain, they rested themselves there, and were soon lost in contemplation of the lovely fading scene.

The soft wind was blowing over the miles of mighty Alp-heads; the glaciers, snow peaks, pine boughs, long curving valley, sparkling Rhine with banks decked with white-housed villages or shining-steepled towns, heights of rocky barrenness like needles pointing to the sky; all were dyed in the rosy hue of sunset.

The drip of the fountain, the vesper hymn of the birds, the voice of some labourer encouraging his oxen on their homeward way, or the song of a bare-legged urchin, were the only sounds that disturbed the evening's stillness.

"It is a time for peace and prayer," said Mrs. Thornton.

"A time for peace," re-echoed Leonard, and stole his fingers round Florence's hand.

Old Mr. Thornton, who was seated on the other side of her, saw the action and remarked:

"My children, I trust you will always pass your lives together in peace. May I not call you daughter in name now, Florence? you have been one in love always."

The trees seemed to fade away, the crimson glory of the dying day to burn her face with its fiery radiance; a great pain pierced through her heart and, for a moment, prevented her speaking. What could she say? how tell those who had been as parents to her that she could never love them as such?

Her embarrassment was relieved by the appearance of some other visitors; one of them so strongly resembled Collingwood that a general exclamation of surprise broke from them all.

"By Jove! I thought that was Owen back again," exclaimed Leonard, when the three figures had passed; the individual whose appearance had called forth this remark evidently heard it, for he turned round and met Leonard's gaze.

"Supposing we make a tour of the gardens, Florence? the mater will wait for us here, I dare say," Leonard made haste to propose, for he felt uncomfortable by the stranger's behaviour.

"Certainly," she answered, only too glad to escape further questioning; and, rising, they turned their backs to the sunset light, and wandered down the narrow paths under the shadow of the trees.

"Your father is unfair to speak to me as he did just now. Aunty promised I should hear no more of marriage for a year to come."

"My mother has not mentioned your unwillingness to become my wife to my father; she knew it would pain him so, and he is not strong," Leonard replied in a weary dispirited manner, very different to his usual happy way.

"You will tell him, Leonard, soon, will you not?

before I go back to school; for I mean to return, I can never be happy at home now."

"Do not say that, Florence; much as your conduct pains me, I will not be the one to drive you from home; let it be home to us both yet awhile, you are young; to please you I will take up my abode in London."

"I cannot stay at Halston, Leonard; oh! I cannot!" she exclaimed, clasping her hands as if in pain.

They walked back to the seat by the fountain in silence. There they found the elders prepared to return to the hotel, and slowly, with sad hearts, they left the rose-named garden.

The next morning they started for Thusis, driving through a series of lovely panoramas. The whole air seemed alive with the joyous voices of animal and insect life: the great golden-bodied bee, the pale-winged butterfly, the long-legged gnat, the steel-flashing dragon fly, the cruel wasp or the courageous blue-bottle, were all fighting their perpetual battle in the sunlight; the lark, linnet, wagtail, finch, thrush, swallow, pigeon, and dove, were sailing on outspread pinions to the sky; the screams of happy children, the laughter of grown men, the rush of the dark river grumbling in its bed, the chime of tiny churches perched upon its hilly banks, took up the chorus in the day's glad matin song.

The dreary pain gradually softened in Florence's heart. This time of trouble would soon pass; Leonard would find a more willing bride, and she—her thoughts went no further, but the tell-tale colour dyed her cheeks, and the brightness of the day pleased her.

On and on they drove, the dust rising in great clouds around them; still away they went, past the open doorways where the matrons sat knitting; past the quiet village, where the dogs were sleeping in the sun; over the wooden bridge that spans the rival Rhines, along the wide road curving through a mountain-bound and river-bedded valley, under the shade of some forest monarchs stretching out their arms to their opposite neighbours and making a green canopy overhead; beside some giant rock rearing its naked limb from out the shallow river, a ruined castle for its altar-piece; forward always until silent Thusis was reached, and the glaring noon sun stood proud in the zenith of his glory.

Oh! who can describe the beauty of that Via Mala roadway, with its background of snowy mountains, its green hill-sides, its vast pine-forests, its half-hidden villages, its twin rushing Rhines, its ancient legends, and its present loveliness!

Our friends were not sorry, however, when their drive was over, for the heat was excessive, and the dust and glare overpowering towards the end of their journey.

Arriving at the hotel they refreshed themselves, then entered the little sitting-room, which they found empty; the green shutters were closed, and the dim light was pleasant after the brilliant radiance outside.

Mr. and Mrs. Thornton were soon nodding over their papers, and Leonard found a book and made himself comfortable in an arm-chair. Florence was the only one who seemed restive, for, after remaining a short time in the room, she disappeared; then, before an hour had passed, came back again, and selecting a low chair sat thinking, with her hands idle upon her lap.

The hours trod upon each other's footsteps, the sun leaned heavily upon his supports of day-beams, when the bell for table-d'hôte brought all thoughts back to place and time, and aroused the sleepers from their nap.

In the moonlight they strolled out into the village street, taking their way across the broad bridge on to the road beyond; the darkness hid the lovely scene of mountain beauty that lay around them, and only the sombre outlines of the giant monarchs and the abyss of shadows below, told of the wonders the daylight would reveal; very slowly they wandered on, stopping every few minutes to finish some discussion or listen to the echo of some distant ox-drawn waggon. Suddenly through the silent air they heard a voice singing; it was rich and full, the soft Italian words ill suiting its wild cadences. As nearer and nearer it approached, Mrs. Thornton and her companions stood still; Leonard watched Florence's white dress glimmer through the moonlight as she approached, with outstretched hands, the advancing shadow; he heard the happy cry, like the coo of a wild dove, that parted her lips as she hastened from his side. A shivering chill came over him, the pale moon's face looked dim, for the first time he felt his love was hopeless, he realised his doom was sealed; he felt his mother's hand creep into his own, his mother's voice whisper loving gentle words. It was but a moment his weakness lasted, one of those bitter moments that come in all our lives, when for an instant the burden of the future is placed upon our shoulders, and, feeling its weight, we stagger blindly like a shot hind.

Florence's voice startled him, and, looking up, he was surprised to see her escort was not Collingwood, but the gentleman whose strange resemblance to him had struck them the previous day.

A short explanation followed, and after a bowing adieu the stranger passed on; they heard him singing away in the darkness, and when the last echo of his voice had died amongst the tree-tops, they retraced their steps, and were soon once more inmates of the noisy hotel.

CHAPTER X.

"Jolly day, is it not?" remarked Leonard, as he joined the interesting stranger in the open doorway of the hotel.

"Very pleasant," answered his companion, puffing a volume of smoke from between his lips.

"I suppose you have visited these parts before?"

"Never left my native Yankee-land until this year."

Leonard looked up surprised; he had not thought Collingwood's double (as he called him) was an American.

"I think we are doomed to meet in unfrequented places, so suppose we anticipate Madame Fate, and make a mutual acquaintance without delay?" saying which the stranger presented one of his cards to Leonard. They were soon good friends, and discussing the merits and demerits of the hotel and neighbourhood.

Mrs. Thornton and Florence appeared dressed for an expedition. Leonard hastened to introduce Mr. Hurst to them, and joined his mother in pressing him to accompany them in their excursion.

Once more they strolled along the open-doored village street, where brown-limbed children were playing in the sun, then across the wide bridge under the vast arches of which the black Nolla flowed; they watched its inky waters hurrying over the rounded stones, and felt angry with it as it tossed its dark liquid into the blue mirror of the fair young Rhine, and disfigured the latter's pure beauty, crushing its white foam into an unlovely death-hue.

Overhead the azure dome of heaven spread out a vast roofage, without one cloud resting upon its breast, the mountain peaks cut the atmosphere with their sharp needle-like heads, and round and about the gentle breeze flew sighing through the forest trees, which bent their stately heads to woo it on its southward journey.

On and on they wandered, stopping often to admire the wondrous beauty of the lovely scene; little brooklets came tumbling down the mountain side to their feet; a short tunnel with limpid walls buried them for a moment in its dim light. Arriving at the first bridge, Florence bent over the low stone wall and threw into the abyss below a small stone; its dying voice echoed, as from rock to rock it bounded until, with an unheard splash, it buried its small body in the blue waters below; the white soft foam sang its requiem, and the happy river flowed on, unheeding the sad chant.

Slowly they moved onwards, a strange silence falling on them all. Florence's eyes wandered from the fair scene around to the handsome dark face at her side: she wanted to know its history, the record of its joys and sorrows. What brought that look of unutterable anguish into the deep eyes? what forced a sigh from between those proud curved lips? He interested her strangely, this new acquaintance of Leonard's, who had so startled her by his resemblance to her love. Longing to know something about him, she at length questioned:

"Have you any beauty that will equal this in America, Mr. Hurst?"

He started as if his thoughts were far away, then after a moment answered:

"I have seen many scenes that most would call more beautiful, but to be frank with you, they did not please my eye so much as this lovely spot; our land is so vast in its wild splendour that you long vainly to take in with one glance the far-reaching grandeur."

"I suppose you would not like to settle in Europe?"

"No, I cannot say I should; I love too well the free life of my own land to care to fetter myself with the chains of a more civilised existence."

"South America, I think you told us, you resided in?"

"Yes, my father has a large sheep farm near D——, and many times I have ridden over a hundred miles between sunrise and sunset."

"Did you not find it very lonely?"

A sad smile swept across his face as he replied:

"I did once, and now all the world is lonely to me; it can make no difference where I live."

She looked at him curiously; what made him answer her so strangely?

"But you cannot be more lonely now than before, since your parents are still with you."

"My parents intend remaining in Europe some years, so I shall return alone."

"You had better marry then."

"I shall never marry," he replied shortly, and, moving from her side, joined Mrs. Thornton, who was a little in advance.

Coming to a lonely house, they seated themselves on the wooden bench outside, refreshing themselves with water from the pump at hand.

Mr. Hurst amused them with some of his American yarns, in which black bears and wolves figured in rather an alarming manner.

The day glided by; its mid-hour was passed before any of the party felt inclined to continue their walk. Leonard, as usual, was the one to give the marching order, and constituting himself their guide, he led the way onward.

Under the covered bridge they paused a moment to purchase some pebbles from the old dame who sat near contentedly displaying her wares. Just when thoroughly tired out, they came upon the view of the long stretching valley all mountain-bound; the richness of the colouring, the beauty of that sleeping landscape, well rewarded them for their hot walk.

Leonard broke the silence by a quotation from Byron, and Florence's cheeks flushed up as she heard his words:

> "Oh! that the desert were my dwelling place.
> With one fair spirit for my minister,
> That I might all forget the human race,
> And hating no one, love but only her!"

Mr. Hurst looked inquiringly at the girl, and as she met his glance, she added quickly:

"I always hate Byron, and I am sure, Leonard, you would soon tire of a spirit companion."

"Will you lend me your spirit to try?" he replied, unheeding her angry looks.

"Thanks, no; I prefer to keep my own spirit;" and a general laugh concluded the subject.

When half-way homewards they encountered a carriage whose inmates on seeing them stopped their horses. Mr. Hurst approached the lady, who bent towards him, and in another moment had begged Mrs. Thornton's permission to present her to his mother; the ceremony completed, Mrs. Hurst insisted upon their all accompanying her home, and both ladies being tired were glad to avail themselves of the invitation.

It was a merry party that assembled in the sitting-room after table d'hôte that evening, and when they had chatted some time Mrs. Hurst, at Florence's request, asked her son to sing.

He complied willingly, and song followed song, the listeners always pleading for more; to Florence it seemed as if her love had come back to her, and with her passionate girl-heart she could have cried out for very joy.

The twilight drew in, and still the rich clear voice filled the evening air with music. He chose the "Earl King" for his final song. The wild cry of the child was like the last pleading words of a lost soul; then the silvery voices of the spirits seemed hardly to whisper through the air; the grief and anguish of the father, as, with a wild cry of despair, he called out, "the fair child was dead!"

There was a silence more eloquent than words, as Mr. Hurst arose from his seat and approached his mother's side. Her eyes were full of unshed tears as she raised them to his face; she knew the cause of the anguish written there, knew the grief that blasted a noble life, the burden that weighed upon those strong shoulders, and sometimes she thought it was greater than they could bear. It was a punishment for her deceit, her heart told her; and with a mother's infinite love she longed to be the one to carry the cross, the one to feel the heavy weight of sorrow, not he.

"Mr. Hurst, you remind me so much of a young friend of ours, I feel quite tempted sometimes to call you by his name."

"Indeed, Mrs. Thornton? You excite my curiosity; for they say every one has a double, and since you know mine, you will oblige me very much by giving me all the information you can about him; tradition runs that our lives will be somewhat similar."

"You have both been in America, that is all the similarity I know of in your lives; but your voice is the echo of his."

"You are putting me on thorns; pray tell me this second self's name?"

"His surname is Collingwood, and his Christian name Owen; do you know the name at all?"

"Owen Collingwood," Hurst repeated, and looked at his mother.

Florence, who was watching his face, was surprised to see his colour rise even to the roots of his hair, and his brows contract.

"Do you know where he lives, Mrs. Thornton? I have heard of a Mr. Collingwood, but I hardly think it will be the same."

"He lives in Wales, near Flint—a place called Owen Lodge. I believe his family have resided there many years."

This time there was no mistaking the evident uneasiness this information gave Hurst, for he bit his lips and pulled nervously at his watch-chain. His mother, too, seemed strangely agitated, and rose to leave the room; but something induced her to alter her determination, and she sat down again by Florence's side.

"Are his parents alive still?" again questioned Hurst.

"No; his father died about two years ago, and his mother I never knew."

It was Leonard who spoke.

"His mother——" began Mrs. Hurst, then stopped, and looked towards her son.

"My mother and his were acquainted when they were young," interrupted Hurst, and turned the conversation into another channel.

Two days afterwards the whole party decided to return to Coire. It was the settled route for Mr. Thornton and family, but on learning the destination of their friends, Mrs. Hurst arranged to accompany them and spend a few more days together.

They were bright pleasant days, long remembered by Florence as some of the most unclouded of her life. True, no fever heat of love made the hours fly quickly or creep on wings of lead; the constant sunshine, the dreamy quiet of the little town, gave her a joyous feeling, and none regretted more sincerely than she when the hour for departure arrived. Leonard, too, had been silent as to the state of his feelings, and the girl began to hope he was already beginning to think of a future without her.

It was the last evening of their stay that young Mr. Hurst and Leonard invited her to walk with them to the Rosenhügel as a short farewell journey; they had been kept indoors by the rain all day, and had watched the lightning pierce the heavens with its fork-like flame and quiver through the heavy storm-laden atmosphere before dashing itself into the green earth; the thunder crashed along the winding valleys and echoed over the mountain tops, resembling a grand concert given by nature to her terrified subjects; the cry of the birds, the low whine of the cattle made itself every now and then audible, they tried in vain to raise their voices in remonstrance against the deafening chorus, but it was like the wail of an infant in the battle fray.

When the storm was over and the sun, breaking through the clouds, shed a warm light over the refreshed earth, all things were more beautiful for their temporary burial; the rain-drops glistened like tears on the grass-blades and tall corn-heads; the birds flew merrily from off their nests, hurrying in search of their evening meal, their carol the while more full of rejoicing now their hour of fear was past; the cattle scampered round the fields, and tossed their long horns high in the air.

The dust was laid on the white road, and the trees, as the wind shook them, shed a tiny shower upon Florence's curls, as she and her companions passed under them.

Mr. Hurst and Leonard were talking earnestly and somewhat sadly, as men talk when a past remembrance of sorrow is brought vividly back to their mind; it was the former's voice that attracted Florence's attention, and the story he was relating soon absorbed her interest:

"I had once a friend whose life was a strange romantic story. It was in a heavy thunder-storm we first met, and ever since the first peals of a coming hurricane remind me of him.

"I had been riding, as was my wont, over the vast prairies looking after our sheep, and returning somewhat later than usual I was overtaken by a storm. I could hardly distinguish the trees that surrounded our domicile, and feared it was too far to arrive there before the deluge came, so taking my stand at my horse's head I quietly awaited my fate: crash roared the thunder, whistle went the lightning; my beast reared and plunged in mortal terror, the bleat of the sheep and lambs was pitiable to hear; I watched them all huddling together, each desirous to be sheltered by his neighbour. Suddenly I saw a general move amongst the flock, and through their midst a black riderless horse came plunging, evidently wild with fear. To have attempted to arrest him would have been madness, and yet I dare not let him thus scamper through my flock. Just as I had decided on what course to pursue the animal came neighing to his comrade; I secured him after a few moments, and waited anxiously for the storm to abate. When the worst was over, I fastened my prize to an immense stone, and mounting my own horse scoured the prairie in search of the fallen horseman. It was long before I found him, and when I did I almost feared I was too late to be of service to him, for he lay quite unconscious, with his face upwards, and covered with blood; he had a wide cut in his head, from which a long stream of blood was flowing. My first care was to bind the wound up, and after a few moments I forced some brandy between his lips. I had at length the satisfaction of seeing his eyes open, and his breath come more regularly. He was very weak, quite unable even to lift himself from the ground; I was obliged to wait some time before I could manage to set him upon my horse; putting my arms around him, however, I secured him there. I shall never forget our ride; every moment I expected to see my companion die in my arms, for he fainted more than once, and time seemed an eternity before we reached our destination.

"Made uneasy by my absence during the storm, my mother was standing in the open doorway awaiting my arrival; when she saw me with my strange burden, she hastened to my side, and bestowed the tenderest care upon our unexpected guest.

"It was months before Gascogne, the rescued man, got well again; we all learned to love him during that anxious time, and when his father, a rich tobacco planter, wrote urging his return home, there was a general mourning over the estate. I had promised him before his departure to visit him in Cuba the following spring."

Hurst paused in his narrative, and his companions noticed the nervous twitch in his lips as he essayed in vain to continue his tale.

They had arrived at the hilly garden, and found their old seat by the dripping fountain; they had rested there some moments before Hurst again spoke:

"Before the spring came Gascogne sent us word he was married, and begged to hasten the time for my visit. Some weeks passed, and the rebellion broke out in Cuba; of its horrors I need hardly tell you; of women hunted by bloodhounds, their tender flesh torn by fierce fangs; of men becoming brutes, respecting neither laws of God nor man: such things, no doubt, you read of secure in your happy homes; how could you imagine one-half the butcheries that took place, too horrible to be printed? God trust you may never witness their equal! You may well shiver, Miss Florence," he said, watching her face blanch and her figure tremble; "women as fair as you found no mercy in their hour of need.

"My friend was in the thick of that brutal war; when it abated his young bride found herself homeless and a wanderer on the earth.

"Two years passed and no tidings were heard of Gascogne; all thought him dead, and before a third was spent his wife had become again a bride. I knew her then, a bright gipsy thing, with the beauty of some rare southern plant, that lived but in the blazing sunshine.

"Months flew by, and sitting one evening with the moonlight all around them, the happy pair were startled from their whisperings by the appearance of a stranger; both looked up: it was the girl's long-lost husband.

"Of their grief and joy I need not speak; such trials come into few men's lives. What was happiness to one, was the other's bitterest misery—they parted.

"I will end my story, for it is getting late, and look! the crimson light of sunset has died out of the sky. Gascogne and his wife now live in Jamaica. I have never visited them there; they are happy, no doubt, a gulf of tears bridged over by their love."

He ceased speaking, and although both his companions were anxious to hear the fate of the unhappy man who had wed his friend's wife, something in Hurst's face prevented them questioning him.

"The Cuban war brought trouble into many a homestead; but all war does; it was fortunate you were not visiting your friend at the time the rebellion broke out," Leonard remarked, desirous to make some comment on his friend's words.

Hurst returned no answer, but rising from his seat proposed their moving homewards.

"You will be sorry to leave Switzerland, Miss Florence, will you not?"

"Yes, indeed I shall, Mr. Hurst; I have spent the happiest weeks of my life here."

He laughed and replied:

"You are so old! I am sure it would not take many seconds to cast up all the weeks of your existence; wait for another five years to pass over your head, and then tell me if your ideas of perfect happiness were realised in this, your first visit to Switzerland."

"Well! if we both live another five years I shall not forget to give you my opinion, although I know beforehand what it will be."

"Ah! you little guess the burning joys or killing sorrows that life may have in store for you; but let us hope there will be no dark days in your almanac, and if there are, remember our own poet's words:

> "'Be still, sad heart, and cease repining,
> Behind the clouds the sun's still shining;
> Thy fate is the common fate of all,
> Into each life some rain must fall,
> Some days be dark and dreary.'"

"You are a great admirer of Longfellow, Mr. Hurst; I suppose it is a natural feeling."

"I suppose it is," he answered, absently.

"Well! it is the strangest thing I ever saw, your extraordinary likeness to Collingwood, Hurst?" broke in Leonard *à propos* to nothing.

"Is it my double you are speaking of, Thornton?"

"To be sure it is! who else could one speak of when you are near? I am always in a mist as to whom I am addressing—a living being or a friend's ghost."

"You are complimentary; one does hope to be an individual in this world, for in the next I imagine we shall all have a somewhat shadowy appearance. Am I only a reflection in your eyes, Miss Florence?"

She blushed a little under his gaze; was it not the reflection that had made him somewhat dear?

"I don't quite agree with Leonard, for I do know with whom I am speaking; still you are very, very much alike I own."

Chatting thus pleasantly they made their way slowly back to the hotel. The pale young moon was hanging in the sky before they went indoors, and they stopped a few moments to admire her dim radiance and shy shadows before they turned their backs upon the lovely sleeping scene and faced the glaring lamplights.

The merry voices of the birds hastening over their matin-song was the first sound that greeted Florence's ears on awakening early the next morning; hastily she performed her toilette, made somewhat thoughtful at the remembrance that to-day she was leaving, perhaps for ever, the hushed quiet happiness of her joyful summer-time.

Under the shadow of those giant mountains, just now ablaze in the rosy dawn-light, her flower of love had bloomed; in the glare of the hot noontide she had taken her first lesson out of the hitherto unopened book of her woman's life, in the bend of the noisy river the first blush of love had mounted in her cheeks, and far away in the sombre pine forest her first tears of grief had been shed. She sighed as she turned away from the reflection of her fair young face in the mirror, and her heart was heavy as she hastened downstairs to join her companions in the *salle à manger*.

Mrs. Hurst and her son accompanied the Thorntons to the station, and at the moment of departure promised faithfully to visit Halston Hall on their arrival in England.

When the train had steamed out of the station and away through the scent-laden air beyond, Mrs. Hurst turned to her son, remarking:

"What a sweet face that girl has; no wonder young Dr. Thornton is in love with her."

"He seemed rather attentive I noticed, but she did not appear to return the compliment."

"No, I hardly think she did; perhaps she is too young to notice such attentions, or at least draw any conclusions from them."

"Women generally think of marriage, from their birth upwards."

"You are severe on our sex, Owen," answered his mother, placing her hand gently on his arm and looking up sadly into his face.

"Have I not reason to judge you a little hardly, my experience has been so bitter?"

"Owen, it is not like you to condemn us all for the misery one sister brought you. You cannot tell how she may suffer; would you respect her more if she proclaimed her feelings to the world, and brought unpleasantness into a home which has been decorated by the hand of a husband who lives but for her?"

"You are right, mother mine, but still you must not blame me for cursing you all sometimes! Think what a wreck my life is."

He pressed the hand that lay upon his arm, and gazed into the aged face that was raised pleadingly to his own.

"Will you never forget her, dearest?" she questioned, her mother's heart torn by the hidden sorrow imprinted on every feature of her dear one's face.

"Forget her, mother! Good God! I wish I could! She was, and is, and always will be, 'my light, my life, my very breath.' Mother, if I knew I should see her but once more, hear her sweet voice whisper once again my name, feel but once the pressure of her lips upon my own, I would live contentedly my life out."

"But, Owen, if you were married, other ties would fill your life up; dearest, forgive me if I pain you, but can I tell you how it grieves me to see how wasted your manhood is!"

"Mother! mother! never speak to me on this subject again; no other woman shall take her place in my heart."

"But, Owen—" again she urged, but he interrupted her.

"I cannot forget her—hush! Do not argue with me, it is useless. Before God I am sinless, and what matters to me the opinion of men? I can brave it for her sake."

His eyes flashed angrily under their thick lashes, and Mrs. Hurst remained silent. She knew it was useless, as he had said, to argue with him, but how willingly would she have sacrificed herself to win back the lost joy of her son's life.

The sins of parents are visited upon their children; so, ye mothers, beware that yours be not the hand to strike the fair blossom when the moment of bloom is at hand; yours the one to snatch the laurel-crown from off the loved head, when the battle of life is won. Guard well your lives that your offspring may not suffer for your follies: will you give them to the world with the seed of crime in them? then when it grows, and spreading out its tendrils, encloses them for ever in its sin-laden branches, can you send them thus before the eternal Judge, and stand by when His mighty voice condemns them to everlasting misery? will not their last cry of despair echo in your ears? Can even the music of the celestial chorus deafen you to its unutterable anguish?

It was dawn, and the sun had risen, looked his first upon the half-awakened earth, glanced admiringly upon the great Alp glaciers and sweet-smelling valleys, upon the dashing noisy rivers and mirror-like cascades, into the face of a tired girl who was watching for his advent from out the window of a stuffy railway-carriage; had smiled upon the Atlantic's white-crested waves, had been welcomed by a dark-haired woman on the shores of Jamaica's hot land, had crept through the sombre shadows of a fir-forest, and lighted upon the grouped figures of a golden-haired child and tall proud man; had listened to the music of a rich full voice, that broke the day-beams' freshness; had sighed over the tomb of a brave young soldier and sorrow-stricken mother; had kissed the green earth into happy bright life; had radiated the atmosphere with glorious blushing splendour; had bathed every atom of the round human world with the light ever ancient, yet ever new, of wondrous

SUNRISE.

PART II.

SUNSET.

CHAPTER I.

THE wind whistled through the frost-whitened chestnut branches, the grass-blades were crusted over with the silvery spray, the sky one mass of grey-hued arches, and the robins with their scarlet waistcoats were pecking the window-frames for a taste of bread. It was winter-time.

In the large comfortable sitting-room of Halston Hall, Mrs. Thornton was seated near a glowing fire; every now and then she looked towards the window, as if to congratulate herself on her own comfortable quarters.

Presently the door opened, and Florence, equipped for a riding expedition, entered the room.

"Florence, I am afraid you will have a cold ride; had you not better send Thomas, with a note of excuse, to the Grange, and pay your promised visit another day?"

"You know I am not afraid of the cold, aunty, and the country will look beautiful with the trees all frosted over; so good-bye, dearest," and, approaching Mrs. Thornton's side, Florence imprinted a hasty kiss on that lady's smooth cheek; then, with a bright smile, tripped out of the room, descended the broad stairs, and stood for a moment in the hall waiting for the groom to bring round her horse.

A pattering of canine feet made her turn round to watch for her old favourite's arrival. Alas! poor Rollo had aged quicker than his mistress, and his approach to her side was slow and painful; she caressed him tenderly, calling him still "her dear old Rollo," and was not ashamed, when Thomas summoned her to mount, to bend down and kiss his black cold nose.

"And sure Rollo can't come after you no more, miss," remarked the grey-headed servant, who had lifted her on her pony or horse since she could toddle.

"Poor Rollo!" was all her answer, as she settled her reins and prepared to start.

The cold east wind made her cheeks tingle as she cut his sharp breath down the leafless avenue, then along through the village street, where, in every homestead, the firelight glanced on the walls. The noisy boys were hurrying back to school and sliding one after the other down the frozen gutter;

their laughter startled her horse, who plunged onwards in frightened haste.

Arriving at her destination Florence dismounted, and, throwing her reins to Thomas, paused a moment at the sight of his purple, cross, pinched face.

"Well, Thomas, I am afraid you have not enjoyed our ride?"

"I never expected to, miss, on such a day; sure I feel half-frozed."

"I thought you liked coming to the Grange, Thomas, or else I might have brought John with me this afternoon."

"They give a good glass of beer at the Grange, miss, and I have no objection to the place."

"I believe you like to see the people, Thomas, and some one in the kitchen, who will give you something better than a glass of ale; so I will not keep you from your reward any longer—don't forget to look round for the mistletoe!" and, laughing at the evident embarrassment of her old servant, Florence entered the house.

A warm welcome awaited her, her friends expressing their wonder at her venturing out. Having assured them she felt no ill effects from her expedition, they fell into a discussion of the gaieties they expected during the holidays.

Nelly and Maude Reede were schoolfellows of Florence's, and a friendship had sprung up between them, owing to their being near neighbours and girls of about the same age.

As they all drew their chairs round the fire and placed themselves each in the most comfortable attitude they could think of, they formed a not unpleasing picture; so, at least, thought a gentleman whose appearance startled them in the midst of their animated conversation.

Florence was the one to spring from among her cushions, and astonished her companions by advancing with outstretched hand to welcome the intruder.

"Oh, Mr. Hurst! how ever did you manage to get here? I thought you were in Italy."

"I feel flattered at your thinking of me at all, Miss Hardman. Mr. Reede is an old friend of my father's, and we met in London three days ago; the next act of the drama was my appearance here."

"Why, Florence! you never told us you knew Mr. Hurst!" interrupted Maude, looking somewhat questioningly into her friend's face.

"I think I might return the compliment, Maude, for I never heard you mention his name."

"I could hardly do so, since I have only had the pleasure of making his acquaintance three days ago."

"Really, ladies, I feel quite bashful at being the hero of such remarks," remonstrated Mr. Hurst;

and Florence noticed his face looked happier than it used to do.

"Bashful!" she exclaimed, her dark eyes sparkling; "have you learned that accomplishment since your arrival in Europe."

"No! no! it is a peculiar failing only acquired in Yankee-land."

There was a general laugh at this remark; then Florence continued:

"Shall I tell when, where, and how we met Mr. Hurst, and entertain my friends for the rest of the afternoon by a full and particular account of our proceedings at Thusis?"

"I am afraid you would only bore them, Miss Florence, and I want an opportunity of inquiring after Mr. and Mrs. Thornton, and the handsome young doctor, their son."

"Thank you, they are all well, and will be only too pleased to welcome you to Halston when you feel inclined to come."

"Is the Doctor with you, then?"

"We expect him to-day; I dare say he will ride over to-morrow when he hears you are here."

"Can you spare him so soon?" he questioned, not sorry to be able to force the crimson colour into Florence's cheeks.

"Spare him! do I look like an invalid?"

"Some diseases are only lodged near the heart, Miss Florence."

Then, drawing another chair towards the fire and seating himself in it, he turned towards the sisters, saying :

"Shall we let Miss Hardman into our secret, and persuade her to join our society ?"

"Oh! I am sure I shall not join any secret society, so do not ask me. I have a horror of secrets of every description, and could never keep one for more than half an hour."

He persisted in his wish to force her into their confidence, and at last obliged her to listen to long programme of carols the sisters and himself had practised to sing in the village on Christmas Eve. They made her promise to join them, and after having fixed their various costumes, Florence rose to bid them adieu.

"I am sure you are courageous to face such a frost, Miss Hardman," Mr. Hurst remarked, as he helped her on with her warm jacket.

"I never feel the cold, and hate being penned up in the house."

"You are a wandering spirit, I am afraid," he replied, and went out bare-headed to assist her to mount.

She laughed, and when comfortably seated in her saddle answered :

"Spirits have wings and I have none, or else I might wander."

Without giving him time to rejoin she trotted

away, kissing her hand to her friends, who were watching her out of the long window.

Mr. Hurst stood for a moment where she had left him, then, as he turned to hasten up the steps indoors he muttered:

"I think I can guess where my lady would wander if she had wings!"

Florence rode thoughtfully along the hard dry road; the pale winter's sun was glancing among the bare branches of the trees, and made their frosty whiteness glitter in his radiance. The house seemed strangely quiet as she entered, and Rollo wagging his tail was the only being visible to make her welcome. Passing slowly across the square lofty hall, Florence found herself in the library, and seating herself in an arm-chair, she gave her fancy liberty to build a thousand airy castles in the firelight.

Outside the merry robins had bid each other good-night, and the red sun behind his frostmist, was gradually sinking to rest; on the far-off sea the fish-laden boats were fast sailing homewards over the angry tossed waves, to the calm, smooth haven under the bay; anxious wives and loving mothers were straining their eyes to catch the first glimpse of the wide-spreading sails; sons and daughters united their voices in prayer for the safety of the dear ones.

More distant, more hushed sounded the twitter

of the robins, less boisterous, less wild the cry of the wind; the room grew darker and darker still, until even the fiery embers were lost in the general darkness. Florence slept.

It was dusk, and the fire burned low when she awoke; a shadow was standing over her, and she rubbed her eyes, then stretched out her hands to drive it into a far-off corner.

They were no shadowy hands that caught her own in a warm, firm pressure, no shadowy voice that roused her from her dreams.

"Why Florence, have you not a word of welcome for me?" pleaded Leonard, as he bent his head to gaze into her wistful eyes.

"You startled me so, Leo, I have not been able to recover my breath yet."

The door opened to admit Mrs. Thornton.

"Well! well! young people, how is it you are all in darkness here? I suppose Master Leonard finds it pleasanter to plead his love-suit surrounded by shadows."

The dim light hid the crimson blushes that spread themselves over Florence's cheeks; before she had time to make any comment, Mr. Thornton continued:

"Florence, my child, I think Leonard has pleaded long enough for your love; remember your union with him was your mother's dying wish, and has always been our brightest hope. You will make us all happy this Christmas time, will you not, my daughter?"

Florence felt an arm steal round her neck, one soft gentle kiss imprinted upon her forehead; she wanted to cry out against this shortening of her liberty; she longed to tell them it could not be, she had no love to give to the companion of her childhood, the playmate of her girlish years; but the words choked her, and she let her hands be placed in Leonard's, let him kiss them and press them in silent gratitude to his heart; then, as the servant brought in lights, she made her escape from the room, hurrying up the wide stairs with flying feet and fast-beating heart.

On entering her own room she flung herself on the couch, and gave way to a passionate fit of weeping.

"Are you ill, my birdie?" she heard her old nurse ask, and felt some one smooth her tossed hair.

"And sure you would not weep without telling Lallah what ails you, my darling? Remember I brought you from your own land, my birdie, and took you straight from your pretty mother's arms. What is it, my white dove?" continued the faithful woman, kneeling down by Florence's side and stretching her arms over the weeping girl.

The tender appeal had a strange effect on Florence; she pushed Lallah from her side, and gaining her feet, paced impatiently up and down the room.

Lallah stood silent, watching her with wistful loving eyes. She had never before seen her young mistress thus, and her heart was bleeding at the sight of that sorrowful, tear-stained face.

The dressing-bell rang, and Florence stopped in her walk, saying with a bitter laugh:

"Deck me in bright array to-night, Lallah, for I am to be led to the altar of sacrifice."

"Oh! my precious, what words are these?" answered Lallah, as with trembling hands she brushed and straightened Florence's long soft curls —for the girl had seated herself before the mirror, and was gazing intently at the reflection of her pained, white face.

She dressed herself in a robe of delicate silvery tint, and roses, like crimson drops of blood, pressed into the folds at her bosom and among her curls. Her lips were quivering, and her dark eyes filled with pain.

When ready to descend she turned to Lallah, and, putting her arms round her old nurse's neck, sobbed:

"Oh, Lallah! I shall never love him, my heart is given to Owen."

"My poor dove, my pretty dove!" murmured Lallah, and the dinner-bell sounding, Florence hurried away.

How she hated the bright light of the drawing-room, the happy words of congratulation, the warm kisses of love that Mr. and Mrs. Thornton pressed upon her lips; then Leonard's low tones of endearment, his bright smile of gratitude for every little word; the sparkling wine with which they drank her health and coupled her name with his. Oh! how her heart ached through it all; how thankful she was when the hour for retiring came, and she found herself once more in her own pretty room, and at liberty to give way to her grief!

Leonard had broken his word to her; had he not promised in Switzerland not to mention his love again? They had forced her into an engagement when she had no time to consult her own heart; the first moment of his return he had taken advantage of. She hated Leonard, she told herself, and vowed she would tell him so without delay, and regain her liberty.

What excuse could she give for her want of love? what reason for unheeding her mother's dying request? what apology for the ingratitude to those who had cherished her all her lifetime?

It was all dark to-night, she said, and sobbed herself to sleep.

CHAPTER II.

THE morning was cold, raw, and bitter; far over the fir-tree tops the river was dashing in, covering the sand-beds and crimpled cockle holes with its rough angry waves; as billow upon billow broke its bosom upon the shingly shore it sent a crash through the air, like the last good-bye of the buried dead who lay sleeping in their ocean tomb.

In the breakfast-room of Owen Lodge a large fire burned, and snoozing in its warm luxury were two handsome setters. A merry voice, singing some simple ditty, awoke them from their early dreamings, and a child, beautiful as a Correggio's angel, came dancing into the room: she stopped just inside the doorway, and looked around as if seeking for something she did not find there; one of the dogs approached her side, and raising his great paws to her bare shoulders licked her face and pretty white neck. She seemed accustomed to the strange embrace, for she smiled and patted his silky head as she gently pushed him from her.

"Find your master, Brutus," she said, and

stretched out her little hand in token of command.

Away across the square hall the animal bounded, and the child, singing, followed him. Up the stairs they hastened, and Brutus, arriving in front of one door in the corridor, paused and barked.

"Well, old fellow, is that you come to hunt up your master? Wait a moment, and then we shall see who ventures to disturb the pasha asleep," a voice called from the room.

"It is me, uncle—me and Brutus," a childish voice replied.

"I suppose me wants her breakfast?" the man's voice answered, and in a few seconds Collingwood came out of the room. He patted the dog's head, who in return jumped upon him, whining with joy. The lovely golden-haired fairy he lifted high in the air, then buried her face in kisses, carrying her downstairs and into the breakfast-room on his back. There he found Miss Eccles, Lilly's governess, waiting for his appearance to pour out the coffee.

"Good-morning, Miss Eccles; you see I am spoiling your pupil as usual."

"Indeed, Mr. Collingwood, I think Lilly will soon be ruined altogether," returned Miss Eccles, but she looked with loving eyes upon the little blue-robed figure. Collingwood took up his letters with a word of apology; the last one seemed to please him, for he read it aloud:

"DEAR COLL,
"The mother bids me command your appearance here for the important morning of Christmas, and begs you to bring all your household gods with you. No refusal will be accepted. There is a trousseau awaiting Miss Lilly's daughter."

"Oh, me must go!" called out Lilly, while her tiny arms stole round Collingwood's neck.

"You little coax, you only want Miss Dolly's trousseau," kissing her rosy lips he replied. Then turning to Miss Eccles, continued: "What is your opinion about our leaving home for Christmas, Miss Eccles? Is it to be the Hall, or not the Hall?"

"I think we would all prefer the journey, Mr. Collingwood," she answered; and looking through the window, something she saw made her smile.

Lilly saw the something too, and jumping down from Collingwood's knee, ran to the window, exclaiming:

"Oh! there is my Doctor! I must run and let him in."

"Stop, Lilly! you don't go near the door this morning."

Lilly arrested her steps in a moment, obedience being the one virtue exacted from her by her indulgent uncle.

Presently Dr. Longford walked into the room, and received a hearty welcome from all its inmates.

"Well! what brings you up so early, Longford? No bad news about my tenants, I hope," remarked Collingwood.

"No, no bad news, decidedly; but a letter I received this morning from Thornton asking me to go down there for Christmas. He mentions your going, so I came up to see what arrangements we could make to travel down together."

"And how about your patients, Doctor? I cannot afford to lose all my labourers."

"I have a friend staying with me who will hunt them up in turn, and dose the old women to perfection; but to the point, do you decide to go or not?"

"Of course we shall go, and have a very jolly time of it; meet us at the station in the morning, and we can catch the down express. And now refresh yourself with some coffee," saying which Collingwood pushed a cup of the steaming beverage to his guest, and rising from his seat took one nearer the fire, making himself comfortable, as he termed it, by puffing away at a very yellow-looking meerschaum.

Lilly flitted about the room, sometimes pressing her pretty head between Collingwood's arms, at others romping with Brutus in and out of the chairs or round the deserted breakfast-table.

After watching her some time, Collingwood called her to his side, saying:

"Lilly, come and show the Doctor your last new trick."

"Now, Collingwood, you know I object to your making the child such a tom-boy; pray do not ask her to perform tricks for my benefit."

But Lilly did not heed the Doctor's words; for she quietly put up her feet one after the other for Collingwood to remove her boots, then, when he had done so, waited until he knelt down; then, with a light spring, she perched herself on his back, and from there to his shoulders; and then, with a gay laugh, alighted upon his head, balancing herself by her outstretched arms.

"Now, Doctor, see how tall I am," she cried, and looked down upon him.

"Come down this moment, child; you will certainly be killed some of these days."

"Now, Lilly!" was all the reply Longford received, whilst he watched anxiously the little girl spring from her high resting-place, and fall somewhat heavily into Collingwood's outspread arms.

"Well, you have a strange way of showing your affection for your little ward, Collingwood, although I must do you the justice to say she seems to appreciate it."

"I want her to grow up a brave, true woman,

able to fight her own battles and know her own mind."

"I thought you did not admire strong-minded females."

"Neither do I; but a pretty woman without a will brings trouble to every heart that loves her."

"Are you speaking from experience?"

"Hardly; I know no pretty women."

"By-the-bye, talking of pretty women, have you seen the girl Thornton is engaged to? She has a sweet little face!"

"You forget I was in Switzerland with them," answered Collingwood, and, catching Lilly, changed the subject of their conversation by saying:

"Tell Doctor Longford how much you love me, Lilly."

"Me love uncle more than all Miss Dollies!"

Both her listeners laughed, and Longford, rising to bid them adieu, remarked:

"And when you become too big to care for Miss Dollies, how much will you love him then?"

Lilly looked confounded; but concluding in her own mind that she would never cease to love Miss Dollies, she answered gravely:

"Uncle will never let me get so big."

"He is a very convenient uncle, small maiden, and a very strange one if he manages to keep you from never loving anything better than Miss

Dollies;" then, with a few low words to Miss Eccles, Doctor Longford took his departure.

An hour or two afterwards, Collingwood was settled in his study, busy looking over his accounts. A gentle tap at the window called his attention from the long columns, and seeing Lilly with her nose pressed against the pane and her eyes gazing steadily in, he rose and, opening the window, let her enter.

"Well, Lilly, what do you want? You see I am busy, and cannot do with you here just now."

"But me will be so good, uncle," she answered wistfully, and followed him meekly to his chair.

"You will have to sit very still for an hour, if you want to stay; do you think you can manage that?"

"Yes, yes," she promised, and pulled her own small chair near his. When ready to begin her task of silence, Collingwood drew her towards him, saying:

"My pretty floweret, you will be somebody's darling some day."

She looked up at him in wonder—the sad earnestness of his voice was new to her.

"Is me naughty, uncle?" she questioned. Her violet eyes brimmed over with tears.

"No, no, my pet! But come, take off this coat of yours, and read this pretty tale; and, remember, no talking for an hour."

He opened her "Grim's" ever-beloved pages, and then, seeing she was comfortable and happy, re-commenced his writing.

The minutes ticked their brief lives out, and the noisy sparrows outside were fighting over their crumbs. Lilly watched them enviously; the letters in her book seemed getting bigger and bigger, and fairies and frogs were becoming hopelessly jumbled together, when at last Collingwood called her. In a moment she had scrambled on his knee, and nestled her head in his arms. He let her remain there; his thoughts wandering back to many years ago, when he had loved more dearly another little maiden with soft brown eyes and waving curls, how when next he had seen her, she had changed into a slight graceful girl, with only her deep dark eyes and waving curls to remind him of his baby-love of years ago. Then came that brief, bright holiday in Switzerland; how with all his manhood's strength he had learned to love Florence as he had never loved before. His face lit up with pleasure as he remembered the many tokens of affection he had won from his coy lady-love. He longed more impatiently than ever to see her once again, to hear from her own lips if indeed she had promised to become another's bride.

He would not steal her from his boyhood's friend he vowed, he could never be capable of such vile treachery; but he must have just one soft word, just one first-last love kiss, then he would bury her with his dead, and only think of her as one who had gone.

His little Lilly should have all his care and affection. Some atonement it might make for her young father's checked life, his own dear mother's sad history. He cursed that cruel sister who by her deceit had caused that mother all her pain. He wondered what had been the after-life of that twin sister, or if children had blessed a union so unhappily begun. He would give much to know her history; if she had suffered as his mother had suffered; if her children had been separated, as he and his brother had been; if poverty had ever knocked at her door, or hunger ever gnawed at her heart? Would he ever hear all these questions answered, or must he leave his revenge to a mightier hand to fulfil?

"Uncle, I hear the luncheon bell," said a small voice; and Collingwood started, for he was living in the past, and had quite forgotten Miss Lilly and the present.

"No, wee-wee, I never heard any bell; but I dare say you are hungry, so we will see what good things are waiting for us in the dining-room."

And he took the little hand held out to him, and walked dreamily out of the room.

CHAPTER III.

"WELL! and are you all here? Let me count you as a hen does her chickens," exclaimed Leonard, as he helped his friends, one by one, out of the railway carriage.

"I think Longford and I are rather formidable-looking chickens, Leonard," remonstrated Collingwood whilst busy dragging out his numerous rugs and wraps.

"Miss Lilly I suppose you have left behind, for I do not see the young lady," again spoke Leonard.

"No; me is here," the small maiden answered for herself, appearing from beneath a large fox rug.

"Come out 'me' then," laughed Collingwood, at the same time burying her again in her hiding-place, and carrying her in the bundle out of the station.

A closed carriage and drag awaited the party outside, and approaching the former, Collingwood was surprised by Florence stepping out of it to greet him.

Having his hands full, he could not take her offered one, and as each glanced into the other's face, both remembered the first time they had met there.

"You see I must pay you back for your refusal of my token of friendship when you first came to meet me here," he said, opening his arms and letting Lilly tumble as best she could out of the rug.

"My little fairy again!" Florence said as she stooped to kiss the lovely child, and laughed heartily at the little woman's composure. "Do you often pack her up in such parcels, Mr. Collingwood?"

"You see she knows how to get out with grace, so she must be used to the business."

Leonard bustling up interrupted their dialogue; and after presenting Miss Eccles and Florence to each other, he settled them in the carriage, and ordered Thomas to drive home.

The Hall was bright with fire and lamp-light as the party drove up; holly and mistletoe decked the wide square hall and hung in long festoons from arch to arch of its grey pillars. Lilly clapped her hands in wild delight at the pretty scene, and danced about in high glee.

"Me love the berries," she explained, when asked by Florence the reason of her joy.

Mr. and Mrs. Thornton were quite in raptures

over the tiny maiden, and still more so when from under her cloak she brought two broken toys, and with perfect gravity presented one to each, saying: "Me brought you these for a Christmas box."

Leonard at this caught her in his arms, and carrying her under the mistletoe, kissed her many times; then, putting her down, asked her to return his embrace.

"Me will kiss you because you is pretty," she said, and waited until he knelt down and placed his face on a level with her own; then she stretched out her arms and clasped them round his neck, whispering in his ear: "You is pretty, like mine dolls."

A chorus of merriment greeted her words; then all separated to dress for dinner.

The gentlemen remained long over their wine; on their entrance into the drawing-room Collingwood was surprised to observe Florence was not there. Taking a seat by Mrs. Thornton's side, he consoled himself chatting to her about their summer trip. Dr. Longford found a corner near Miss Eccles, and, judging from their faces, their conversation was deeply interesting to both. Leonard amused himself with Lilly, showing her various picture-books and other treasures he had hunted up for her benefit from amongst the relics of Florence's babyhood.

Presently they were all startled by the sound of

voices singing outside. Leonard went to the window, and opened it wide. Through the frost-bound air the words of the "Adeste fideles" echoed, that sweet, glad welcome to a suffering child-God: they heard every accent in the hushed night air, and the full tones of the human voices seemed mingled with others, whose cadences were not of earth.

"Well, mater, I bet my hat that was Hurst's voice," remarked Leonard when the voices ceased and the hymn was ended.

"What Hurst do you mean, Leonard? I never heard you mention a friend of that name before," Collingwood questioned.

"Yes, we met the fellow at Coire, and a very jolly parti too; by-the-bye, he is the image of you, Owen; we nick-named him your double."

"Thanks for the compliment."

"By Jove! it is a compliment, for he is a handsome fellow; I only wish I could make myself his double," saying which Leonard jumped through the window, and followed the retreating figures of the singers down the avenue.

"Hurst, I know it is you, so come and wash your face clean, and let us see how many pounds of soot you have managed to paste on it," he exclaimed, clapping a tall individual on the back. "The mater says I am to take you all prisoners, so please turn to the right-about and march."

These words were greeted with a laugh by all except the one to whom they were addressed.

"You shall escort the ladies, Thornton, but I must beg you to excuse me this evening as I have a particular engagement to fulfil."

"Oh! Mr. Hurst! you promised to try that duet with me; how mean of you to leave us now," remarked Maude Reede. Then turning to Leonard, she continued: "Just imagine, we have been singing in the village, and not one of the bright inhabitants recognised us."

"I am not surprised at that, Miss Reede, for I fancied you were Macbeth's witches taking their midnight rounds rather earlier; if you ask the mater, she will tell you how whitish I became round the fangs when I saw you. I assure you I felt a sort of feeling, all-over-all-under kind, generally gained by reading ghost-stories before tumbling into Murphy's arms."

"Leo, what tales you do tell," interrupted Florence; and then they retraced their steps to the house.

In the brilliantly-lighted hall they certainly looked a very deplorable trio; long black dresses, tattered shawls, peaked bonnets, which covered their hair and half-hid their faces, made them appear not unlike the witches to whom Leonard had compared them.

"And where is my wonderful portrait?" Collingwood demanded from his post under the swinging lamp, round which a bough of mistletoe was twined.

"Hurst declared he had an engagement, and refused to come up at present; mind you give it to him, mater, when next you catch hold of the animal, for I meant him to help me to win some gloves."

"Perhaps I might help you in that office, Thornton," suggested young Reede, a tall youth with an eye-glass, who thought himself a man before his jacket-term was ended.

"I am afraid the gloves you would help in winning might be a little tight, Reede," answered Leonard, not well pleased with the youngster's impertinence.

Reede, who did not see the joke, looked sulky, and consoled himself by dislodging from his pocket an immense cigar, which, after several vain efforts, he succeeded in lighting, and fumed himself away to the billiard-room.

A little later in the evening Florence had occasion to pass through the hall on some message Mrs. Thornton had sent her. She had almost reached the centre, where the mistletoe hung, when she felt herself lifted in some one's arms, carried under the inviting bough, kissed upon her cheeks, lips, eyes. Angry, mortified, vexed, she endeavoured to extract herself from the unwelcome embrace.

"I think I have won my gloves fairly," said a voice whose tones she had learned to love.

Over her cheeks and neck the crimson blood rushed, but the anger had died out of her eyes as she raised them to Collingwood's face.

"You have taken an unfair advantage of me, Mr. Collingwood."

"Why unfair, Florence? I think, on the contrary, I have been most patient, considering I have been standing behind that pillar for the last hour in hopes of seeing you."

"You will let me go now," she pleaded, for he still held her hands.

"Why should I let you go? I have waited for you so long," and his eyes spoke of another waiting, longer than the hour behind the pillar.

"I am in a hurry," she said, unable to meet the passionate love-glance he fixed upon her face.

"Answer me one question then—"

"And that is?" she interrupted.

"Are you engaged to Leonard, or not?"

She tried to draw away her hands to hide her poor flushed face, but he held her in an iron grasp until the pressure hurt her.

"You have no right to ask me such a question," she urged, driven to bay.

"I have a right, Florence. The right of a man who loves you with all his strength, who has hungered for the sight of you all these months with the hunger men feel when adrift on a plank on the ocean, no vessel in sight, no food at hand; with a longing, child, you, in your weakness, cannot understand. Without you all the world is a hell! with you—near you—it is paradise! Tell me now, have I no right to ask you such a question?"

Florence remained silent, his strong love frightened her, and yet drew her near him. Like the strength of the oak makes the ivy cling round him, so the fierce passionate love of the firm strong man drew the girl's heart from her and made her cling to him with all her sex's weakness.

"Do you love Leonard?" he asked, and bent his head until his lips almost touched her hair.

"Oh! let me go," she cried, fearful of revealing her own secret.

"Do you love any one," persisted he, unheeding her efforts to get free.

"Do you love me, my darling?" once more he questioned, his voice low and mellow with hushed hoped-for joy.

With one quick effort she freed her hands and sprang from his side, away through the grey tall pillars. He followed her more slowly, and laughed softly to himself as he watched her enter the library and heard her lock the door behind her.

"Does she think bolts or bars could hide her when I seek?" he muttered.

Arriving at the door he knocked and asked gently:

"Let me in."

No answer was given, then he knocked again, still the silence in the room remained unbroken; a third time he demanded an entrance, and said in a voice less gentle:

"If you will not let me in I shall burst open the door."

He waited a moment, then throwing his whole weight against the oaken panels, burst open the door and entered the room.

Florence was half kneeling on the rug before the fire, her head buried between her arms, which were stretched across a chair near; her slender frame shook with passionate weeping, and among the long curls of her hair the fire-flashes glimmered.

Collingwood approached her side and raised her tear-stained face from its bent attitude.

"What have I done to grieve you so? Tell me, is it I, darling, that has caused you this pain?" he questioned, wounded by her tears.

He put his arm about her neck, and raised her face until the fire-light danced upon all its sorrow shadows.

"You must tell me all your troubles, dearest; it is I who will carry all your burdens now. Do you think my love is a fair-weather feeling that cannot brave all storms of sorrow for your dear sake? Look into my eyes, darling, and promise me no secret in the past or future shall ever stand between us; only trust me, Florence, and all will be well?"

Oh for the strength to tell him of her treachery, of the request made by the voiceless dead! Must she lose his love, or stand perjured before that unseen tribunal? Half wild with joy and pain she could but weep tears whose bitterness were drying up her heart-strings.

A form stood behind the closed window, and, through the parted curtains, watched the pair standing silently in the glow of the bright fire-light. He noted the girl's tears and the man's love-bent form, and shivered as he saw the gentle caress that so vainly sought a return.

"Good God, are we all accursed? Could not his mother's sufferings save him? Must his life be wrecked as cruelly as mine has been?" he muttered between his shut teeth, and then sighed a heavy life-weary sigh, so laden with misery that the frost refused to freeze it, and passed it onwards down through the white tree branches, which, in their turn, tossed it over the dead cold heather and away to the far-off sea, where the mermaids heard it and ceased their song, and let it drift and drift until a warm island caught it, and there its ice-breath melted and a woman's heart pitied it, and amongst the golden orange boughs it found a home of rest. And the pair stood silent, and the Christmas night strode on!

Suddenly the sound of footsteps entering the room startled them. Glancing towards the door Florence saw Mr. Hurst approach them with a candle in his hand.

He walked straight to where Collingwood stood, with the light falling full upon his face, revealing its strange resemblance to the one it accosted.

Collingwood started, and Florence heard the mad beatings of his heart; his voice was strangely altered as he questioned:

"Who are you who thus trespasses upon our privacy?"

"Have you no idea who I am, Owen Collingwood? My name must bring sad remembrances to you."

"Tell me, pray, who are you?" impatiently demanded Collingwood; and he drew his giant form up to its full height.

"My name is Owen Hurst; my mother was your mother's twin sister. Hush!" he said, seeing Collingwood was about to interrupt him; "Hush! I have come to ask forgiveness for a mother's weakness and a father's folly; will you grant it, Owen Collingwood?"

"You *her* son, then?—the woman whom I curse every day of my lifetime; she who brought my mother all her sorrow; sent her out into the world homeless and penniless; caused a brother to die by a stray shot for a stranger country's glory. You are her son?—that base, deceitful woman who embittered all our lives! Do you think me a fool that you dare come and ask my forgiveness? Ah! I will have my revenge now."

"Hush! hush! Collingwood, you speak like a madman.

"I am mad at this moment, Hurst; for I could kill you where you stand."

"My life is of no value to me, Owen; you can take it if you will. Remember, that act will not bring your mother back to you, or give you another brother."

Florence, in her terror, dare not speak, but looked with admiration on the cold proud face of Hurst. Fear was certainly not a weakness pictured there.

There was a strange silence for a moment, both men seemed to have forgotten the girl's presence.

"Owen," she said at length, her courage returning, "Owen, will you forgive the past for my sake? You say you love me."

She put her hands about his arm, and looked up pleadingly into his face. The strong frame shook, the proud face whitened as with the whiteness of death, and the voice that answered was hoarse and thick as of one who was conquering a death-agony.

"For your sake, Florence, I would face almost hell! but, child, you do not know what wrongs you ask me to forgive; think of my mother sent adrift on the world, her death-hour so lonely without a child to hold her head; think of my father's pride all crushed in the dust, of his silent anguish when he found out his terrible mistake, of the long years spent in seeking that wife whom he never found, of her grave in a far-off land unknown, uncared for. Oh! my darling, do not ask me to forgive these wrongs."

Before he had finished speaking, the chimes of the Christmas night sounded; they rose and fell in joyous happy cadences, telling of a redemption won for man that night.

Could hatred or revenge live through those moments, when even the earth was white at the remembrance of a man-God's love?

It was Hurst who broke the silence:

"Collingwood, you talk of revenge; God has struck me a blow your hand would have been powerless to deal. Have patience with me for a few moments, for I must tell you what a sad-paged history my manhood's life has been. You will have no cause then to bemoan your young brother's death, for to me death would be but happiness. I once saved a man from an untimely end, perhaps the only good deed I have blest my years with. We nursed and tended him, my mother and I; and in return he loved us. He resided in Cuba, and when well again returned to his native home; soon he married, and I, his dearest friend, went to visit him, to become acquainted with his young bride. Whilst I was with them the rebellion broke out, and never shall I forget the few last hours I spent in that unhappy island—men became as brutes, and chased their fellow-creatures with hungry hounds. In the midst of the fray Gascogne came to me leading his young wife by the hand; his face had grown old in that short time, and despair was written upon its every feature.

"'Take her and save her, Hurst; it is the last favour I shall ever ask you. If I live, in six months' time I will come and claim her; and if those brutes cut me down, you will cherish her for my sake.'

"Then taking the weeping girl in his arms he kissed her, and bade her save herself for his sake; then turning, left us. In the bright moonlight we hastened out, creeping in the shadows and tearing our hands with the cruel cactus leaves, or trembling through the long straight grass where the snakes lay sleeping.

"On and on we wandered, bent upon reaching the shore before the daylight greeted us. The hours flew by, and I saw my companion's strength was forsaking her. I watched her as she gasped for breath and pressed her hand upon her heart to still its weary beating. At length she sank down, utterly exhausted.

"'Leave me here, and save yourself; it is not right that we should kill you.'

"Through the night air I heard the fierce growl of the bloodhounds as they tracked our footsteps. This was no time for argument, so without a word I raised her in my arms and hurried onwards.

"The dim dawn-light illuminated the sky before we sighted the shore. The sweat of a great agony stood upon my brow, my eyes were heavy with the constant strain to catch a glimpse of the distant ocean. I stumbled at every step.

"Nearer came the footsteps of our voiceless pursuers. I seemed to feel the fumes of their hot breath. With one last effort I pulled my strength together and ran for very life.

"The shore was reached, and on the crested waves a pleasure-boat was tossing. Waist-deep I dashed into the water, placed my senseless burden hastily in the little vessel, jumped in myself, cut the rope that bound us to land, and the strong current drifted us quickly out to sea.

"The hounds, with their blood-red fangs, lay exhausted on the beach; shots came pouring from the thick foliage of the trees, and broke the surface of the water around us. One struck my arm, and stunned me for a moment with the agonizing pain.

"Farther and farther we drifted, until the island was but a speck upon our horizon, and our world was bounded by vast ocean billows.

"The day wore on; the rays of the noon sun

scorched our uncovered heads. I tried to shield as best I could the girl's upturned face from its hot breath; her little hands lay all blistered, crossed upon her breast.

"Many times I thought her dead; but a low groan or a gasp for breath assured me that not yet had the great reaper mowed her down. I prayed wildly for help in our distress; but no sign of sail or funnel answered my appeal.

"The hours passed, a deadly sickness came over me. The ocean looked one vast mass of burning waters. Every nerve in my body quivered with pain; every muscle was strained to its utmost. Hopelessly I sculled on with the one oar the boat contained.

"The great heaving billows mocked my parched throat by their blue cool depths, and I longed madly to bury myself in their lofty tombs.

"The sun was setting. I watched the sky crimson and the day-god sink to rest; then a dagger seemed to pierce my brain, and with a wild cry, I fell I knew not where!

"When I came back to consciousness, the scene was strangely altered. I was lying in a berth—a young doctor binding up my injured arm, and a pale, dark-eyed girl standing by his side.

"Need I say more than we were saved? Gascogne's wife was warmly welcomed by my parents, and her sad history won her the love of many hearts.

"The months passed by, and still no husband came to claim the pale young bride. One year sang itself to death among the golden orange boughs; another followed close upon its heels, and when a third had aged the world with its changeful seasons, Gascogne's widow had at last become my wife."

He paused a moment in his narrative, and his voice had a pleading accent in it as he continued:

"Collingwood, I loved her with all my soul! Heaven and earth were nothing to me; she was my all—my idol—and God punished me for my sin.

"The time flew by, and the happiness of Paradise seemed mine—to sit and watch my beloved in her dawning womanliness, to hear her sweet voice whisper words for which my heart had so long hungered; to feel her little hands clasped about my neck, her blushing dark face pressed against my bosom. Oh! good God! how blissful were those hours!

"Just when my cup of happiness was full to the brim, a hand came up and snatched it from my lips.

"Gascogne came to claim his wife and my new-made bride!

"We looked into each other's faces and each

wished the other dead; then Gascogne, turning to me, said:

"'It seems but base ingratitude to take her from you now. Owen, forgive me the sorrow I bring you this night.'

"The brave true words shamed me. I thought of the long years of suffering he must have endured, with only the hope of claiming again his bride to comfort him, and surely I, who had saved them both from death, would not part them eternally?

"The unhappy girl stood between us, with her face buried in her hands. I put my arms about her and kissed her once—her tears lay wet upon my cheek—then I looked deep, deep into her sweet eyes, then turned away and sped swiftly through the bright clear moonlight. All the earth was dark to me just then."

He ceased speaking, and a great silence fell. The Christmas chimes sounded their last warning, and the morn of Christ's day had dawned upon the earth.

Florence's memory went back to Hurst's tale in the scented Garden of Roses. She had never guessed that he was the hero of that sadly-ended drama, his the vessel wrecked upon the shore of joy.

"My brother is revenged!" at length spoke Collingwood, his eyes fixed upon his cousin's face.

"And your mother?" asked Hurst, in his sad mellow tones.

"You must give me time to think—"

"Owen, you have promised me the past should be forgotten," interrupted Florence, leaning her head against his arm.

Merry voices, joyous laughter echoed through the hall, and in a few seconds the Misses Reede, their brother, and Leonard entered the library.

"Well! you are nice people to go and hide yourselves on Christmas-eve; and you, Hurst, declaring you had a particular engagement, and then turning up after midnight! The mater says we are all to march straight off to bed, having a hard prayer-day in prospect. Ah! by-the-bye, Collingwood, you see your double at last. What do you think of him? I suppose Florence has introduced you by this time, for you all seem as if you had had some secret meeting here."

"Mr. Hurst, I find, is my cousin, Leonard, so you see family ties have drawn us together quickly."

"By Jove! Your cousin? I never knew you possessed such an article—however, I wish you joy of him;" then approaching Florence's side, Leonard continued in an undertone: "What makes you look so pale? How is it you have been so long here with Collingwood?"

"I am tired, Leonard, so will follow your advice and say good-night without delay," she answered, not willing to take any notice of his last question.

It was Collingwood who lit her candle, and as he placed it in her hand their eyes met.

"You will forgive the past?" she murmured.

"For your dear sake," he replied, and noticed the diamonds flash in her *porte-bonheur*, as she stretched out her hand to be clasped in his.

Once in her own bedchamber, Florence seemed to have forgotten her desire of retiring to rest; pulling a low chair to the fireside, she seated herself in it, and, with her eyes fixed upon the glowing embers, began to think.

How could she face Leonard, and tell him of her treachery? She had never loved him, that he knew, but of her own free will she had let him consider her willing to become his bride. Her dying mother's request—dare she unheed it?

She covered her face with her pretty white hands, not even the fire eyes must see the sorrow written there.

CHAPTER IV.

THE air was breathlessly still. Above in the blue dome of the angels' gallery, the pale queen moon was seated on her nightly throne; one or two planets glimmered weakly, as if ashamed of their less brilliant light. The tall stately chestnuts cast long shadows upon the white-frosted ground; the robins, with heads nestled under their wings, huddled together amongst the ivy-leaves, now and then a little death-cry of one, as he fell frozen from his perch, saddening the hearts of his red-coated brethren.

The Christmas chimes had long since ceased, and far away in the vast cities the organ pealed out the joyous Hallelujah Chorus; a thousand voices re-echoed the glad strain, and the Gothic pillars of Nôtre Dame shook and quivered in sympathy with that strong human joy. Candles and flowers decked the gorgeous altar, and Mary, a virgin and a mother that night, raised her eyes with a more pleading look to the throne of her Saviour Son. Other churches were teeming with the happy praise-hymn, other altars luminous and bright flashed into faces lit up with earnest prayer. Here the aged, the poor, the sad, the sorrowful; there, the young, the gay, the rich, the happy—all sending up that night petitions to their Babe-God.

And the breath of the great family prayer swept past the pale queen-moon, who smiled her watery smile, and shed more brilliant beams upon that white-robed earth, for she loved it, with its tall cathedral towers and joyous organ-prayer, its snow-crowned and shadowless hill-tops, its river-bends and valleys so fair.

Yes, she loved and smiled upon it all; upon the great heaving billows that tossed angrily under her glance; upon the swaying hill-tops, that were singing still their death-chant; upon the frozen lake where the shining fish lay buried; upon some happy lover, who lingered to whisper last words in her shadows; upon one tall form, who paced impatiently up and down the long avenue of Halston Hall, who recked not of her beauty, of her cold pitiless smile. Collingwood, for it was he, noted naught of the night's hushed loveliness; his heart was too full of contending passions, his mind too fixed upon its own bewildering thoughts for him to heed the faint call that Nature made him to gaze upon her face and find comfort in its beauty. In a weak moment had he not forsworn his revenge? for the love of a girl he had forgotten the wrongs of a mother. Whose the brave heart that had beat its last beat for a soldier's glory? whose the true honour that had sacrificed life to put one leaf in a nation's laurel-crown? whose the pure love that had given its all to win a last blessing from a lonely woman's lips? Was the history of two ruined lives to be washed out by tears from phantomless eyes? No! no! he would sacrifice his love but have his revenge; that voiceless past should not haunt him with its black-lettered page; he would efface those cruel words with his own heart-blood, or Hurst should be the one to give an account of his stewardship.

The moon hid her face behind a sombre-bosomed cloud, and Collingwood, hating the darkness, entered the house.

He paused in the hall a moment to procure a light to guide him to his room.

A sound, a rustle, the softest, lightest footfall arrested his attention; he listened—again it came, pitter patter, down the oaken stairs, so light, so ariel, that it seemed like the fall of one stray snow-flake.

Nearer and nearer it crept and paused close to where he stood.

The moon peeped out from behind her veil, and shed a long stream of light athwart the grey pillars and across the stone floor.

In the pale glory a girl stood.

Long curls swept over her shoulders, and the thin cashmere of her dressing-gown clung closely to her figure.

Collingwood started and caught his breath. It was Florence bathed in that moonlight glory— Florence, who with clasped hands and head uplifted, invited the gaze of the night's fair queen upon her sweet face.

Collingwood thought she was dead, and this her ghost come to upbraid him for placing aught between her love and him; then her low voice breaking the silence reassured him; and again he scarcely breathed for fear of waking her.

"I will promise you, Leonard, but it will break my heart. Ask me anything but that."

Then she turned a little, as if influenced by his presence, and continued:

"Yes; I love Owen Collingwood!"

The look that swept across her face, the flush that crept into the marble whiteness of her cheeks, broke down the barriers of Collingwood's self-restraint. He forgot the danger of awakening her from this her strange life-sleep; forgot the stain he might place upon her name; forgot the past, present, or future; and with one passionate love-word, clasped her to his breast, kissing her lips and sightless eyes until, her limbs trembling, she awoke.

Awoke in the quivering moonbeams, encircled by the arms of the man she loved so truly. Stunned, bewildered, she uttered not a word, but raised her eyes wonderingly to his face.

Collingwood felt the uncertain beatings of her heart, felt her whole frame shiver as if with some deadly chill; then her head dropped like a bird's shot on the wing, and he guessed she had fainted.

He cursed himself for his mad folly in having awakened her, and lifting her in his arms, he carried her to her room.

Having placed her gently amongst the soft pillows, he aroused Lallah, who always occupied the room adjoining her young mistress's.

The old woman listened to his tale, then shook her head, saying:

"Thee will bring sorrow to my babe," and shut the door angrily in his face.

For more than an hour Collingwood kept his self-imposed door-watch; at the end of that time he knocked softly, and on Lallah's turban-bound head appearing, inquired news of Florence.

"You'll be off to your bed, if you please, and not be disturbing people; the maid's better," she replied, then quickly shut the door.

With weary steps he traversed the long corridor, and entered his own room. How could he sleep or rest with the past misery and present love fighting their deadly battle in his heart?

The early Christmas chimes aroused him from his troubled reveries. Refreshing himself with his usual cold shower, he descended to the breakfast-room, where he was somewhat surprised to find Florence already seated.

Glad greetings poured upon him from every side, and Lilly insisted upon his attention being given to the various wonders she had discovered in her stocking.

As soon as the meal was over there was a general move to prepare for church, and Collingwood failed to find an opportunity of speaking to Florence about the night's strange adventures. He noticed she was paler than her wont, and dark circles shadowed her deep eyes. He loved her better thus than when the flush of health dyed her cheeks, and the flash of happiness danced in the depths of her brilliant eyes.

When hastening to join the rest of the party ready to start for church, Collingwood was accosted by Lallah.

"You will please follow me in here for a moment, for I must speak with you."

Following her into a small work-room near, Collingwood impatiently awaited her tidings.

"You'll not mention about the accident of last night to my babe, for I have persuaded her that all was a bad dream; and if you upset her with your tales, look out for the consequences."

"Then does Florence often walk in her sleep?" he questioned.

"And what does it matter to you if she does? Is it your business, I wonder?"

"It is my business if I choose to make it so, Lallah; and you will be good enough to answer my question."

The old nurse turned upon him like a tigress upon one who attacks her young.

"Yes, you have made it your business to come and steal the peace and happiness of my wee white dove! to break her heart, and ruin her beauty with the tears you make her shed! Before she met thee at that out-of-the-way hole in the summer-time she was as bright and happy a little lady as one would wish to see; but now there is nothing in her face but them big eyes, that pierce one's very heart with the pain that is in them; and it's you that have done this business."

Covering her head with her apron, Lallah wept, swaying herself backwards and forwards.

"Lallah, you do me a great injustice—"

But Lallah interrupted him passionately:

"Injustice indeed! Them that's not just to other people cannot expect justice for themselves. And how about our young master, Leonard?"

"Lallah, Lallah!" a sweet voice called in the corridor; and Lallah, fearing to be caught in the midst of her grumblings, hastened out of the room.

Collingwood was not well pleased with the old nurse's speech, and lit a cigar to strengthen his nerves after it. Descending to the hall, he found the rest of the party awaiting his appearance to accompany them to church. Being monopolised by one of the Misses Reede, he was forced to offer himself as her escort.

Later on in the day, whilst endeavouring to kill time by looking over the stables with Thomas, Collingwood was again forced to listen to a somewhat unpleasant truth. He was expressing his admiration of a young filly that Thomas was training for Florence when the latter said:

"And sure Miss Florence ain't looking herself this many days back."

"No, she is changed from the little lady you brought to meet me nearly eight years ago, Thomas."

"It ain't the years that have changed her so much, master, for she's but a young thing yet; but you see them dainty things have 'arts, as my old woman says, and if Miss Florence's hain't gone astray, my name's not Thomas Patter," saying which Thomas posted himself opposite Collingwood, and looked him down with his cunning small eyes.

"But all young ladies lose their hearts sometime, Thomas. You do not expect to keep Miss Florence here always, do you?"

"And why should we not keep her here, sir? Ye don't know perhaps that her and the young master is to be made one some fine day?"

"I certainly did not know that they were engaged."

"Sure and I don't know the meaning of that there word 'engaged,' but I do know they were made express for one another; and it would be a sin to part um."

There was a moment's pause after Thomas's speech; then he took up his argument again, saying:

"And sure I knew Miss Florence's mother before she went to that there India; and she and Mrs. Thornton they were a deal fond of one another, just like two sisters."

"Well, Thomas, I hope I shall see you at the wedding," was all the reply Collingwood made, and with a passing remark about the filly, quitted the stable.

Thomas, left to himself, made his meditations aloud.

"But 'tis a thousand pities such a fine young gent as that should go hankering after another chap's bride. But them rich folks do strange things sometimes; and he looks like one of the clean-limbed ones that win of a sure in the race. Oh, my old woman, sure she is a wise one; for ever since Miss Florry came home she has been a-saying as her 'art's left behind. Well, well! them are fools who bother their brains about women. To my fancy, they are much of a muchness—one as good as another any day."

Then he marched himself off home, where he found his old woman enjoying her forty winks, whilst awaiting his arrival for tea; pussy, too, was on the hearth, and following her mistress's example.

Collingwood, as he walked briskly to the house, did not feel in the most amiable mood; even his well-loved meerschaum, smoked every shade of yellow from the bright amber to the dusky brown tint, failed to soothe him. Having settled himself comfortably in the library, with Rollo for a companion, he puffed away for an hour or more.

"All is fair in love and war," he argued, not feeling satisfied with himself for running the gauntlet against his old college friend. He loved Florence with all the passionate force of his nature, and the very difficulty he found in gaining her rendered her doubly dear—the way with all men.

Then his thoughts wandered to Hurst's story, and his even white teeth bit hard the amber pressed between them, and some words (not a blessing) were muttered in his throat.

He was certainly not a pleasant companion Rollo thought, as he received several discomforting kicks which disturbed his agreeable dreams.

The early winter twilight set in, and in the corners of the room strange shadows flitted; but Collingwood did not heed them; what were shadows to a man who had such painful realities to deal with? And yet how true are the words, "Coming events cast their shadows before;" if he had heeded the shadow of months ago, that love-shadow that was tarnishing his shield of honour and casting a dark stain upon its surface, that no sunlight in the future could ever brighten—ah! if he had heeded that shadow, what might have been?

If we all would but heed the harmless shadows, how different would our lives be; when the time for battle comes what one amongst us does not remember the shadow of the enemy afar? but we trust to our arms and raise our shining shields to the dazzling sunlight, and laugh our reckless laughter to think that the smoke of any enemy could ever tarnish the brilliancy of that polished steel. And yet the enemy unperceived draws nigh; without warning he attacks us, and we, unprepared, drop our shields in the dust, and never, never more can their brightness be regained.

And thus it was with Collingwood, he had seen the shadows and recked not of them; had watched the enemy from afar, and laughed as he tested the strength of his shield. What enemy powerful enough to put one dint into *it?* what arm strong enough to cast *it* in the dust? Blind in his proud confidence, he had slept when he should have been watching, and the enemy came and found his arm powerless, and before the love-bandage had dropped from his eyes, his shield was tarnished and his honour lost.

And the Christmas twilight gathered in; the darkness crept around him, and he saw in the fire-glow that skeleton shield, and bowing down his head, he gave up the ghost of that honour once so real, and deafening himself to the low whispers of his better angel, he vowed he would sacrifice all—all! to win for his bride a girl with a sweet pale face and matchless eyes.

And a great black spot was dropped upon his life-book, and a sigh swept among the choirs of the silver-winged hosts, for they knew that one soul the more had forfeited his birthright to a golden-seated throne; one song the less was printed in brilliant letters upon their celestial programmes.

CHAPTER V.

"And what is my little woman doing here?" inquired Leonard, as he came upon Lilly dancing with Miss Dolly round the grey pillars in the hall.

"Me is learning mine steps," she replied, continuing her exercise.

"And pray why is me learning mine steps?"

That question brought her to a standstill, and required Miss Dolly to be well shaken before a reply could be discovered.

"Me is going to the ball to-morrow."

"And if me is going to the ball nobody will ask me to dance," retorted Leonard.

"You must," the child replied, running up to him and raising her face to be kissed.

"I! why I could never dream of dancing with such a tow-stick," he answered, pulling her hair.

"You don't like mine curls?"

"Not at all. I think mine curls very ugly, and would cut them off if I were Lilly; but does *me* like mine curls?"

Lilly remained silent for a moment, her great

violet eyes fixed steadily upon Leonard's face, at last she answered with a considerable amount of determination in her baby-voice :

"Yes, me thinks mine curls very pretty."

Leonard laughed at this, and told her she was a conceited little puss; then swung her round the misletoe and left her.

When he disappeared out of sight the small maiden began talking very seriously to Miss Dolly.

"He does not like mine curls, Dolly—me cut them off," and she walked gravely up to the nursery where Madame Lucas was busy preparing a dress all silver and blue for her darling's use the following evening.

"C'est joli, ne c'est pas?" she questioned, her French heart in raptures over the tiny Parisian toilette.

"Oui, c'est joli," answered Lilly, looking at it with a critical eye, and wondering if it would fit Miss Dolly. She had no vanity in her, the pretty fairy Lilian; accustomed to flattery from every side, she had grown weary of the comments upon her wondrous beauty, and had ceased to heed them, and often drove Madame Lucas to the bridge of despair by her utter disregard of all dainty toilettes.

Florence, entering the room, was surprised to find Lilly so quiet, and asked her if she would like to come and help in decorating the ball-room, which everybody was busy preparing for the morrow. Lilly assented with delight, and after placing Miss Dolly in her tiny bed, she trotted after Florence downstairs.

The two drawing-rooms had been thrown into one, and formed a very handsome apartment; long garlands of holly and mistletoe, mixed with rare flowers, hung from window to window; coloured lamps were hid amongst the green in the winter garden beyond; a scented fountain sang its weak ditty in the centre of tall fern-heads, and an inviting bench was hidden behind the tiny spray.

Leonard, Collingwood, and the Misses Reede were busy decorating the room when Florence and Lilly entered.

What made Collingwood's wrist tremble as he heard Florence's voice? What brought that streak of dark blood across his forehead as he watched Leonard approach her side and whisper something in her ear.

Unable to bear suspicion of her for an instant, he descended his ladder and moved towards them.

"Have you come to help us, Lilly?" he questioned of the little girl, and toyed with her hair.

"Yes, we have both come to offer our services," Florence answered for her, and looked up at him; but there was no happiness in her glance.

"If you offer your services we shall all claim them, so you had better select a master."

"Must I?" she replied, and a dreamy sorrow crept into her face.

"Or perhaps you are a slave already bought?"

"With what a price!" she retorted, and dew-like tears welled up into her eyes.

He bent his head and lowered his voice until his words were only audible to the one to whom they were uttered.

"No price could be too heavy to pay for such a slave."

She shuddered and passed on. Leonard, watching her, sighed: she was so young, so frail to suffer so, and now he knew her pain; how he had learned it, he alone could tell. Ah! that hoped-for Christmas-tide, what agony it had brought him! and yet his face was as bright and his laugh as gleesome as ever. Much as he loved her, he would not give her back her liberty.

Why could she not trust him? Why become a traitress to herself and him? If only she had had the courage to avow her love and throw herself upon the generosity of a noble heart, what bitterness would she have saved herself and him from— what long years of after-regret and pain. But alas! she too had watched unheedingly the shadows, and although she had no shield to guard, yet she sat sleeping when the enemy was at hand.

The long garlands were all hung, the picture-frames all decorated, the gold and silver globe-balls glittered among the dusky leaves; and the workers declared their task was done.

"Mr. Thornton, will you come and have a game of billiards with me? I am sure Miss Eccles and Mr. Longford must have ended their battle long ago, for they have been cannoning away all afternoon," remarked Maude Reede to Leonard, who stood near.

"Of course I will, with pleasure. I dare say we shall find that lazy dog Hurst there; he is always turning up in unexpected corners."

"Take me too," pleaded Lilly.

"Come away then, small maiden, and mind I don't put you in a pocket instead of a ball, because you have a very roundish appearance."

"May I fetch Dolly?" she asked anxiously.

"Dolly! why, what for?"

"Because you know you could not put us both in your pocket," very gravely answered the child.

Leonard took her hand, and ran with her to the billiard-room, his companion following more slowly.

Florence and Collingwood were alone.

"I have brought you a little present; I want you to wear it the day after to-morrow, to please me."

She turned her face towards him, and it cut his heart to see the pain that was written there.

"Owen, Owen! do leave me—leave me for

ever. I cannot bear to have you so near me, for I dare not break my promise to Leonard. How can I be so ungrateful to them all?"

There were no secrets now between them. She had told him all; but late, too late! He had vowed to win her, and he would.

"You do not love me, Florence," he answered coldly, and walked towards the fountain's side.

She followed him, her long dress rustling among the fallen leaves, crushing many a bright-cheeked berry; yes, at every step killing something more precious than the green-tongued holly or the crimson seedling that adhered to its stem.

"You know that is not true; accuse me of anything but that. Oh, Owen! you do not know how weak I am. Owen, do trust me; let me give you a sister's love."

And she clasped her hands about his arm, and glanced pleadingly into his face.

"Child, child! can I never persuade you I must have all or nothing? Do you wish me to leave you now, and never, never in this world again to look upon your face? If you wish it tell me, and here let me bid you an eternal farewell."

He was cruel to test her so.

"Stay but a little while; do not go just yet," she pleaded, and bent her head until her lips pressed against his hand.

"Good God! Do you think I am made of iron,

that you tell me to stay and flit away my manhood's hours in base ingratitude, in foul dishonour? Be true to him or me, child; but, for both our sakes, do not trifle with us any longer. Once my bride, I will win their forgiveness for you. Yea, even if I bend upon my knees to gain it. But send me away from you, or promise to be mine. Florence, dearest, for the last time I will ask you to decide."

How could she decide?—a weak, frail girl, hardly past her childhood's years, with not the strength of a reed in her whole nature. Ask the frail lily to stand stiff in the breeze, the rose to hold together her petals through the storm, the rudderless vessel to sail straight homewards, the shot deer to elude his fierce pursuers.

Florence was silent. How could she speak?

At length Collingwood continued:

"Darling, listen to me for a few moments, and remember if my words sound cruel, it is because I dare not make them tender. I see this life is killing you, blasting the fair floweret I found so blooming on its stalk; and even I, dearest, will not be the cause of its utter decay. Nay, sooner than watch you suffer, I will bury myself in some far-off region, from whence my name shall never reach you, and pray that in your heart its letters may be effaced. For your sake I have forgiven the wrongs of all past years, those wrongs of a mother and brother, which you know. If you decide that we shall part, the past shall remain in dark oblivion; for never could I take back my word to you. My little Lilly you will cherish for my sake, and Hurst, perhaps, will remind you of one that must be numbered among your dead. For dead I shall be to all earth's joys from the hour I look my last upon your face. In time you may forget me, and live content and happy as another's wife—you women change so. Children will brighten your life-path, and their laughter be the only sound your ears will care to hearken to."

She had listened to his words with her head bent low, and her long curls just touching the hand that clasped her own. No tears dimmed her eyes as she raised them to his face; no quiver stirred her lips as they parted to answer him. His speech had borne her into womanliness, and there was no hesitation in her voice as she replied:

"Owen, I will follow you to the world's end! You have only to give the word."

"To home and happiness, my darling!" he answered, clasping her tightly in his arms, and pressing kisses upon her face.

A great, glad, triumphant smile lit up all his features. Yes, his slave was truly bought at last.

CHAPTER VI.

It was New Year's Eve; that strange, half-sad, half-joyful day that has quite a beauty and a history of its own; from the first blush of the late, dull sunrise to the death of the fiery orb in the fading moon the hours sing naught but their own requiem. Its three hundred and sixty-four brothers are dead, and alone it remains, the last lingering life-hour of the dying year.

To some the heavy breaths of that day-breathing monarch have been but one delicious gasp of joy. The snow, the frost of misery, the weary rain of trouble, or the great storms of life-wrecks, have passed them untouched by; and with unbent brows and unclouded eyes, they look fearlessly forward to the advent of the unborn king. But to others, who have felt the bitter frost of adversity, have been dashed from rock to rock by the angry billows of fate, whose eyes are sunken with weeping, whose lips are white with pain, whose hearts are rent with sorrow, these shiver as they watch the last sunset of the expiring hero, for its pale, uncertain blush reflects in their eyes that blood which has dropped in slow drops from their heart-wounds until the gap is so wide that none but a Divine hand can heal it. In the dim future lie still those shadows of past agonies, and the ghosts of buried griefs will haunt that unborn year, perhaps with even greater ghastliness than before.

Leonard, as he walked impatiently up and down the hall, and tapped angrily the face of the weather-glass, heeded not any sorrows that the new year might have in store for him.

"By Jove! I do believe King Frost means to trouble us again, hang him!"

"Well, Thornton, what chance do you think we have of sport? or do you mean to reserve all your energies for to-night?" questioned a voice behind him.

"Ah! Hurst, is that you? The scent will lie a bit, I dare say, for it thawed last night; but we must have a sharp run if we want one at all."

"Is the meet any distance from here?"

"No, only a mile or two away. Have you attended to the inner man yet?"

"Hardly! I have only just this moment put in a presentable appearance."

"Well, let us be off then, for I saw Florence wandering about a short time since."

They found Florence at her post, and Leonard

suspected she had been reading a letter, for on their entrance she hid something hastily in her dress.

"A thousand pities Coll disappeared to Ipswich yesterday, for he so thoroughly enjoys a run with the hounds, and I know none better to follow than old Sir John's pack," Leonard remarked carelessly as he seated himself at the table.

"I think Mr. Collingwood is sure to return in time for the ball; he expected he would only be detained a few hours, but I suppose something prevented him getting back last night," answered Florence, and hid her blushing face behind the urn.

"You seem to know Collingwood's movements well, Florence. Has he made you his confidante?" questioned Leonard.

Lilly entered the room and drew all attention to her. She wore a riding-habit of dark green velvet, a hat to match rested on her golden curls, and her face was sparkling with anticipated pleasure.

"Well! Miss Lilly, you mean to favour us with your company, do you?" Leonard remarked, as she approached his side.

"Yes, uncle said me might go, and Tiger is all ready, so me must," replied the little maiden, composing herself to her breakfast.

"But uncle is away, so me cannot go, for no one else will take care of me," Leonard rejoined.

"I know you will," turning her face to him, she replied.

"No, indeed I won't, Lilly; so you had better ask Hurst here; he is surely big enough to look after you."

Lilly continued eating her breakfast for a few moments in silence, then she turned to Leonard again with a move of her pretty head, indicative of childish scorn.

"You is rude; me take care of mine self."

"Mine self will come to grief then, I am sure."

Florence, from behind her screen, watched the crimson blood rush up the rounded cheeks, and the tears of anger dim the violet eyes; but Lilly controlled her feelings, and with little hesitation replied,

"Me no friends with you any more," and turning her back decidedly to Leonard, she went on with her meal.

"We'll see about that, my proud little beauty; only wait until you are in want of a friend, then you will hunt me up pretty sharp, I reckon. For the present, however, *au revoir;* for I am off to the stables." Then as he passed by Florence's side he asked in a would-be light tone, "Do I do, Florry?" claiming as a right a look of affection, although in his heart he knew that right existed no longer.

"Yes, you do do," she laughingly rejoined, mocking his ungrammatical sentence.

He bent his head and snatched a kiss from her

parted lips, then made a hasty exit from the room.

Hurst, who had watched the little scene, wondered. "Whom was she playing false?" he asked himself, as the girl's face went first pale, then scarlet, under his fixed gaze.

"You seem to be on very familiar terms with Thornton," he remarked, indifferent to the impertinence of his words.

"We have been brought up like brother and sister, Mr. Hurst," she replied, her eyes seeking anything but the cold proud face opposite to her; then turning to Lilly, who had sat silent and preoccupied, she continued, "Come, Lilly, Leonard will be waiting for you in the hall. He will take care of you, I am sure; you must not mind what he said just now."

Lilly arose from her seat and shook the crumbs from her dress, then taking Florence's extended hand, they walked out of the room together; in the hall they found Leonard all impatience to be off.

"I will take Thomas with us to Sir John's, in case Master Reynard leads us over the dykes; but if he chooses the meadows Lilly can accompany us with safety, I will keep my eye on her. And now, good-bye," he said, whilst holding Florence's hand in his own and looking wistfully into her face; he looked so handsome and so bright in his pinks that the girl's heart beat painfully at the remembrance of her treachery to him. Was she the one about to quench the laughter from those clear eyes, to crush all the happiness from out that fair frank face? Ah! the old year was dying and her young sinless life with it! What would the new year bring?

And Hurst watched her with his questioning eyes and judged her harshly; forgetting her youth and frail nature. His voice was bitter as he bade her in his turn adieu.

"You will be anxious for us *all* to get back safely, no doubt? so mind and pray for us whilst we are away."

How elastic men are where their own honour is concerned; how thick the rope that must tie a woman's!

Florence found no words with which to answer Hurst's words, but her face showed plainly the pain they gave her.

Lilly's calling her for a last kiss brought her thoughts back to time and place, and throwing a warm shawl about her shoulders, she went out into the cold morning air and gave the small amazon the wished-for embrace.

Years afterwards, when all scenes of earth were fading one by one on the panorama of her life-stage, Florence gazed once again upon the one illuminated by the pale streaks of the dying year's sunrise; and the two figures, of the golden-haired child and frank-faced man, came out of the past and moved together onward down the slanting path of life. Ah! yes, other eyes than hers would look back upon that winter morning, and through quivering lips broke words that told of griefs half buried and happiness hoped for.

"Out of sorrow cometh forth joy."

It took long years to be cured of that blindness of sorrow; but the joyous sight came at last.

The house sounded very still and quiet as Florence re-entered it, so calling Rollo, she hastened to her own small sitting-room, where, drawing her desk to the fireside, she seated herself before it and began to write.

Her letter seemed to progress slowly, for ever and anon she laid down her pen and sat gazing absently into the midst of the glowing embers. It was a favourite attitude of hers to sit thus with her elbows on her knees and her chin buried in the palms of her hands, her eyes looking deep down into the fiery tombs which King Flame with his red tongue was making.

Sometimes a tear stole between her long dark lashes, and rested there as if reluctant to stain the pale fair cheek with its salt breath; sometimes a smile parted the scarlet lips and a gleam of intense happiness swept across the delicate features; for, as she sat there, a world of joy and sorrow shook the girl's heart and left her stunned and bewildered by its force.

Some one entered the room; Florence thought it Lallah and did not look up; but they were not Lallah's eyes that were fixed upon her face when at last she raised her own from the study of the burning embers.

With a glad, low cry, like the coo of a wild dove, she sprang from her seat and nestled herself in Collingwood's outstretched arms.

"And what makes my birdie sad?" he asked, for he had seen the tear-stains.

"I am not sad now you are here, Owen," she answered, looking into his face, whilst her own told only too plainly the great love that was at once her blessing and her curse.

"I want my birdie to let me clip her wings to-morrow; do you think she will consent to be so shorn?"

"To-morrow! so soon?" was all her reply.

"Florence dearest, listen, and forgive me if I have done wrong, but I feared so to lose you, that other influences might come and draw you from me, that I have been cruel, and taken you at your word; forgive me, dearest!" and he kissed the dark liquid eyes, and continued in rapid tones as if repeating a lesson he would willingly have left unsaid:

"I have arranged for us to be married at Ipswich

to-morrow morning, about five; we can easily escape unnoticed during the ball, and return before the guests have left. Once my wife, we can keep the secret until you are of age—which will not be so very long, little one—then I will bear all the blame of our hasty action, and my dove shall have no thorns in her nest."

"Owen, could it not be otherwise, how can I deceive them all so long?" she urged, the frank, fair face of the morning forcing itself upon her memory.

"Do you regret your promise, wifie?" he whispered, his whole face lit up with passionate love.

"Regret! I cannot regret anything that will give me to you."

Collingwood shivered, and all the light faded from his face, but he answered in the same low, mellow tones:

"How can I ever forgive myself, dearest, if I bring sorrow or trouble on you?"

"I will take sorrow with you rather than all joys with another, Owen."

He took her face between his hands, and gazed eagerly into it. He wanted to assure himself of her great love.

The luncheon-bell summoned them downstairs, and as they passed through the hall it seemed like years to Florence since the night when Collingwood had pressed his first love-kiss upon her lips under the berried mistletoe, and doomed her girlhood to eternal burial.

She chatted and talked with Maude and Nelly during the meal, wondering what they would think of her if they knew the part she was enacting. She agreed to join in their plans for the coming spring, and could have cried out for mercy as they alluded to her marriage with Leonard.

Towards dusk, Lilly and her cavaliers returned from the hunt, all looking better for the day's sport. Leonard had long tales of the small maiden's bravery, of how she and Tiger had managed to clear Dennison's brook and spin over the hurdles in Gray's farm.

Collingwood, looking on the child's fair face, sighed. Would her wondrous beauty, her brave, fearless nature, save her from treading the thorny path wherein women's feet seem ever to wander?

"Well, Lilly, would you rather have Leonard or myself for a companion after the hounds?" he questioned, for Lilly was standing very silent by his side.

"Me would rather go with him," she answered, nodding her head at Leonard, who stood some little distance off.

"You are an ungrateful pussy. I am sure I take far more care of you than he."

"But me likes to take care of mine self," urged Miss Lilly, who was always independent.

"Look here, Leonard — a new specimen of womankind! one who likes to take care of herself. I trust she will hold to that excellent idea all her life; save any amount of bother to us unlucky dogs."

"Me take care of him," interrupted Lilly, not understanding the argument.

"Are you contemplating the weather, Leonard, that you make a post of yourself in front of the window? Remember you are not transparent," continued Collingwood, as he approached Leonard's side. The object of his companion's gaze he found was the figure of a girl coming slowly up the avenue with her long fur cloak drawn tightly around her.

"Ah!" he exclaimed, recognising Florence, and followed Leonard to the hall door to welcome her in.

"Have you been gathering holly for your personal adornment?" questioned Leonard, being the first to reach her side.

"Do you think I require adorning?"

"Not with holly, certainly. I would choose you leaves more soft and tender."

"Supposing I prefer the prickles," she returned, as Collingwood joined them.

"Where have you been though, Florence? you have not yet told me," Leonard still urged.

"I want to know where you have been, and what sort of sport you had; and how Lilly got on, and what escapes of death and danger you were saved from; and a hundred other things besides. So please allow me my privilege of lady, and satisfy my curiosity first."

"Ask Hurst; he will give you a full and particular account of the day. Lilly won the brush, and old John, as he presented it to her, declared his eyes had never been blessed with a prettier sight than my lady as she came galloping in at the death; and really, John has more than half an eye, for she did look bonny."

"She is as fearless as she is pretty," answered Florence, mounting the steps wearily one by one.

Lilly was standing at the top, and held in her hand her well-earned prize. On seeing Florence she advanced to meet her, and offering her poor Reynard's *débris*, said:

"Me kept it for you all the day, so you must not say no."

"Indeed, I cannot take it from you; it is quite a treasure to be guarded. Think how proud you will be when you grow big and go to school, to be able to tell your friends you won the brush when you were seven."

"Me would rather you have it," persisted Lilly.

"No, no, darling! I would not rob you of a single prize," answered Florence; and, bending down, imprinted a warm kiss on the lovely little upturned face.

Leonard felt uneasy and unhappy. There was a nameless something in Florence's look and manner that he could not account for; he had seen her look pale and miserable before, but that wistful, startled look in her eyes was a stranger to him. He was hardly surprised when, as they all stood in the hall, she turned to him and said:

"Leonard, can you spare me a few moments? I want to have a talk with you."

"Certainly. Will you have me as I am?"

"Yes, yes," she answered quickly; and as their two companions quitted them, Leonard followed her upstairs to her work-room.

Arriving there, she seemed in no hurry to commence the conversation she had sought, for, after removing her cloak, she stood silent before the fire.

"Sit down, Leo; I suppose you are not in a hurry. It is hardly four, and so we have plenty of time before dinner-hour."

"I am in no hurry, but prefer standing, thanks, Florence," he replied, resting his arm on the chimney-piece and gazing absently over the room.

Again there was a silence, and the girl locked and unlocked her hands in sudden nervousness.

"You remember the promise I made you?" at last she said, her voice unsteady and her eyes pleading.

"Yes."

"Do you mean to keep me to my word, Leo? Do you think it best?"

"Yes," again he replied, and gazed still into vacancy.

"Oh, Leo! release me, I pray you."

"Why?" was the sharp rejoinder.

"Because—because I do not love you."

"I knew that before, Florence."

"But, Leo, you do not wish to force me to marry you when I do not love you?" she urged, keeping her eyes fixed upon his face.

He moved his arm from off the chimney-piece and withdrew his gaze from vacancy to encounter hers.

"I know you do not love me, Florence; but you are young, and cannot have formed any affection strong enough to blast your life, if you marry me, later on. 'Love begets love,' they say, and I think I can trust to the strength of mine to win yours in return some day."

"Leonard, I can never marry you."

"Why? why?" he asked again, knitting his brows.

"I cannot! I cannot!" she only murmured, her eyes sad.

"But there must be a reason. I do not ask you to marry me to-day or to-morrow; and time will change your feelings."

"Oh no! Time will never make me love you,

and if you really loved me, you would be generous and release me from my promise."

"You promised to be my wife of your own free will. I will not release you, Florence."

"Your father forced me into my engagement. Leo, Leo! for all our sakes, set me free."

It was pitiable to hear the wistful pleading of the girl's voice.

Leonard was roused at last, and Florence, who had never seen him so moved before, trembled as she looked into his face, all white and drawn by the strong passions that were fighting for mastery over him.

He was vexed and pained, and would have no pity on her; she had played him false, and should suffer for her treachery. Whilst he lived none other should claim her for his bride.

"Since you are so sure you can never love me, your heart must be given elsewhere. Are ten years of love to be thrown out of the balance-scales? Will they count for nothing in your estimation?" Then his voice softened, and he seized her hands, and almost forced some of his own passion into the girl's cold frame. "Florence! my little Florry! that I cherished, and guarded, and loved, and tended; my jewel, whose worth I have but just discovered; my precious little seedling, whose roots are in my heart! Oh! my darling! can I never warm your heart with some of my own deep love? Is all the long future to be to me one endless blank? Have I not been patient enough, gentle enough, kind enough? Have I done nothing that can ever win your love? Am I so repulsive to you that no change I can make will enable me to creep into one small corner of your heart? Let me be your servant, your friend, your protector—anything so that your life may be but joined to mine. Ask me to work and wait for years, and I will do it; though God knows how long those years will be to me! Ask me anything —to be burned in hot climates, tossed on rough seas, frozen in glaciers—anything but to give you up; for I swear to you, Florence, it is beyond my power to do it!"

"You know not how to be generous, Leo," was her quivering reply; for her lips were white with pain, and her throat dry with the salt of her unshed tears.

"Generous! What a woman's taunt! Generous! You know not the meaning of the word. I offer you a lifetime of work and waiting; a lifetime of constant love—for what? A claim upon you, however weak, a right to guard your honour and your name, a thread of gold to bind your life with mine. And you tell me to be generous! Generous you would think it to release you from a promise made to the dead; to let you bask in another's love—one who will never love you as I do, never cherish you as I do, never prize you as I would. You think I do not know who is my rival in your heart; not know the false friend who has stolen my jewel from me; not know the man whose hand is raised to strike a blow more deadly than Brutus gave to Cæsar; not know who has driven the laughter from your eyes; killed the music in your voice, crushed the happiness from out your features, taught you the lesson of deceit and falseness, you who were so pure and true. Do you think I have been blind and deaf, not to see and learn these things? Wait, wait, Florence; I shall have my revenge some day."

"Hush, Leonard! you must not speak so of one I hold so dear; you are unjust in your anger. Knowing all this, would you still wed me?"

"Yes! and rather than see you his bride I will hold you to your word until my death-hour."

She started as if stung, then moved quickly towards him.

"Leonard, I love you as a brother!—trust me as a sister—but ask me not to be your wife; anything but that. Oh! forgive me the pain I have caused you, the sorrow I have brought you; take my gratitude, but give me back my freedom?"

She tried to take his hands, but he drew them from her, and his tones were stern and cold as he replied:

"Never! never! I will never set you free!"

Then she knelt before him and clasped her hands about his knees.

"Leo! Leo! for the love you profess for me, unsay your words!"

He stooped to unclasp her hands, and with gentle tenderness forced her into the low cushioned chair; but his voice, though kind, was firm, as he answered:

"Florence, it is useless to urge me further; I will keep your secret faithfully, it would break my mother's heart to know of your cruel treachery, but never, never, I say again, will I give you back your freedom. You are my plighted wife, and I will hold you to your word."

He walked towards the door, and had his hand upon the handle, when Florence's words arrested him.

"For the last time, Leonard, I beg—I implore of you to release me from my bondage! I am asking you for something more precious to me than life."

He turned, and caught her hands roughly in his own.

"And you love that villain so?"

"With all my life!" and even in the dim winter's twilight he saw the blush that dyed her pale pained face.

"Then I shall learn to hate you both," he answered, and pushed past her through the door.

The despairing look in her dark eyes as she heard his words haunted him for ever. Years passed, and still when the twilight of the dying year drew in he saw again that slight young form standing between him and the last gleam of sunset, with the misery of a half-wild despair gleaming in the depths of her fathomless eyes; and he would have given half his lifetime to efface that scene from his memory.

So it is with us all. We commit a deed in the white heat of passion, and when we look back at the misery we have brought, at the burden we have taken on our shoulders, we curse our blind folly and eat up our lives with endless regrets. If we had had but a few moments' patience, but made one weak effort at self-control, what a dark cloud chased from our life-sky, what a heavy billow saved our little barque from breasting! but no! we hasten on: and the rain of sorrow overtakes us, or the shipwreck of life awaits us; then we look back to that little black spot, or to that blue smiling wave, and cry out with such salt tears in our eyes, "What might have been!" Ah! what might have been if that temptation had not assailed us, or we had not fallen so easily to its vile power! And other voices, with tones too sweet for earth, echo back the words as white wings sway backwards; in their spirit-lives regret exists not, but their sympathy is roused by the unutterably pathetic sentence, and pleading for us, they too murmur,

"What might have been!"

* * * * *

And Florence sat alone in the dim winter's twilight.

CHAPTER VII.

THE strains of a Strauss waltz echoed through the scarlet-blushed or pale-cheeked berries; the gold and silver lamplights shivered in their nests of green; the tender beauty of some rare exotic faded and died as one loud chord crashed out its death-knell. The ball of New Year's Eve was at its height, bright eyes flashed into bright eyes, dark lashes drooped to hide some half-told love-glance; voices soft and low, deep and melodious, answered one another in words whose meaning only two could tell. Many a young heart beat high with pleasure, many a brave one stood still to hear one word from a woman's lips. The swell of the bewildering music, the swift play of tiny feet, the gorgeous light, the heavily-scented air—all combined to hasten the death-struggle of the slowly dying year; laughter greeted its agony-cry, and its death-rattle was the tinkle of dancing feet.

Leonard, hurrying through the hall to welcome his guests, saw a little figure half buried in the shadow of one oval window.

"And what is my Lilly doing here?" he questioned, approaching the child's side.

"Is me nicer?" answered the little lady, running into the centre of the hall and placing herself directly under the lamplight.

"Why Lilly, what have you done?" exclaimed Leonard on seeing a perfect shower of golden curls fall from the child's lap.

"You said you did not like mine curls," she pleaded, with her violet eyes opened wide.

For all answer Leonard caught her in his arms and kissed her many times under the hanging mistletoe.

Years afterwards he knew that under that white-berried bough, his own love had been betrayed, and the seed of another love sown in a little childish heart—a seed that grew and strengthened until it blossomed into a fair sweet flower.

"Well, my shorn beauty, you must come and dance with me now, for I am afraid no one else will look at you, notwithstanding your dainty robe," continued Leonard, as he put Lilly on her feet again.

"Me is very glad," she replied, and trotted contentedly by his side.

On arriving at the ball-room, they joined the dancers, where, despite Lilly's rugged head, there were many admiring eyes fixed upon her.

When the dance was over Leonard went in

search of Florence, leaving Lilly in charge of Hurst, who had taken a strange fancy to the child, and was always willing to become her slave—perhaps he guessed her history; but Collingwood and he were almost enemies still, only conversing with one another when politeness obliged them to do so.

Leonard found Florence standing in the pale gleam of a rose-hued lamp. The expression of her face reminded him of Guido's Magdalen, and he arrested his steps a moment to wonder at the strange deep sadness that was written upon its every feature. Collingwood's tall form was by her side, and Leonard's anger gathered as he watched his rival caress with his hand the girl's long curls; there was no mistaking the deep red love-blush that swept across her features, or the passionate love-glance that beamed from her dark eyes as she raised them up to Collingwood's face.

"Florence, will you dance this waltz with me?" he petitioned, glad to break in upon her reverie.

She started and went pale again as she heard his voice, and the eyes that encountered his had a world of pleading in them.

"I believe I am engaged to Mr. Collingwood."

"I think I may plead a prior claim to you as partner."

"For the dance, certainly," Collingwood replied, with a strange smile.

"We are missing the best part of the music,"

Florence interrupted, afraid of some bitter words passing between her lovers.

In a few moments they had joined the circle of dancers, and as they swung lightly round and round, some of the girl's lost youth-joy came back to her; the music sounded so gladsome, the brilliantly-lighted room with its scented air and Christmas holly seemed so filled with happy laughter and merry voices. Ah! could she bury all the past, shut out from her life-story the event of the coming dawn! stand once more free upon the bank of her destiny, and cross with less unwilling feet that tiny strait where maiden and womanhood meet!

Many eyes turned to look upon her face, and there were some who, in after-years, remembered the pure fairness of its young beauty; one who, when next he looked upon it, recollected its present charm and almost cursed the hand that had blasted all its features and placed the seal of death upon its white smooth brow.

The midnight chimes sounded—not with the solemn peal of the Christmas day-dawn—but merry and joyous, like the voice of a thousand Cupids set free from their golden fetters to pierce with poisoned arrows a million human hearts.

The aged sighed as the chimes concluded; their year was passed, their spell of life shortened, and blind with the blindness of earth, they did not see through those starry apertures which, hanging in the sky, give us a peep of heaven.

Each peal of the merry chimes struck an arrow sharp and painful into Florence's heart; for each told a tale of vows half-broken, of sin unrepented, of honour lost; and under the silken splendour of her spotless robe the girl's heart bled.

The hours flew by on their winged and soundless feet, and the dawn of the glad New Year was breaking.

"Florence, you will come now?" said Collingwood, approaching her side and bending his head to look into her face.

"I am ready," she answered, and pulled leaf by leaf to death a crimson rose she held in her hand.

Together they left the ball-room.

Through the hall Collingwood hurried her, and arriving in the library took a heavy cloak from a chair, placed it upon her shoulders, and lifted her through the low window into the moonlit air beyond.

No word passed between them as they hastened down the avenue; once or twice Collingwood pressed a little closer to him the girl's slight form, or imprinted a hasty kiss upon her uncovered head. Beyond the gates some distance they found the carriage that Collingwood had arranged to meet them, and when once its inmates both seemed to forget all but the other's presence.

The long uncertain moon-shadows caught their pathway, and, glancing into Florence's fair face, saw written there the characters of a boundless love.

It was dark still when they arrived at Ipswich; the church, with its flickering candles, its pale sanctuary lamp and cold stone pillars, seemed filled with awe-hushed whispers of angels' voices. The priest and the old clerk looked inquiringly at them, and one warned them gravely of their hasty action. He was young, but had known sorrow, and long-buried thoughts of the world's cold joys brought back energy to his words. Florence trembled, and fain would have returned unwed, but Collingwood urged his love, and unwillingly the girl consented to the ceremony being commenced.

How solemn in their simple wordings sounded those eternal marriage-vows! From the dark corners, how they seemed to echo! The uncertain light of the swinging lamps flickered upon Florence's pale face, or caught the flash of the jewels that bound back her wealth of hair. Some one, standing in the shadow of one grey pillar, watched with angry eyes the strange, sad wedding group. It lay imprinted upon his memory like the features of some horrible dream.

It was his boyhood's friend that stood at that altar, with the girl whom he had looked upon as wife! It was the woman whose love had been his life-joy, whose silken robe glistened in the dim dawn-light. Ah, God! was this his reward after all his years of waiting? Those two whom he had loved and trusted, is it they who have betrayed him? He heard the few low words that bound them until "death should us sever," and ground his teeth in fierce passion, and cursed them bitterly below his breath.

He waited until the priest's last words had echoed through the Gothic arches; waited whilst the vessel of his life was wrecked; whilst the glad New Year sung out its first matin song, and the old, with its priceless joys and burning sorrows, lay buried in the tomb of time. Yes, he waited until those two dishonoured ones came together down the silent nave; behind them the pale lamp glimmered, on the altar the candles still burned. The hush of the sacred household was around them, the quiet of the new-born year was abroad. Only in his heart was the uproar of the battle of a thousand angry feelings; only in his eyes was space filled with hideous forms.

They had almost reached his side when from behind his hiding-place Leonard stepped out and accosted them.

Collingwood started, and pressed his hand against his heart, his face whitened and contracted with a deadly pain, and he gasped as if in great agony; his lips parted, and his voice was hoarse and thick as he used it in defence of his bride.

"Blame her not, Leonard," were his words, whilst he clasped more tightly the trembling figure that clung so hopelessly to his arm.

"I have cursed you both, and may shame and sorrow ever darken the portals of your home!" was Leonard's reply in a voice all broken with bitterest anguish.

Florence gave a little cry, then fell forward as if struck by an unseen hand. Collingwood raised her in his arms, and pushing past Leonard without a word, carried her out of the church.

Once seated in the carriage with his loved burden, the man's grief gave way. Hot tears like rain fell one by one upon Florence's face. He kissed passionately her parted lips, so white and cold, and prayed wildly that his sin might not be visited upon her.

The first pale radiance of the awakening morn was resting on the horizon as they drove up to the Hall gates. Lights still blazed in their glittering splendour, and bright forms flitted across the pillar-supported hall.

Taking Florence once more in his arms, Collingwood hastened up the avenue and entered the house, as he had left it, through the library window; the room was quiet and untenanted, with but one shaded lamp to illuminate its corners. Gently he placed her upon the sofa, and knelt down to gaze anxiously into her cold set features.

He put his arms about her, he pushed the long curls from off her broad smooth brow, he kissed her hands, her face, her lips, her eyes, and called her by every endearing epithet his trembling lips could utter, but still she lay like one dead, heedless of the voice that had been her life's sweetest music.

The guests departed one by one; the music ceased; the holly and mistletoe dropped their shining balls, and tried to hide with their withering leaves their departing beauty. Far away among the foam-crested waves of an angry sea the New Year's morn was breaking.

The birds sang more merrily, for the frost was leaving the earth; the snowdrops and crocuses shook their hidden heads, knowing the hour of their short bright life was at hand; the tiny elves that lay under the grass-blades opened wide their sleep-unbound eyes to gaze once more upon the released earth; the frost-fairies flitted away on their shivering wings and lost a few stray gleams of their snow plumage on their northward journey. The joy of the glad young king was brightening the earth's fair surface, and with the roar of the sea and the whistle of the wind he proclaimed his kingship, with fearless eyes and smiling brow ascended the steps of his throne, little recking how soon all his kingdom would lie in the dust, how short would be the hour of his kingship.

CHAPTER VIII.

"YOUR wife is paralysed; you had better seek further medical assistance, I can do nothing for her," said Leonard, moving from Florence's bedside and casting a cold hard look into Collingwood's face. He had no pity for the pain he was inflicting, for the deep cruel wound he was piercing his late friend's heart with; even the sudden pallor and the shiver of agony that shook the strong man's frame did not move him; and although he would have died to save the girl from all sorrow or pain twelve hours ago, now he felt glad that her girlish beauty and pretty ways would never give pleasure to any heart.

"Florence," murmured Collingwood, kneeling by her side and pressing his hot lips upon her stiffened fingers.

Mrs. Thornton entering the room found him thus.

"You have yourself to blame for all this misery, Owen; how could you have been such a traitor to us all?" she said, laying her hand upon his shoulder and speaking in a weary, heart-broken tone. How could she forgive the wrong he had done her darling?

He never answered, for all his pride was buried in the dust—nay, he would have blessed her could she have killed him with one blow; he was so dishonoured, had proved himself so worthy of the title she had given him.

"Go now and fetch Dr. Drew, Collingwood; you can do no good here."

Silently was the command obeyed, and Collingwood left his new-made bride to the care of those from whom he had stolen her. Good God, what a bridal morning!

The village doctor came, shook his head and sighed; the great M.D. from London gazed long on the pale, still features, and told them he could do no good; his patient had received a dreadful shock, and he doubted if those rounded limbs would ever move again.

Collingwood, as he heard the words, rushed from the room, and wandering through the park lost himself among the damp bare forest trees.

What mattered if the earth was clothed in her garment of brown or verdant green; never more would he look upon her face with gladness; never more listen to the distant chimes of the village church as the wind carried their sweet music over the sleeping vale; never watch the red-robins plume themselves in a stray sunbeam or flutter their dainty wings in some tiny streamlet; never wonder at the beauty of the stately hyacinth or the rich red blush of the poppy's head; never reach from on high the scented honeysuckle, or shake a shower of rosy petals from their airy perch. The summer's loveliness, the winter's frost would never be aught to him again; the earth with her thousand beauties, her million graces, her wondrous music, was as a thing dead, with the decay of nature disfiguring her; for his eyes were blinded with unshed tears, and at his heart the fangs of a giant wolf, despair, were gnawing.

Wherever his sad eyes rested, he saw that senseless figure, the pure pale face, that cluster of curls, those matchless eyes with their silken fringe. As the wind swept past him he longed for the pressure of two soft arms, for the touch of warm rosy lips; as the robins twittered he listened for the sound of a low sweet voice, for the laughter of girlish glee—and he knew they were all gone from him, slipped out of his life, blotted out of his history, passed from beneath the shadow of his pathway, buried in the tomb of the past. He had sacrificed his honour, his friendship, every true feeling that his manhood's life had been decked with to win his bride, and this was his reward!

"The wages of sin is death," were the words the wind sang to him, and half maddened by his pain and shame he wandered recklessly on in the cold pale winter's sunlight.

And Leonard, what of him?

When dismissed from Florence's sick-room he had descended to the library, where, pulling a chair to the fireside, he sank into it exhausted in mind and body. Over and over again he reviewed his lifetime: what sin had he committed to merit such punishment as this? his life had been pure as few men's lives are pure, and his shield of honour stainless! He cursed Collingwood with a deep passionate curse, and vowed to be revenged. He drove himself wild by letting his angry passions master him, and sat gazing into the firelight until his eyes were bloodshot, and the palms of his hands bleeding with the wound his nails made as he buried them through the flesh in his heartbreaking misery.

He did not hear the door softly opened, he did not heed the patter of tiny feet across the carpet; the twilight hid a white-clothed figure from his gaze, and he started as Lilly pressed her pretty head against his knee, weeping out her sorrow for him.

He pushed her away and arose from his seat, speaking to her in cold indifferent tones. The little one looked up, her violet eyes wide with wonder. His anger did not frighten her, but her voice was sad and strangely serious as she answered him.

"Me love you all the same, but you is unkind."

Her tears were all gone, and with steady steps she passed quickly out of the room.

In the great wide window-sill of the hall she found a resting-place, and, hiding her tiny figure in the shadow, gave way to her grief.

Hours afterwards, when night had drawn her thick veil over the unhappy household, Hurst found her there weeping softly to herself; he coaxed her from her hiding-place, and with tender words soothed her sorrow, but his heart was too sore to give much comfort; and when Madame Lucas came for her little charge, he wandered out into the cold night air.

CHAPTER IX.

FIVE years have come and gone; five times has the earth changed her annual vestment; five times the snowdrop and crocus have greeted the glad young king with their low-voiced chorus; five times the roses have wept themselves to death with their leaflet tears; five times have the snow-fairies visited the earth.

In one household a young mother has lost her first-born; has closed two blue eyes with trembling fingers; has wept with wild, sad weeping as she gathered to her bosom those tiny stiffened limbs; has wondered why God so cruelly tortured her! why give into her keeping so fragrant a blossom, if before the moss on its bud had parted the floweret in the heart lay dead ı

In another home a proud father has read the long printed columns that tell of a son's brave deeds; looking back into the far-distant years when his darling, with locks of gold and eyes of azure, had played soldiers at his knee; remembering the wooden "hobby" that carried the young hero to imaginary combats, the noisy trumpets that drove poor mamma distracted, the strange reports that so startled cook and Anne the nursemaid, the unaccountable deaths of a pet rabbit or a favourite pigeon, the storm of a little sister's tears as a Miss Dolly was found headless. Alas! he remembered them all as his eyes read again and again those long small-printed columns that praised his boy's brave deeds, and told of a soldier's glory and a hero's death; big tears fell one by one on that wrinkled cheek, and through their dim mist the tall straight form, the handsome, haughty head, the soft womanly eyes looked back at him, and the father's grief was stilled and soothed as it carried him over the bridge of death, and his strong love burst open the iron portals of eternity!

Five years! full of change—full of sorrow—full of joy—full of hopes—full of trusting—full of misery —full of crime, what an eternity they seem!

Florence, what had her life brought her during those five years?

She had known naught of joy, the spring's brightness, the summer's wealth, the autumn's glory, the winter's snow—they had come and gone, and she had never noted their advent or their death. From maiden to womanhood she had passed with no feeling but the strange heavy weight of her pulseless limbs that was killing her. The golden bracelet, with its diamond stars, rested still upon her arm, but she felt it not—for it was her left side that was paralysed. Stiff and motionless had lain her pretty limbs, once so full of vigorous young life; the delicate features of her face seemed softer and more delicate than before; the wondrous beauty of her matchless eyes had deepened, until looking into them seemed gazing into a well where naught but sorrow lay.

Collingwood, as he sat reading to her, or carried her, or wheeled her in her bath-chair from place to place, or kissed her, or caressed her, could only hope for the look in her eyes to thank him—for during all those five years the music of her voice had never gladdened his ears. Sometimes she would twine her fingers in the silvered threads of his hair, and a tear would drop amongst the thick curls; she could give him no sympathy in his sorrow, never by one single word encourage him to bear patiently his pain; she was his wife, his love, his slave that he had bought with such a price; and as he looked upon her face, held her in his arms, he cursed the mad passion that had blasted so fair a floweret, wrecked so dainty a vessel, robbed the earth of so precious a burden. Yes! but it was too late now to repent; too late to take up that shield which he had cast so carelessly in the sand; too late to place the stolen flower upon the withered stem; to set the little vessel rudderless upon the surging sea! "Too late!" and through the June's scent-laden air the words were ringing.

"Florence, shall I wheel you to the shore, my darling? The air is soft and warm, and soon the sun will set."

Florence looked up and bent her head, her usual reply to all Collingwood's requests. He lifted her gently from her sofa, half buried as she was in rich rare rugs and costly-covered cushions of down.

Wealth had been lavished upon her, even the house in that small common fishing-village was filled with gems of art and costly playthings; rich Turkey carpets, in which your feet lay buried, covered the wooden boards; strange birds with gorgeous plumage chirped in an aviary, green as a miniature forest; flowers of every shape and hue decked the tiny garden with their beauty; trees bent their graceful heads to the wild sea breeze, moss, green and fresh as from some stony cavern, stretched its velvet covering over the lawn. Every beauty that the eye could wish for and wealth procure was lavished upon that little home, whose mistress lay so still and white like one just dead; no wealth, no love could bring joy into her checked life; the hand that she loved had struck her her death-blow, and the deep wound would never heal.

Yes, the air was soft and the wind was lulled, lulled to sleep far away amongst the blue depths of the ocean's tomb-house; the birds had gone to rest, and if a stray gull screamed its night-cry it was the only sound that disturbed the hushed hour of the crimson sunset.

Far away the waves were rocking the mermaids' babes to sleep. The purple mist lay thick over the mountain-mother's head; the tiny crabs or white-shelled cockles were sporting in the pools among the red rock-beds; the long stretch of sandy banks in the Dee's bare bosom were covered by tiny billows, for the tide was full; the fishing-boats were slowly sailing home, their dark hulls making black spots on the crimson bordering of the sky; the shrimp-fires gleamed and paled as the sunset light just caught them; the reeds bent their stiff heads as a white-breasted rabbit jumped lightly over them; the butterflies and bees lay sleeping amongst the clover-leaves or under the golden glory of the broom's bright head.

Amongst her thick rugs and soft cushions, encircled by her husband's arms, Florence listened quietly to Nature's sweet good-night; she pointed with her frail white hand to the great red sun, sinking lower and lower into his watery bed, she signed to Collingwood to sing, and in the still, hushed hour the rich full tones of his glorious voice echoed.

He had sung it once before, in the years gone by, in the forest glens among the Alpine shadows, Schubert's sad-worded "Adieu." The late gulls rested on their outspread wings to hearken to that music; the rabbits stopped in their hasty scamper to listen to that wondrous voice; the bees and butterflies awoke from their early slumbers to catch the last stray echoes, and the wild sad pleading of the great master's soul seemed to have power to unloosen the girl's stilled tongue.

"Owen," she said, and he caught his breath and bent his head until his lips rested upon her brow. Did he hear aright? could his sense deceive him? once more the music of her voice would gladden his hungry ears! He hardly breathed, for fear of losing one whisper of those precious words.

She saw his face light up with a strange wild joy, watched his eyes become dim with passionate longing, and she pressed her head closer into his bosom and whispered, but so low, so low that the sigh of the breeze almost drowned her words.

"Owen, I shall be with you always."

Yes, he had heard aright; the music of his life so long hushed had come back to him, and again in possession of that precious joy he would forget all other joys that might have been.

The sun sank lower, the rose-hue crept far and farther over the sky, a golden glory rested upon the waves and buried itself among the peaks of the blue misty mountains; the white-sailed fishing-smacks were pink and crimson, or gold or rose-hue, just as a flitting beam caught them; the awed stillness of the earth's deep joy, as her king cast his last love-look upon her, rested in the atmosphere; Nature was breathing still her sweet good-night.

Florence withdrew her eyes from gazing on the day's dying hour to fix them upon Collingwood's face. Oh! the deep true love in their dark depths, the undying longing under their silken fringe. Collingwood seeing it blinded it with kisses; he dared not breathe all his idolatrous worship, dared not tell of the wild agony-prayers he had besieged Heaven with to spare him his darling.

He pressed her closer and closer to his breast, he felt her shiver as if with a sudden chill, he gazed anxiously into the fair sweet face; he watched, as his heart stood still, a gradual mist steal over those matchless eyes; he saw the curved lips part, the small white teeth glimmer. The last ray of sunset blushed the transparent cheeks, and as the sun dropped into the sea Florence's head, with its clustering curls, fell back upon his bosom; one sigh parted her whitened lips, one tremble quivered through her senseless limbs, one tear glistened on her silken lashes, and the pure young soul took its flight with the white-winged gulls to heaven.

It was June, and her sun was set.

* * * * *

"Owen, I shall be with you always." The words were ringing all through the still night air; he felt no cold, heeded no darkness; would she never speak again? never look into his face? smile into his eyes? never press her curl-crowned head upon his bosom? never twine her tiny fingers in the rings of his silvered hair? Ah, God! was it all past! even the bliss of calling her wife. He had killed her! and all his strong limbs shivered.

He pressed her senseless figure tighter to his breast; what mattered how deadly cold it was? what mattered the ashy whiteness of that upturned face, the dreadful stiffness of those tender limbs? Oh! she was not dead, but sleeping!

He lifted her gently in his arms, covering her with her costly rugs; then carried her back slowly to his little home.

She was surely with him, with him in that soft June twilight which no darkness ever kills, with him as he sat kissing her soulless clay until the warm breath of his own love-words seemed to put a spark of warmth into the cold stiff limbs.

She had promised to be with him always, she would not leave him now; he called her by her name; he tried to put her dead arms about his neck, and when he felt their stiffness, great tears of a man's salt agony fell one by one from his burning eyes. The long hours of that twilight summer night, the hushed stillness of those slowly fleeting moments! would the day never dawn? would the deep-hued clouds of night never part? Oh for daylight to drive away this horrible nightmare! Oh for one ray of light to look into that beloved face, and see the gleam from under those silken lashes! The suspense was torturing agony, one wild longing was bursting his brain, and still the night wore on.

He pressed his precious burden more passionately to his bosom, great tears were buried in thousands among the rippling curls; the strong man's heart was breaking in the lonely silent hours, and when the day did dawn, he could no longer see the white set features, no longer feel the pressure of those slender stiffened limbs.

Other fingers closed those sightless eyes, other arms lifted from his the precious burden; for under the long suspense Collingwood's mind gave way, and in the early dawn his servant found him faint and delirious.

Hurst had been a wanderer during the long five years; but, returning to England some months before, had at length succeeded in discovering Collingwood's hiding-place.

He had taken up his abode in the one solitary hotel the village contained, and on the morning after his arrival heard from his host the sad history of Florence's death.

Without hesitation he hastened to the assistance of his cousin, thinking of the last time he had seen him under the shade of a rose-hued lamplight in the scented atmosphere of a crowded ball-room; and the girl now stiff and dead, her fair sweet face, the wealth of her glorious hair, the matchless beauty of her wondrous eyes—they haunted him even in the glare of the noonday's glory.

His own sad history came vividly back to his memory. All the years that had come and gone since the night when, under the broad clear moonlight, he had looked his last upon his lost love. Collingwood and he were indeed suffering for their parents' sin; the hasty action of the one, the long deceit of the other, had brought a bitter punishment upon their children.

So it is often, dear reader; the innocent suffer for the guilty, the children for their parents; and the world and the suffering ones ask—why is their life so wretched? Let them ask the question of the father who tossed them upon his knee, or the mother who lulled them to sleep upon her breast! They will answer, with tears in their eyes and heads bowed down with shame or sorrow—Alas! repentance to them has come too late, and their punishment through their darlings is so bitter!

In the long silent hours of his first night-watch, Hurst had time and opportunity to notice the dreadful change in Collingwood's countenance.

The dark hair was silvery white, the cheeks hollow and worn; the heavy brows contracted, as if with perpetual pain; the deep grey eyes sunk and dim, as if salt tears were frozen in them; the mouth hard and set, closed against all murmurings of a sad fate. To look at that face, so old and haggard in its prime, was to see a proud spirit humbled, to feel that that man's heart was broken.

Too often was the stillness of the night broken by piteous pleadings for a loved one's presence, by heart-breaking requests to a dead one's ears, by words of passionate endearment, or fevered calls for the pressure of a dead woman's lips. Hurst shivered as he heard them, and prayed that the fearful awakening from that dream of misery might be spared to the suffering man.

But the soldier who has deserted his colours must be punished by death. Great Michael, as he passed the decree, grieved that so bitter a death as the death of all life's joys must be passed upon one of his legion; but the command was issued and the sentence passed; and when the punished soldier takes up again his shield, once more spotless, washed, and shining, a greater joy than earth can give shall await him, and although his pathway of life may be stony, the end will soon come, and out of the agony and sorrows of a lifetime cometh forth the joy of everlasting bliss.

Then, reader, why murmur at great Michael's decrees?

CHAPTER X.

"LILLY, my dear, cannot you stay with us a little longer? Leonard sends me word he may be home before the end of this month."

It was Mrs. Thornton who spoke, addressing Lilly, now a tall girl just entering upon her teens. Miss Eccles, her ancient governess, was recently married to Doctor Longford, and Mrs. Thornton had invited Lilly to come and pay her a long visit. Owen Lodge, with its sombre fir-trees and lonely halls, was hardly a fitting residence for so young a girl, and although Lilly resisted strongly any suggestion to leave it, her friends were anxious for her to do so.

"I should like to stay," at length answered Lilly; then turning to face her hostess, she continued, in her usual determined tone: "but you know Uncle Collingwood may come home any day, and I must be there to welcome him."

"Your uncle will never come home again now, Lilly; he has forgotten or ceased to care for you or any of us."

"No, no! you wrong him; it is his sorrow and

his shame that keeps him from us; Miss Eccles told me all the sad history of his marriage, and now you have learned to love me, dear Mrs. Thornton, I want you to forgive him for my sake." She knelt down by the elder lady's side, and few could have resisted the earnest pleading of her violet eyes.

"My Lilly, you can never know all the sorrow your uncle brought us; think of how long the years have been since our boy left us to be a wanderer over the world—my Leonard, who was so bright, so true, so loyal, who would have preferred death to dishonour; and trusted your uncle above all others; dearest, do not ask me to forgive just yet, perhaps some day when my boy comes back and is happy once more, I can grant your request, but not just yet, darling, not just yet;" and bending her head Mrs. Thornton kissed the girl's lovely face.

"Uncle only loved Miss Florence too much," murmured Lilly, whilst she submitted to the caress.

"You are too young to understand this matter, Lilly: if you were older I should quarrel with your words."

There was an answer on Lilly's lips, but the entrance of a servant arrested her words.

"A telegram, please, madam, and only I thought master was here, I should not have fetched it," said Thomas, approaching Mrs. Thornton's side, and lingering there, using his privilege as an old and faithful domestic.

"Lilly, read it to me, dear. I trust it is no bad news of my boy," holding the yellow paper towards the girl, Mrs. Thornton said, her voice hesitating with fear.

Lilly took the offered paper, and read out in her clear girlish voice :

"Mrs. Collingwood is dead. Collingwood dangerously ill. Send Leonard." The paper dropped unheeded on the carpet, and both the girl and woman's face blanched with horror.

"Oh, my poor little one!" exclaimed Mrs. Thornton, and gave way to her grief; but Lilly stood transfixed for some moments, then said sadly, but firmly :

"I must go to him."

Then she tried to soothe her weeping companion.

Old Thomas shuffled out of the room, grumbling to himself as he went along :

"Did you ever know such a scamp of a fellow, now?"

Mr. Thornton's entrance disturbed the sorrowing pair, and Lilly, leaving the husband and wife alone, hastened to her own room, where she found Madame Lucas. Making known to her the sad news, Lilly insisted upon her escort to the north that night. Madame Lucas remonstrated, but seeing it was useless to argue with her young mistress, she commenced her usual task of packing, and when all was ready, Lilly descended to acquaint her host and hostess of her plans. They were grieved at her thus hastily leaving them, but did not try to persuade her to alter her determination.

The long June twilight was drawing in when the girl and her maid departed. During the journey Lilly sat thinking of the fair sweet face so soon to be hidden in a dark tomb. It was not so many years since she had first seen it in the peerless city of France's flower-land, and now she was going to look upon it for the last time on earth. The mystery of death was too awful for her to dwell upon, and forcing her thoughts into other channels Lilly soon fell asleep.

The short summer night was soon over, and before many hours of the next day were spent Lilly and Madame Lucas arrived at Collingwood's home. The sun had set again, the rose-light had faded from the sky, and the strange stillness that always announces the advent of night rested in the atmosphere.

Motionless Lilly stood by Collingwood's bedside; the twilight gathering all around draped her in its misty veil, but about her head her hair shone like a golden glory.

For hours had the invalid lain, seemingly without pain, silent and still. Suddenly he opened his eyes, and fixed them upon Lilly's white-draped figure.

"Lilly," he murmured, so low and weak that the girl half guessed his word.

She bent her head over him, and a look of such

exquisite joy swept across her features that Hurst, who saw it, was startled. He had not given her credit for so much feeling—that bright-haired girl, with her proud fair face, fit for the centre of a Raphael's picture.

"My dear, dear uncle," she uttered again and again, kissing his thin hands and pressing them to her heart. Collingwood moved his head to look into the bent face, but his eyes were blind to its wondrous beauty. To him nothing in life could ever bring into his heart again that "joy for ever" of which our great poet tells us. His joy, his happiness, his life, were all blasted, and despair was written upon his haggard features.

"Did you love her?" he questioned, for to none but those who had loved *her* would he ever speak again. So he had resolved.

"You know I loved her, uncle, and have grieved for you so much," was Lilly's reply, whilst her lips quivered and the dreadful misery expressed in his deep eyes almost made her tears flow. With a strong effort she checked them, knowing how injurious to him the indulgence of her grief might be.

"Lilly, if you love me you will help me to see her once again? I am so weak," and the wild look came back into his dull eyes.

She saw it and knew how dangerous it would be to thwart him, so with gentle words assured him his wish should be granted; then he insisted upon its being gratified at once, and Lilly, summoning Hurst, left them to cast a hasty look on the white-draped room of the young dead wife. She soon heard the heavy tread of the invalid, saw him stagger into the flower-strewn room, and watched the first glance he cast upon the peaceful pure face. Never in her lifetime did she forget the hoarse, wild cry that parted his lips, as, with delirious strength, he shook himself free from Hurst's supporting arms, and, with one bound, cast himself on his knees beside the motionless figure. He never touched her, never attempted to kiss the white, still features, never called her by her name. His agony was too great to be soothed or conquered by these few actions; he writhed as if in pain, his breath came thick and fast, great sobs of anguish shook his frame. Hurst, unable to witness such grief, left the room, but Lilly knelt weeping on the other side of the bed. There was a look of almost divine pity on her young face, as she tried to sympathise in a grief too deep for her comprehension. After a time she approached his side, and clasped her little hands about his neck, her tears falling in cooling streams among the curls of his silvery hair; she pressed her lips upon his cheek, and whispered some low words of endearment into his deafened ears; but he heeded not her presence or hearkened to her words, so utterly mastered was he by this cruel blow.

The time passed on. A summer shower beat a thread of music on the window panes, the tide flowed back into the ocean's bosom, the men and maidens sought their cottage homes, and many stopped a moment on their way to cast a passing glance, or murmur a short prayer, before the little rose-decked cottage, so sacred to them now that the pale young wife lay dead within its walls. The early crescent moon rose up from her bed of golden gorse or drooping heather, and slowly along the heavens she pursued her way; the night hours were numbered and the earth lay sleeping her wearied sleep, when Collingwood rose from his lonely watching. By the dim silvery light Lilly saw the unutterable anguish written upon his face, as white and set as the dead one on which he gazed. His grief was buried in his own heart now for evermore; and as he looked his last on the pure sweet face so calmly sleeping in that sleep that knows no waking, he stooped and kissed the cold white lips and closed sightless eyes; then reverently, and with tenderest care, he gathered the slender limbs once more to his bosom, and whispered a low passionate farewell. Having placed his dead darling again on her flower-strewn pillow, he moved out of the room without venturing to look back.

Out of her hiding-place then Lilly crept; he had not noticed her, not felt grateful for the loving sympathy the girl had proffered him, but she forgave him all the pain he caused her, and only lingered to utter a short prayer for peace to come to his troubled heart.

CHAPTER XI.

THE wind was blowing through the dark green oak leaves, over the tops of stately elms, amongst the deep underwood, where the snakes and lizards slept, coiled round and round like bands of shining steel.

In the midst of the wondrous beauty of a vast Canadian forest, two men were walking.

One had a letter in his hand, which, however, he seemed in no hurry to read, for he continued his recital of a wild adventure he had had during the past season, and quite excited his friend by his vivid, eager words. At length the latter reminded him of his epistle, saying: "Well, Thornton, I think, if I was you, I would see what the old lady says to your disappointing her about your arrival."

"Poor old mater. I know she will be upset, but I cannot face England yet; let them wait a short time longer; I must have some treasures to back myself up with; it would never answer to return empty-handed. By Jove! the fat would be in the fire." And as he spoke he opened his letter carelessly, and perused it somewhat slowly.

Over the sun-brown of his face his friend noticed a strange pallor creep; then it surprised him to see

Leonard stand still and lean against the trunk of a grand old forest monarch, which had no doubt seen many scenes of horror enacted under the shade of his wide arms; death had lain at his feet, grief had been wept out beneath his leaves, despair had sheltered itself under his shadow; the wild, dark chief had bent his bow, and shot swift through the air his poisoned arrow, whilst he knelt behind that wide, knotted bark; the white man had levelled his rifle, and shot to earth some graceful deer, whilst the leaves above him quivered—and still the old monarch lived on, year by year casting his green coverings, and burying in his leaf-tears a thousand insect lives; time would not change him, seasons could not harm him, it was only the hand of man he feared, only the eyes of man he hated to look upon his royal beauty.

Leonard's was but one more story told into his wide bark ears, one more heart pierced in the depths of the wondrous forest home; surely it was better that this white-faced man should bend and shiver, than that stately young sapling with its brown-tinged leaves and graceful, slender stem!

The forest monarch judged so.

After a while, Leonard tossed his letter to his companion, saying:

"I have had bad news, Wilson; I will get over my grumps alone," and turning on his heel he hastened away from the great oak's side, and was soon lost in the green-domed wilderness beyond.

Wilson took up the fallen letter, and hastily glanced at its contents; he knew nothing of Leonard's history, although they had been comrades for some months, sharing the dangers of the endless frosts, and the delights of fishing in the deep, clear lakes.

"Lilly, a bonny name," he exclaimed, as he read the signature of the letter, and discovered it was not from the "old lady," as Mrs. Thornton was termed by the friends.

"I wonder who this Mrs. Collingwood is! Odd her death should upset Thornton!"

Well might he wonder, as many of us do, when we see a face grow pale, or lips quiver, at the mention of an unfamiliar name or the look on an unknown face; each one of us has some secret which we guard carefully, as the miser does his gold; what a chaos the world would be if it were not so!

Leonard stumbled onwards; many times he bruised his head against a tree, or cut his hand with the prickly brambles; but he felt no pain; the end had come; his boy's love, his youth's idol, his manhood's promised wife, she was dead! and never would he look upon her face again. The bitterness he had vowed should fill every hour of his rival's life, the revenge he had sworn should be his task to fulfil, they must be relinquished now.

He felt the strong Hand that rules each of our destinies, and for the first time for five long years bent his head in supplication to Him Who can heal our deepest wound, or soothe our bitterest sorrow.

The wind whispered softly over his head, and wafted upon its breath a few sweet words from his dead love's lips; the graceful ferns, as they fell beneath his feet, whispered out a low chorus of loving sympathy. Then he stopped and, opening the large locket he always wore at the end of his watch-chain, gazed long and earnestly at the painted image of the pure girlish face, with its waving curls; he pressed the senseless picture to his lips, and murmured again and again that name which in years gone by had been his talisman of joy; he wept great burning tears, then wandered on and on until his grief was spent, and from off the tall tree-tops the sunbeams hastened; until the birds ceased their joyous vesper hymn, and the wind had sung the sun to sleep—the hush and silence of the coming night creeping over all.

Then he returned to the log-house which he and his friend occupied, and found Wilson awaiting him to sit down to their evening meal.

It was all so strange and saddening to him, this death of his baby-love. He left his meal untouched, and sat silent and pondering by their open wooden door. Wilson wondered more and more who this Mrs. Collingwood could be, that her death should have such an effect upon the usual light-hearted Leonard. At length, when the glorious summer night had shed her soft silvery veil over the miles of forest wilderness, Wilson took courage and addressed his companion.

"Thornton, your letter of to-day contained sad news; do you object to tell me if Mrs. Collingwood was any relation of yours?"

Leonard started; his thoughts had gone back to that New Year's Eve of long ago, when he passionately refused to listen to Florence's pleading. He was picturing her to himself as he saw her then, with the dim winter's twilight gathering round her, and her deep eyes filled with unshed tears. Ah! could he ever forget the earnest wistfulness of her low voice? How he blamed himself now for his harsh words! how he regretted the cold tones with which he had answered her, the shock his presence in the church had given her—it was he! it was surely he that had struck her her death-blow!

"Mrs. Collingwood was my father's ward for many years, and my betrothed wife; but we will not speak of it," at last Leonard answered; then, after a moment's pause, continued: "We must part to-morrow, old fellow. You will not forget your promise of hunting me up when you return to the mother country?"

"You may rely upon my doing so, Thornton. We shall have many a jolly chat together, I hope, before long," Wilson replied, his thoughts busy filling in the picture of his friend's life.

"Turn in now—never mind me, I mean to keep watch over Madame Moon to-night, for I dare say I shall never see her queening it over these parts again, and I am anxious to recognise the scene in the happy hunting-fields the old chief used to tell so about."

Wilson shouldered his chair, and disappeared into some inner regions.

Leonard took up his pipe again, and soon lost himself in his deep sad reveries. He was revenged, how fully! he pondered, and Collingwood's haggard face, as he had last seen it, rose before him. How bitter must have been his sufferings! what a loss was his! what a lifetime of pain must he have endured, with his young wife always dying before his eyes! Surely he could forgive him now?

The wild night-cry of the round-eyed owl startled Leonard from his thoughts; but when all was still again, they returned grieving him once more.

Was it only the moonlight quivering on the bending graceful ferns that cast that strange mysterious shadow into the air? He thought it a white-draped figure from the spirit-world! The low whisper of the wind swept past him, laden with the scent of honeysuckle; surely it was the first chant of that spirit's praise-hymn? Gradually his anger died away, and the revenge he had so craved to vent upon his rival faded from his heart.

As the moon and her silvery shadows were eclipsed by the more brilliant radiance of the day's golden king, Thornton rose from his seat a wiser and a better man.

CHAPTER XII.

THE autumnal glory had decked the woods with its brown and crimson dyes, the blustering winds were chasing the dead leaves from their temporary homes under the bare hedges, the great heaving billows came crashing up the stony shore, and the fishing smacks were tossed here and there on the angry sea, like rose-leaves in a summer storm.

Owen Lodge, with its dismal fir-trees, looked desolate in this advent of winter-time. A girl walking impatiently up and down the sloping avenue noted the lonely look of the quaint old mansion. She knew its history, and loved its ancient grandeur; often she raised her eyes from the book she held in her hand to fix them upon the weather-beaten pile, pondering over the many joys and sorrows its thick stone walls had been silent witnesses to. Only a few days ago she had learned her own history, and the sorrows of her young parents were pressing like burdens upon her shoulders. She was thinking too of her first meeting with the man whom she had so soon loved as a tender father, and a rosy blush spread itself over her features as she remembered the guise he had found her clothed in. Another's eyes had seen her then, and the proud little head reared itself up as the thought of those other eyes came back to her. She drew her cloak more closely around her, and shut up her book with a quick sharp gesture; then calling her favourite dogs "to heel," wandered through the open gates along the broad white roadway. The dust was flying in clouds, turning the brown hedges grey; her curls were blown into her eyes until she was almost blinded; baffled, she turned homewards again, and had not gone many steps before some one from behind overtook her, and addressing her, said:

"Can you direct me to Owen Lodge? I think I ought to be somewhere in its neighbourhood."

Lilly turned and faced the stranger; his eyes struck her as cold and piercing, his long brown beard was almost white with the dust from the road.

"You have only to go through those gates, and you will see the Lodge in front of you, sir," she answered.

"A Mr. Collingwood lives there, I believe?" again questioned the bearded stranger.

"Yes, he does," shortly answered Lilly, and turned to face the dust again, for his familiarity vexed her.

She felt her curls caught, she thought by the

wind, but usually the wind does not retain his victims. Angrily she moved her head, but before she had time to remonstrate her hands were clasped, and her cheeks kissed by her unacceptable companion.

"Why, Lilly, have you forgotten me?" said a voice which seemed to come out of past memories, softened and altered since a few moments before.

Then when she looked up and saw the smile light up the clear eyes, and flash like a sunbeam over the sunburned face, Lilly recognised Leonard. She returned his smile with words of hearty welcome, and let her hands lie pressed in his.

"Why what a tall young lady you have grown, Lilly; all legs and wings, I see!"

She blushed again more deeply than when a few moments before she had thought of their first meeting in Paris. What girl likes to be told she is all legs and wings?

"I never heard any one compliment me so highly as to tell me I was all legs and wings, Mr. Thornton."

"Very rude of me to make the observation you think, no doubt, but roughing it in the backwoods does not improve one's manners, Lilly. I must beg you to drop the Mr. Thornton; I mean to be Leo to you still."

"What are you coming to the Lodge, for?" she replied, too much vexed to take notice of his words.

"I have come to see Collingwood."

"He will not see you."

"Not see me, after all these years! Is he made of stone?" he replied, and his lips curled with impatient scorn.

"Let me go first to tell him you are here; he is so changed. You must have some pity on him."

"Pity! Nonsense, child; men don't waste pity on one another. I have come to settle all old debts, and the sooner my mission is over, the better for us both."

"You do not know how much he has suffered; you cannot imagine how altered you will find him. Pray, for the sake of old times, Mr. Thornton, refrain from raking up all the miseries of the past."

"I mean to rake up no miseries, Lilly, and I will not forget the past. I wish to God I could." Then he paused, and continued more calmly, "If you like to warn him of my presence, do so; perhaps he might kick me from his door like a dog."

"You are unjust, Mr. Thornton, but if you will await me here I will speak to my uncle of you;" and without more words she hastened into the house, leaving Leonard some little distance down the avenue.

He looked around him on the cold bleak scene, and wondered how the owner of it would receive him. Before his wonderment had spent itself, he saw Lilly returning.

"My uncle is waiting for you in the library; you will be gentle with him for her sake," she said, and raised her violet eyes full of pleading to his face.

As he returned her gaze, her wondrous beauty struck him as it had never done before; even the ungraceful age of girlhood could not mar the loveliness of that perfect face. He sighed as he passed onwards, thinking of the lives that might be wrecked to win a smile from those red pouting lips.

The library was a dark dismal room, and the bright fire burning on its hearth did little to enliven its sombre corners. Leonard, on entering, failed to perceive the form of a man seated in an armchair close to the burning embers; but as Collingwood rose to greet him, even he, warned as he had been of the change in his boyhood's friend, started back in horror at the wreck of the man that approached him. Could this be Coll?—tall, handsome Coll! who had nursed him at College, fought his battles, puzzled out his verbs?—that bent form, those sunken hollow cheeks, that silvery hair? Good God! was it indeed he? All his anger died away, and a pitying love sprang up into his heart as with outstretched hands he hastened towards his companion's side.

"Coll! Owen! let the past be forgiven? She shall be our judge in the world above."

They looked into each other's faces; no words passed between them, only the strong pressure of those firmly-clasped hands told of wrongs forgotten and a friend regained.

The bleak wind blustered about the dead leaves, and the fire-glow was all of light that remained in the room, while still the long-estranged friends sat side by side with only a word now and then to tell of the troubled feelings that were making sad havoc in the hearts of both.

"Uncle, dinner will be in directly; had you not better persuade Mr. Thornton to share it with us?" said Lilly, coming into the room.

Her presence aroused the silent friends, and Collingwood, turning to Leonard, begged the favour of his company at their board.

Somewhat hesitatingly Leonard agreed to remain, and before long found himself breaking bread with the man against whom he had sworn an eternal hatred.

So it is often with us all; some great misfortune, some heavy trouble overtakes our enemy, and all that is true and brave in our nature asserts itself, and forgetting our past grievances, our vowed revenge, we stretch out our hands to plead for forgiveness, wondering how aught but pity and love could enter into our hearts for a brother so less fortunate than ourselves.

When the gentlemen entered the drawing-room after talking some time over their wine, they found Lilly seated before the piano, and Leonard was considerably surprised at the evident talent the girl possessed.

Collingwood found himself a cosy corner by the fire, and motioned Leonard to take an arm-chair opposite. Silently they listened to Lilly's music, which echoed through the long old-fashioned room and lost itself among the heavy foils of the window curtains.

"Lilly," Collingwood called, and with swift feet the girl obeyed his summons.

"Yes, dear uncle," she said, kneeling by his side and bending her head so that his hand might caress her hair.

"I wish you would run down and see how Hubert's child is getting on. Jones told me her arm was paining her a good deal this morning."

Lilly regained her feet, and left the room quickly; re-entering it, however, almost immediately, equipped for her walk.

"Take Rollo with you," Collingwood said, as she bade the gentlemen good-night and was proceeding on her way.

"Surely, Lilly, you are not going alone?" remonstrated Leonard, escorting her through the hall.

"Yes, of course I am; besides, Rollo will take care of me."

"Are you not afraid, child? the night is dark, and the moon up late."

She laughed, and her eyes flashed scornfully, as she answered:

"I have not learned to be afraid of the dark yet, Mr. Thornton! Do you wish to give me a lesson in that art?"

Receiving no reply, she stooped to pat Rollo's head, saying:

"You do not know this Rollo, do you? I will tell you his history." Her voice was wonderfully soft as she continued: "When uncle was travelling with his wife abroad, she saw this doggie in a poor little cottage; she signed to them to stop the carriage, and eagerly pointed to the dog, who lay sleeping lazily in the sun. Of course uncle persuaded the peasants to part with the animal. When Mrs. Collingwood knew the dog was hers, she put her one arm about his neck and wept bitterly, the only time they ever saw her grieve. Uncle called him Rollo in remembrance of her favourite of long ago. And now, of course, Rollo is quite master here—uncle would not part with him for untold gold; he lets me take him out sometimes, but not very often. And now, good-night," changing her voice, she concluded.

"Not good-night just yet; I mean to see you to your destination, wherever that may be," and opening the door, they made their exit together.

It was indeed a dark night; even the fir-trees were but a black mass, only a shade darker than the surrounding atmosphere.

"Now you must tell me what is the cause of our

little invalid's wounded arm. You remember I am a medical man myself, and can perhaps help you in your charitable mission."

"Dr. Longford attends all uncle's tenants, and he was with Hubert's child this morning."

"Well, never mind, I should like to prescribe for her too, and Longford is an old chum of mine, so we are not likely to quarrel over the patient. By-the-bye, is not Longford married? I have a vague idea I heard of his committing some such folly."

"Yes, he married Miss Eccles nearly two years ago."

"Have they any chicks then?"

"One little tiny boy, such a dear little fellow, and I am his godmother."

"I suppose you admire wee babies then, Lilly? although to me you seem a baby still."

"I am not a baby, Mr. Thornton! indeed, I think I never was."

"You had a hard time of it when you were; had you not, my Lilly?" His voice was singularly sweet as he put the question, for the thought of the little ragged-clothed figure in the Parisian garret came back to him, and he wondered what strange history the girl's had been.

There was a silence for some moments; then Leonard broke it.

"Lilly, do you know who your parents were? it

was strange Collingwood taking you as he did, and adopting you as his niece."

She hesitated before answering him, but at last replied: "I know my own history, but cannot tell it to you. Ask uncle if you wish to hear it; perhaps he will tell you."

"I shall never ask Collingwood anything about the past or the people concerned in it; he is not in a fit state to be put out by anything or anybody; therefore, unless you can trust me, Lilly, I suppose I must let my interest in you die." Again she did not answer, and he felt somewhat piqued. "Well! so you will not trust me?" he questioned as they arrested their steps in front of a cottage door.

"It is not my secret to confide to your keeping, Mr. Thornton."

"I told you not to call me Mr. Thornton. I can praise you for your caution," and he followed her through the opened doorway.

Amongst the children Lilly was in her element; she took the little invalid and another upon her knee, and rocked them to and fro in a most ungraceful manner, singing snatches of Welsh songs that she had picked up during her long residence amongst them; then her pocket was emptied, and found to contain many treasures all very acceptable to the rough youngsters around. The elders of the family looked on pleased at the notice their younger members were gaining, and Leonard found himself quite a secondary personage in the noisy group. After a time, however, Lilly remembered his presence, and his wish to prescribe for her little invalid; she rose from her chair, and with the colour deepened in her cheeks begged him to excuse her thoughtlessness, and showed the injured arm of the wounded girl; Leonard looked at it, felt it gently up and down, then having pronounced his opinion upon the extent of the injury, proposed their returning home. At this there was a general outcry, and hands not very clean seized Lilly's dress, and voices not low pleaded very earnestly for just one little tale before she left them. Leonard added his voice to the general chorus, and succeeded in persuading Lilly to comply with their request. So in her clear ringing tones the girl commenced her story.

"It was long before the forests on the mountain sides were cut down from the wild wind's love words, long before the deep blue rivers were walled in the wide white towns, long before the little birds with their bright plumage were shot dead whilst they sang on the wing, long before the timid hare or white-breasted rabbit were netted in the dark, starless nights; it was quite when the world was young, when every bird, beast, and fish was happy, being free from the cruelty of man, when tiny little fairies and transparent small elves inhabited the sunny earth, and the summer time lasted always, and no frost, or snow, or storm, or shower dimmed the clear, bright atmosphere.

"Amongst the large family of fairies there was one who was elected queen. She was fair and beautiful, like those pretty white butterflies you so often see in the summer weather flitting from flower to flower. She was much loved by her subjects, and the most delicate rose or most spotless lily was selected for her scented throne-room. I must tell you the elves were deadly enemies to the fairies; they were small black-winged sprites, with eyes of fire and voices whose softness quite enthralled you if you listened to it. The first law in fairy-land forbid any communication being held with the elves, and many and severe were the punishments inflicted on the disgraced little fairy who ventured to disobey the command.

"One day, when the wind was soft and warm and rocked gently to and fro the tall lily in which the fairy-queen slept, an elf roaming from flower to flower struck his wings against the fairy's throne-room. Quickly the body-guard, consisting of some dozen fairies, all ablaze with cowslip shields, rushed out to entrap the venturous enemy, their swords of grass blades were lifted high in the air, and in an instant the elf would have been cut into a thousand pieces if the queen had not been awoke by the scuffle, and looking over the lily-leaf saw the unequal combat; she took pity on the elf, for her judgment told her one against twelve was hardly fair-play, raising her wand of primrose-stalk she commanded the swords to be sheathed and her guards to bring the prisoner into her throne-room.

"'What has brought you into our dominions, sir,' she said, trying to look very angry at the little fire-eyed elf.

"'He must not speak! he must not speak!' shouted the body-guard, and in their earnestness they shook the lily so that its stalk cracked.

"'Silence!' ordered the queen, and having by this time worked herself into a rage she turned two furious eyes upon her trembling subjects, then addressed the elf, saying, 'Answer now my question, sir, or I shall have you drowned in the dew to-night.'

"Then the elf shook his dark limbs from their cob-web fetters, and fixing his eyes on the white-winged queen, replied;

"'I have heard of your beauty, fair queen, and determined to feast my eyes upon the vision I flew against your throne-room.'

"At the sound of his voice all the guards trembled, and their grass-blade swords and cowslip shields fell drooping by their sides. The queen called them to order, but they quivered and shook so that the poor lily's-head being unused to such a commotion broke off from the stalk and sent the queen and all her court right into a dandelion's bosom. It just happened to be the dandelion selected by the elves for their assize-court, and a great divorce case being on, all the men of law were solemnly seated each on a separate leaf. You may imagine the confusion that arose when the queen and her guards came plunging in—the wigs flew off the councillors' heads, and the judge losing his balance fell into the witness-box. However the naughty elf, whose voice had been the cause of all the trouble, managed to save the fairy-queen from injury, and when order was somewhat restored he commanded the court to adjourn, and a special jury to be selected to pass judgment on the case of the queen and her court having invaded premises not their own. Each of the unfortunate body-guard was sentenced to become a stuffed ear-wig; they pleaded hard for mercy, and begged at least to be allowed to adopt a butterfly's body for their own; but after a long and serious consultation the verdict was pronounced against them. Then the queen's turn came; as she stepped into the witness-box all the jury lost their heads by her beauty. Her case was heard, but no sentence pronounced; for each elf was dying of anxiety to claim her as his elfess. Just then up popped the naughty prince-elf, who had ventured to invade her throne-room.

"'I mean to wed the fairy-queen,' he called out in a voice of thunder, and made such a commotion that a cow who was grazing near turned up her tail and scampered away through the field and out into the roadway, where meeting a little doggie she tossed him on her horns into a large pond, where he fell upon a gold-fish and killed the shining tiny mite.

"'I mean to wed the fairy-queen,' and all the jurymen bobbed their heads together, and a little murmur of dissent or assent—it was difficult to distinguish which—ran through their ranks.

"'It is forbidden by the law,' at last ventured to remonstrate the most courageous.

"'Hang the law, and all of you too, if you presume to apply any law to me!' proudly answered the fire-eyed prince, and stalked out of that leaf back into the court-house one, where, addressing the poor little queen, who still remained in the witness-box, he said, 'You are to marry me and be my queen.'

"'I won't!' she exclaimed, and even her wings went green at the thought.

"'You must!' commanded the elf, and produced a tiny ring made out of a shrimp's leg, and putting it upon the unwilling queen's finger he proclaimed her queen of the elves.

"Then there was a great war, but neither party being strong enough to exterminate the other a mighty peace was signed, and ever since the elves and fairies have been one people."

Leonard, as he watched the group as Lilly finished her tale, thought he had never looked upon a more picturesque scene—the tallow-candle which was short at the commencement of the story flashed out and died down in its socket; the logs burned brightly in the wide hearth, and their flames lighted up every face in the circle; the younger members of the party had eyes opened wide with intense interest and delight, their rough little hands clinging to some portion of Lilly's dress, and the two upon her knee had their heads upon her breast, with lips wide apart as if longing to echo her words. Her own lovely face and golden curls caught many a fiery glow, and the sweet gravity and childish earnestness that hovered about her lips made her appear like some young angel dropped from the sky, and a little fearful of its more ancient comrades.

Standing against the rude-cut chimney-piece, and by the side of Lilly's chair were the elders of the family, they were smiling at the happiness expressed in the faces of the little ones, but in their eyes too the love for the young reciter was plainly visible.

"Now I must really go," said Lilly jumping up and giving a hasty kiss on each dirty cheek.

"Oh! no, no, no!" a chorus of voices answered, but their mother coming in silenced the little pleaders, and Lilly was permitted to depart in peace.

As they sauntered slowly back to the hall, for notwithstanding the unpleasantness of the night Leonard felt reluctant to part with his companion, he was speculating as to the character of the girl; she was certainly different to any other of her age, and he felt somewhat at a loss how to address her; at length he remarked carelessly:

"I suppose you learned that little story you have been telling the children at school, Lilly?"

"I have never been to school, Mr. Thornton; and don't suppose I should be likely to learn stories there, if I had."

"You have learned to be uncommonly sharp somewhere."

"Paid a visit to my uncle's razor-box yesterday, sir," and she laughed.

"I dislike sharp young ladies."

"But you consider me a baby, so that you cannot expect me to comply with your rules for young ladies."

"Well, whatever you are, you have grown very impertinent and forward."

"I am sorry you have formed such a bad opinion of me, but, unfortunately, I cannot diminish into a baby again for your sake."

"I do not imagine you would if you could, Lilly."

Here they arrived at the Lodge, and when admitted, Lilly, with a careless shake of the hand, bade her companion good-night, and disappeared up the wide stairs.

Perhaps it would not be treason to follow her and watch her, as she stood looking earnestly at the reflection of her face, in her mirror. Her cheeks were flushed and her eyes sparkling, and as she turned away she stamped her foot, exclaiming:

"Let him wait a few years yet, and he shall love me!"

CHAPTER XIII.

It is once again sunrise: once again, as of old in the years past and gone, the sun casts his first warm glance on the face of Halston Hall; now, as of yore, the flowers open their bright eyes, delighted to welcome the first love-glance of their fiery king; the geraniums and stocks are all ablaze in their brilliant coverings, and the pale blush rose or sweet-smelling pink throw out a wind of scent into the summer air.

There is no child dancing round the flower-beds, no canine friend playing with a baby-mistress; the little head "running over with curls" lies pillowed by earth in a cold bed-tomb; the rough four-footed playfellow has his resting-place under that bending willow—it weeps perpetually, though others cease to grieve.

The silvery mists of early morn have faded quite away from the valley; the flowers, accustomed to the sun's warm glance, are tossing their pretty heads to the flighty butterflies, who, in their turn, dash their dainty wings against some old oak trunk, and thus ruin their brilliant beauty.

The day was still young, and its early freshness not quite faded, when through the open doorway of the Hall a girl stepped out.

The sun could look into her face and find no flaw, the stars could gaze into her eyes and see their rivals there, the willow might bend to the soft breeze and not equal her in supple gracefulness, and a stray warm sunbeam that fell amongst the heavy coils of her hair lost itself in the golden splendour.

As her young father had walked out of the white foreign city ready to die for a stranger country's glory, as the sunlight danced in his hair and caught the look in the depths of his eyes, perhaps then he resembled her! her, his wee unseen babe, the only offspring of his lion-hearted wife; perhaps then he resembled her! All those who looked at Lilly's face turned quickly to look again; it was not the fine chiselling of her perfect features, not the soft fairness of her transparent skin, not the deep violet of her superb eyes or the wealth of her golden hair; it was not all these that made her "a thing of beauty" or "a joy for ever;" grief for others' woes often dimmed the brightness of her eyes, love for the forsaken was in every whisper of her clear voice, pity for the sinful in every movement of her supple form. The rich praised her beauty, the poor her charity, the suffering her patience, and the crime-stained her gentleness.

And yet Lilly was not perfect; in the smooth

well cared-for life she had led since Collingwood had taken her to his heart, after the death of his wife, she had few troubles to contend against; there were those, however, who called her cold and proud, cruel and indifferent, men who had laid their lives and fortunes at her feet and received a scornful laugh or a few indifferent words for all thank-offering. She was a puzzle to all, even Collingwood was surprised by her haughty manner and careless words to those who sought her love, but to him she was ever the obedient tender child of long ago.

"Miss Lilly, they are waiting breakfast for you," said Thomas, now very old and grey, coming up to her side as she stood admiring the morning's freshness.

"I will be with them in a moment," she replied, turning to smile into his wrinkled face; then, pulling a few flowers with the dew like tears on them, she entered the house.

Mr. and Mrs. Thornton and Collingwood all rose to greet her as she joined them at their meal; and as she bent her stately head to offer her usual kiss to the elder lady, Collingwood turned his eyes away—it was a new pain to see her thus winning the love that had once been his dead darling's, taking the place which only she should have occupied. Alas! in life there is no time to mourn the dead; they are gone, passed out of our pathway—why seek after them?

When breakfast was over Collingwood offered to take Lilly for a ride, an exercise she was passionately fond of. As they were leaving the house Mrs. Thornton detained them, saying:

"Mr. Hurst and Leonard are coming this evening. Will you be back in time to welcome them?"

Lilly looked inquiringly into her uncle's face. It was the first time since his marriage he had visited Halston Hall, and she knew not if now he would like this meeting with his ancient rival.

"Both Lilly and myself will be in good time to welcome your son, Mrs. Thornton; Hurst is a favourite of ours, too, I think?" Collingwood answered quietly, with some slight hesitation in his tone.

Then along between the green hedgeways and under the flowering chestnuts, the girl and the man rode; she, noting the beauty of it all, and feeling thankful for the wealth of youth and health she enjoyed; he, thinking of the dead past, putting in every corner of the summer scene that little figure with its brown, rippling curls that in the years gone by had made the earth his Paradise; surely his love had been as deep and true as Abelard's for Eloïse, or Dante for his ideal Beatrice?

Readers, how many of us ride side by side down the roadway of life, some looking with happy eyes upon the fair, peaceful landscape, others—and those, perhaps, our nearest and dearest—seeing it all through a mist of tears?

The day wore on, and the silence of the twilight hour hushed the birds and winged insects to sleep.

Lilly was seated by the low window, looking down the long avenue of chestnut trees. Collingwood in a chair near her, reading, dropped his book to criticise her face. He was proud of her beauty, yet it pained him, for never had he seen the colour deepen in her cheeks, or the thick lashes veil the brilliancy of her eyes. Was she as cold as she appeared to be? Or who had taught her thus to mask her feelings? He sighed as he watched her, and wished she had resembled more his pale, timid bride, who lay buried far away by the wild, rushing waters.

Oh God! what might have been if she had lived her life out, and smiling babes had danced about his knees and laughed into his face this hushed twilight June-tide? What might have been if his recklessness had not killed her?

There was a rush of horses' feet, a dash of a heavily-laden carriage; a scuffle of many people in the hall; then the door was thrown wide, and two figures entered the room.

Hurst's tall form was the first visible, as he seized Collingwood's outstretched hands; his voice was full of gladness at their meeting. Leonard soon followed his companion; he was little changed from the brown-bearded stranger Lilly had met in the dusty Welsh highway, more than four years ago.

"Well, Lilly! you have managed to grow into a young lady at last," he remarked, retaining the hand she had offered him in welcome.

She had her back to the window, or else Collingwood might have seen the crimson colouring that overspread her features as she answered, laughingly:

"I believe I am considered something better than a baby now."

"Miss Lilly, it is my turn to have a look at you," interrupted Hurst, joining them, and turning Lilly facewards towards the light.

His gaze was long and earnest, and he, too, sighed as he let go her hands, saying:

"You are as dainty as your namesake; but beware, child; beauty is a dangerous gift in a woman's hands."

Tell-tale blushes again dyed her cheeks, and this time Collingwood, seeing them, wondered at the cause.

After dinner, when all were assembled in the long drawing-room; Collingwood and Hurst deep in conversation, and Leonard, as usual, by his mother's side; Lilly, thinking herself *de trop*, slipped out of the room and sought refuge down the shaded avenue. She felt restless and unlike herself; notwithstanding her ride of the morning, she wished she dare venture alone on her favourite's back over the sleepy valley, and away, away, she cared not whither.

"Lilly," said some one by her side, "how is it you always run away from me? Surely you can treat me to some news after all your travels! I quite expected to find you a chatterbox."

"I was never given that way, Mr. Thornton; but why have you left your mother? she must want you this first evening, I am sure."

"She sent me to hunt you up; we are all waiting for you to come and pour out our coffee. Do you feel inclined to curtail your ramble for our sakes?"

"I am always willing to sacrifice myself for the public good."

"Not for an individual's good, then?" he questioned, looking inquiringly into her half-averted face.

"How?"

"How, Lilly? Would you marry a man to be a comfort and help to him if he offered you everything but love?"

"No! never! never! I would rather die first; for I should learn to hate him." Then, restraining her excitement, she added in her usual calm tones: "How foolish we are to talk about subjects that cannot interest us! I am afraid the coffee will be the sufferer, or rather, the unlucky ones who mean to drink it; for you have kept me out until, I am sure, it is cold. What will Mrs. Thornton say?"

Retracing her steps, she soon found herself in the drawing-room again.

All the evening she tried to avoid Leonard's company, but he managed to secure her at last in a quiet corner quite out of ear-shot of the others.

"Lilly, do you believe a man can love twice in his lifetime?"

"How can I tell? I am not a man!" she answered, not looking at him but playing with the bracelet on her arm.

"I suppose you would object to marry a widower?"

"No widower has ever been fool enough to ask me—but, Mr. Thornton, do talk sense? I am sure I do not want to anatomise widowers' hearts."

"For argument's sake, I want to know if you think you would marry a widower, supposing you were in love with him?"

"If he had not loved his first wife, perhaps I might; but I must be before and beyond all things and all people to the man whom I choose for my master," and she looked up at him with a proud defiant light in her superb eyes.

"'Before and beyond all things and people!' You are ambitious," he repeated after her; then, rising, continued somewhat sadly: "Some men are doomed to lose the race, however hard they ride."

"Leo!" she called, her lips parted with a happy smile; but he did not hear her, and had joined Collingwood and Hurst in their discussion.

Later in the evening, Hurst and Leonard found themselves together in the smoking-room.

"Well, Thornton, what do you think of our production in the way of females? Better than the mixture over the Channel, eh?"

"An improvement certainly in the right direction. Collingwood's importation resembles her namesake:

"'Divinely tall and most divinely fair.'"

"Don't be overcome with surprise when I tell you Collingwood's importation, as you entitle Miss Lilly, is his niece."

"By Jove! you don't mean it, surely!" answered Leonard, in his surprise dropping his meerschaum.

"'Truth is stranger than fiction' sometimes, Thornton; pray digest the news between your bedclothes!" with which wise advice Hurst quitted the room.

Leonard, left to himself, recovered his pipe and pondered so deeply on the intelligence he had just heard that he fell asleep. With a start and a shiver, he awoke long past midnight; with a few grumblings he then beat a hasty retreat to bed.

CHAPTER XIV.

We must pay our last visit to Owen Lodge, for the first time to look upon it in the full glory of the summer-time. The old grey walls are smiling into the day-god's face; a thousand dancing beams glitter among the casements of its Gothic windows; the birds, with happy voices, sing among the dark fir-trees, and make the woods re-echo with their gleeful strains.

Far away down the hill-side the corn in golden glory is bending its graceful head to the salt-burdened breeze; the poppies, too, toss a bunch of scarlet nosegays into the balmy air; the dog-daisies, blue-bells, buttercups, and heather are laughing at one another over the wide-spreading hedge-top; the cattle are hiding under the shade of some friendly tree, whipping the teasing flies from their freckled backs with their long tails; the little streamlets are having it all their own way up in the mountain passes.

It is broad, broad noonday. Lilly is standing in the cool picture-gallery, gazing steadfastly at a painting of herself, painted by a hand feverish with the heat of love, criticised by eyes blind to all beauty but that of the fair-haired girl's. She remembered but too well the quiet, shaded studio in the bright Italian city; the fair, sloping city, with its emblem of spotless flowers—well loved both in history and romance—where Correggio had died under the shaded tree-tops, and Tasso had pictured with vivid words his wondrous armies with their brilliant banners all swaying in the sun.

Her thoughts troubled her, and with a little impatient stamp of her foot she moved onwards down the gallery; she had not gone far, however, when another painted image of herself arrested her attention; the memory of the dear wrinkled hands that had lingered so tenderly over every shade of that baby face made her heart ache; it seemed but yesterday, that day so long ago when she had lain in the dazzling sunlight and warmed her shining limbs in its bright rays. Was it really more than ten years ago since a tall stranger had darkened the door of her poor garret home and taken her to his heart for all eternity?

"Lilly," said a voice behind her, and she started and blushed as she turned to face Leonard.

"Do you want me for anything, Mr. Thornton?"

"If I did not want you should I be seeking you?"

"I really cannot tell. You say you have learned

many odd things in Yankeeland; perhaps one of them may be to seek after unwantable things."

"Are you a thing?" he retorted, laughing.

"I am a noun, which, according to Murray, signifies the name of any person, place, or thing."

"But you come under the head of persons, don't you."

"Oh, never mind bothering me! I come under my own head, I imagine."

"Women are never logical, Lilly, but I always considered you an exception to the rule. By-the-bye, I suppose you have given up all school ideas now."

"I only attend the school for scandal, being perfect in the other branches of education." Then she laughed and walked towards the entrance of the gallery.

"Don't go away, Lilly; you seem to forget that I came in search of you, and I want to talk to you before this picture."

"The sun hurts my eyes there," she answered, and stood still, irresolute whether to go or stay.

"The sun is not more powerful now than he was a few moments ago, and you did not seem to object to his presence then."

"I have some letters I must write before lunch."

"Lilly, I want to speak to you. Will you listen to me for a few moments?"

"Yes," she replied in a low soft voice, and approached his side again.

"Do you remember cutting off your curls to please me one New Year's Eve?"

"My memory is not short," and the crimson blood dyed all her face.

"Would you destroy your beauty now for my sake?" he questioned eagerly, bending his head until his face almost touched hers, and involuntarily seizing one jewelled hand in his own.

Her lips quivered, and as she slowly met his gaze she questioned:

"Leo! Leo! are you sure that you love me?"

Her exquisite beauty acted upon him like a spell; all his indifference to her vanished in a moment; he caught her in his arms, his limbs trembling with wild excitement.

"Above and beyond all things and people, my darling; can you doubt it?"

She felt his hot kisses upon her lips, and her heart beat madly with intense happiness and joy. The love of her life was not wasted, after all!

The noonday glory was fading away, the flowers and grass-blades were reviving, and standing once more in the sunbeams. Lilly blessed the radiant light, and thought it would last always; the earth was surely rejoicing with her now in the brilliant glory of her noonday love.

In the silent, moonlight hours of that summer night Leonard related his broken life story; Lilly listened with all her woman's sympathy aroused;

reason questioned, would he ever love her as well as he had loved his promised bride of years ago? What mattered it? she would not be jealous of the dead, and now he was all her own.

Collingwood was sad and silent as his wont. Another heart had forgotten his dead darling. She knew how they would all forsake her, surely, when she had promised in the glow of the summer's sunset "to be with him always." He felt she was with him now, only her thin spirit-veil hid her from his sight.

CHAPTER XV.

THERE were many sad hearts, many sad faces, on the brave boat's deck; many passionate words passed the portals of quivering lips. True lovers looked their last for years to come into eyes that were dim with tears. Wives and husbands uttered many times over the caution each gave for the other's safety; brothers and sisters clung about each other's necks, never feeling so united as at this moment of perhaps eternal parting.

A pale-faced woman there, with hands clasped tightly and great sobs shaking her slender frame, look! she is gazing at that slight boy with his tattered clothes and unkempt hair; he is her only one, "and the son of a widow." She has stitched her fingers to the bone, she has tried her eyes until their sight is almost gone; but her labour has procured those few pounds that will serve to help her darling in his start of life far away on the western shore.

Let us hope those salt tears will not be shed in vain, those fevered worded prayers will reach the eternal throne; and that, when trembling age seizes those slender limbs in his withering grasp, the parted ones will be united, and on a loving and beloved son's breast that patient widowed mother will find her rest.

There is another figure we notice in the group of poorly-clad figures. Again it is a woman, a woman with little tiny children clinging round about her skirts; their baby-voices are calling for their "Daddy," follow their eyes and you will see him there amongst the steerage passengers. A tall dark man, with a frame that might serve for a Hercules model; eyes dull and heavy, for sleep has been a stranger to their weary watching for many a long night; cheeks sunken and pale, hunger has found a victim there; hair damp with the sweat of pain: truly a wreck of one of England's greatest treasures.

How hard it is to keep those tears from falling as he looks on that little group gradually disappearing from his sight—will he never look upon their faces more? never feel the warm clasp of their little arms about his neck, or toss them upon his knee when his day's work is done? They are pulling at his heart-strings with their soft wee hands, and he almost thinks he hears their pleadings for their "Daddy." Let us hope he, too, will prosper, and make a home for all in that far-off western-land.

There is still another group I would fain draw your attention to, dear reader, before I close my story.

They are looking over the tall ship's side, those parting friends; they are gazing down into the brown-hued water-depths, and the sunlight dances amongst the woman's golden hair, or touches tenderly the silvered threads of her companion's.

She has her hands clasped upon his arm, her violet eyes are running over with tears, some linger still upon her long lashes as if loath to disfigure her fair face with their stains.

"My darling, you will be happy," said Collingwood, bending down to kiss again and again the trembling quivering lips.

"Oh! how I wish you were not going!" between her sobs Lilly gasped out, and pressed her head upon his breast and hid her face there.

"My Lilly, I am so weary of my native land, you would not have me stay? But, darling, I shall think of the welcome you will give me when I come back again," and he pressed his arm more firmly about her.

The great bell rang.

"All visitors ashore!" called out a sailor, going from group to group and hastening friends away.

"Leo, take your bride, and guard her well," said Collingwood, unclasping Lilly's arms from about his neck and pushing her gently towards Leonard, who was standing with Hurst near.

There was a last hurried kiss and hasty blessing; then Collingwood and Hurst were standing silently together looking over the boat's side at the tug and her few sad passengers. Lilly's blue dress fluttered in the breeze, and she waved her handkerchief to them until they were but part of the dark hull side.

The noon-day passed and the eve-hours drew in, night's dark veil was hanging in the sky waiting to be drawn across the earth's green face; it was the hour for silence and meditation, for thoughts of the dead or absent to come stealing into our memory.

Lilly and Leonard were seated side by side on the sandy hills, whereon, in years gone by, Florence had looked her last upon an earthly sunset; their voices were sad and low, for the dead and absent were the subjects of their conversation.

But there was a bright dawn of love and happiness awaiting them on the morrow, and knowing this they lingered tenderly over these last sad hours.

* * * * *

The sea boarded the horizon; the rose light of sunset was creeping from cloud to cloud, and brushing the foam on the crested waves; the fishes caught the crimson glory on their silvery scales, and the mermaids pulled out their harpstrings and twined their locks to be ready for their evening gambols.

Hurst and Collingwood were standing side by side watching the dying hour of the day-god's king.

Hurst noticed the deadly pallor of his companion's face, noticed the fearful shiver that shook his strong limbs, watched him press his hand against his heart, as if to still the pain that was gnawing there.

"Owen, are you ill?" he said at last, and turned his face away from the rose light to look more earnestly into the sad one at his side.

He received no answer to his question, but Collingwood swayed backwards, murmuring a long loved name, and would have fallen if Hurst had not caught him in his arms.

One glance revealed the dreadful truth. Collingwood was dead! dead in the crimson glory of the sunset hour; the ripple of the waves and the cry of the sea-mew for his death-chant.

The remembrance of that sunset hour of long ago had come when his tired frame was too weak to bear its pain, and without a murmur, without a sigh, the tired soldier had dropped in the field where the battle of life was fighting; and the sun of earth, that sun that had brightened his noonday love, that sun that had watched at his hour of agony, was set in the rosy west; and his shield, now cleansed with his tears of pain, is awaiting his arm to uplift it; and his love, whom he loved on the green earth's bosom, is standing there in the crimson light, and opening wide with smiling lips the portals to eternal happiness. He is dead, but he has ceased his weeping, he has passed the bridge over the eternal river, and stands safely on the shore of everlasting bliss. His work is done, and his prize awarded; his dawn of joy is breaking, and the sunset of his life is past.

Reader, it was June, and the sun had dropped into his tomb of crimson and golden splendour.

THE END.

LONDON: R. WASHBOURNE, 18 PATERNOSTER ROW.

R. WASHBOURNE'S CATALOGUE OF BOOKS,

18 PATERNOSTER ROW, LONDON.

NEW BOOKS.

From Sunrise to Sunset. By L. B. 12mo., 3s. 6d.

Pius IX., his early Life to the Return from Gaeta. By Rev. T. B. Snow, O.S.B. 12mo., 6d.

Three Sketches of Life in Iceland. By Carl Andersen. Translated by Myfanwy Fenton. Dedicated to H. R. H. the Princess of Wales. 12mo., 2s. 6d.

Rest, on the Cross. By E. L. Hervey. 12mo., 3s. 6d.

The Faith of our Fathers: Being a Plain Exposition and Vindication of the Church founded by our Lord Jesus Christ. By Rt. Rev. James Gibbons, D.D., 12mo. 4s.; paper covers, 2s. nett.

"The author is not aggressive; is never bitter, never sneers, nor deals in sarcasm or ridicule; does not treat his reader as a foe to be beaten, but as a brother to be persuaded. His sense of religion is too deep to allow him to make light of any honest faith. We perceive on every page the reverend and Christian bishop who knows that charity and not hate is the divine power of the Church; the fire that sets the world ablaze. It is not necessary that we should say more in commendation of this treatise. It will most certainly have a wide circulation, and its merits will be advertised by every reader. Bishop Gibbons has written chiefly for Protestants, but we hope his book will find entrance into every Catholic family."—*Catholic World.*

The Panegyrics of Fr. Segneri, S.J. Translated from the original Italian. With a preface by the Rev. William Humphrey, S.J. 12mo., 5s.

"Happily eloquence was not the only great excellence of Segneri. His matter is always most valuable, for he was a thorough theologian as well as a wonderful preacher."—*Month.*

My Conversion and Vocation. By Rev. Father Schouvaloff, Barnabite. Translated from the French. With an Appendix by the Rev. Father C. Tondini, Barnabite. 12mo., 5s.

"This is a very edifying and a very readable book. Some books are readable without being precisely edifying, and many works are edifying though not at all readable, but this work has both good qualities. It is an autobiography, the record of the trials, struggles, temptations, doubts, fears, calls to grace, and the final victory of a Russian nobleman. It is founded, perhaps not altogether unconsciously, on one of the greatest works ever produced by a human pen—'The Confessions of S. Augustine.'"—*Tablet.*

Men and Women of the English Reformation from the days of Wolsey to the death of Cranmer. By S. H. Burke, M.A. 2 vols., 12mo., 10s.

"The author produces evidence that cannot be gainsaid."—*Universe.* "Interesting and valuable."—*Tablet.* "A clever and well-written historical statement."—*Month.*

*** *Though this Catalogue does not contain many of the books of other Publishers, R. W. can supply all of them, no matter by whom they are*

The Story of the Life of St. Paul. By M. F. S., author of "Legends of the Saints," &c., &c. 12mo., 2s. 6d.

"That delightful writer for the young, the author of 'Tom's Crucifix,' 'Catherine Hamilton,' 'Stories of the Saints,' 'Stories of Martyr Priests,' and many other works of similar excellence and interest, has found a most attractive theme for her prolific pen in the wonderful and edifying story of S. Paul. The Story of S. Paul thus written will be a favourite with those juvenile Catholic readers who have already so much cause for gratitude to M. F. S."—*Weekly Register.*

Fluffy. A Tale for Boys. By M. F. S., author of "Tom's Crucifix, and other Tales." 12mo., 3s. 6d.

"A charming little story. The narrative is as wholesome throughout as a breath of fresh air, and as beautiful in the spirit of it as a beam of moonlight."—*Weekly Register.*

The Feasts of Camelot; with the Tales that were told there. By Eleanora Louisa Hervey. 12mo., 3s. 6d.

"This is really a very charming collection of tales, told, as is evident from the title, by the Knights of the Round Table, at the Court of King Arthur. It is good for children and for grown up people too, to read these stories of knightly courtesy and adventure and of pure and healthy romance, and they have never been written in a more attractive style than by Mrs. Hervey in this little volume."—*Tablet.* "Elegant and imaginative invention, well selected language, and picturesque epithet."—*Athenæum.* "Full of chivalry and knightly deeds, not unmixed with touches of quaint humour."—*Court Journal.* "A graceful and pleasing collection of stories."—*Daily News.* "Quaint and graceful little stories."—*Notes and Queries.* "There is a high purpose in this charming book, one which is steadily pursued—it is the setting forth of the true meaning of chivalry."—*Morning Post.*

The Eucharistic Year; or, Preparation and Thanksgiving for Holy Communion on all the Sundays and the principal Feasts of the Year. 18mo., 4s.

Life of S. Angela Merici, Foundress of the Ursulines. From the French of the Abbé G. Beetemé. 12mo., 4s. 6d.

Catechism Made Easy. By Rev. H. Gibson. Vol. 3, 12mo., 4s.

A Hundred Years Ago; or, a Narrative of Events leading to the Marriage and Conversion to the Catholic Faith of Mr. and Mrs Sidney, of Cowpen Hall, Northumbrland. By their Granddaughter. 12mo., 2s. 6d.

The Franciscan Annals and Monthly Bulletin of the Third Order of S. Francis. 8vo., 6d.

The Angelus. A Catholic Monthly Magazine, containing tales and other interesting reading. 8vo., 1d. Volume for 1876, cloth, 2s. 6d.

Vespers and Benediction Service. Composed and harmonized by Leopold de Prins. 4to., 3s. 6d. nett.

Catholic Hymnal. English Words. For Children, Church, Convent, Confraternity and Catholic Family Use. For one, two, or four voices, with accompaniment. By Leopold de Prins. 4to., 2s.; bound, 3s. nett.

Captain Rougemont; the Miraculous Conversion. 8vo., 2s.

ADELSTAN (Countess), Sketch of her Life and Letters. An abridged translation from the French of the Rev. Père Marquigny, S.J., by E. A. M. 12mo., 1s. and 2s. 6d. *See page 11.*

Adolphus; or, the Good Son. 18mo., 6d.

Adventures of a Protestant in Search of a Religion. By Iota. 12mo., 2s. and 3s. 6d.

AGNEW (Mme.), Convent Prize Book. 12mo., 2s. 6d.; gilt, 3s. 6d.; calf or morocco, 7s. 6d.

A Hundred Years Ago; or, a Narrative of Events leading to the Marriage and Conversion to the Catholic Faith of Mr. and Mrs. Sidney, of Cowpen Hall, Northumberland; to which are added a few other Incidents in their Life. By their Grand-daughter. 12mo., 2s. 6d.

A'KEMPIS—Following of Christ. Pocket Edition, 32mo., 1s.; embossed red edges, 1s. 6d.; roan, 2s.; French morocco, 2s. 6d.; calf or morocco, 4s. 6d.; gilt, 5s. 6d. Also in ivory, with rims and clasp, 15s. and 16s.; morocco antique, with two elegant brass corners and clasps, 17s. 6d.; russia, ditto, ditto, 20s.

—————— **Imitation of Christ; with Reflections.** 32mo., 1s.; Persian calf, 3s. 6d.; Border Edition, 12mo., 3s. 6d.

Albert the Great. *See* Dixon (Rev. Fr. T. A.).

Album of Christian Art. Twenty-three original compositions of Professor Klein, in Vienna. 4to., 6s.

ALLIES (T. W. Esq.), St. Peter; his Name and his Office. 12mo., 5s.

Alone in the World. By A. M. Stewart. 12mo., 4s. 6d.

Alphabet of Scripture Subjects. On a large sheet, 1s.; coloured, 2s., on a roller, varnished, 4s. 6d.; mounted to fold in a book, 3s. 6d.

ALZOG'S Universal Church History. 8vo., 3 Vols., each 20s.

American Life (Forty Years of). By Dr. Nichols. 12mo., 5s.

AMHERST (Rt. Rev. Dr.), Lenten Thoughts. 18mo., 2s.; red edges, 2s. 6d.

Amulet (The). By Conscience. 12mo., 4s.

ANDERSEN (Carl), Three Sketches of Life in Iceland. Translated by Myfanwy Fenton. Dedicated to H. R. H. the Princess of Wales. 12mo., 2s. 6d.

Angela Merici (S.) Her Life, her Virtues, and her Institute. From the French of the Abbé G. Beetemé. 12mo., 4s. 6d.

Angela's (S.) Manual: a Book of Devout Prayers and Exercises for Female Youth. 2s.; Persian, 3s. 6d.; calf, 4s. 6d.

Angels (The) and the Sacraments. 16mo., 1s.

Angelus (The). A Monthly Magazine. 8vo., 1d. Yearly subscription, post free, 1s. 6d. Volume for 1876, cloth, 2s. 6d.

Anglican Orders. By Canon Williams. 12mo., 3s. 6d.

—————— A few Remarks in the form of a Conversation on the recent work by Canon Estcourt. 8vo., 6d.

Anglicanism, Harmony of. *See* Marshall (T. W. M.).

Anti-Janus. *See* Robertson (Professor).

Apostleship of Prayer. By Rev. H. Ramière. 12mo., 6s.

AQUINAS (St. Thomas), Summa Summæ. By Dr. O'Ma-

Association of Prayers. By Rev. C. Tondini. 12mo., 3d.
Augustine (St.) of Canterbury, Life of. 12mo., 3s. 6d.
Aunt Margaret's Little Neighbours; or, Chats about the Rosary. 12mo., 3s.
BAGSHAWE (Rev. J. B.), Catechism of Christian Doctrine, illustrated with passages from the Holy Scriptures. 12mo., 2s. 6d.
────── **Threshold of the Catholic Church.** A Course of Plain Instructions for those entering her Communion. 12mo., 4s.
BAGSHAWE, (Rt. Rev. Dr.), The Life of our Lord, commemorated in the Mass. 18mo., 6d., bound 1s.; Verses and Hymns separately, 1d., bound 4d.
BAKER (Fr., O.S.B.), The Rule of S. Benedict. From the old English edition of 1638. 12mo., 4s. 6d.
Baker's Boy; or, Life of General Drouot. 18mo., 6d.
BALMES (J. L.), Letters to a Sceptic on Matters of Religion. 12mo., 6s.
BAMPFIELD (Rev. G.), Sir Ælfric and other Tales. 18mo., 6d.; cloth, 1s.; gilt, 1s. 6d.
BARGE (Rev. T.), Occasional Prayers for Festivals. 32mo., 4d. and 6d.; gilt, 1s.
Battista Varani (B.), *see* Veronica (S.). 12mo., 5s.
BAUGHAN (Rosa), Shakespeare. Expurgated edition. 8vo., 6s. The Comedies only, 3s. 6d.
Before the Altar. 32mo., 6d.
BELLECIO (Fr.), Spiritual Exercises of S. Ignatius. Translated by Dr. Hutch. 18mo., 2s.
BELL'S Modern Reader and Speaker. 12mo., 3s. 6d.
Bells of the Sanctuary,—A Daughter of St. Dominick. By Grace Ramsay. 12mo., 1s. and 1s. 6d.; stronger bound, 2s.
Benedict (S.), Abridged Explanation of his Medal. 18mo., 1d.; or 6s. 100.
────── **The Rule of our most Holy Father S. Benedict, Patriarch of Monks.** From the old English edition of 1638. Edited in Latin and English by one of the Benedictine Fathers of St. Michael's, near Hereford. 12mo., 4s. 6d.
Benedictine Breviary. 4 vols., 18mo., Dessain, 1870. 26s. nett; morocco, 42s. nett, and 47s. nett.
Benedictine Missal. Pustet, Folio, 1873. 20s. nett; morocco, 50s. nett, and 60s. nett. Dessain, 4to., 1862, 18s. nett; morocco, 40s. nett, and 50s. nett.
BENNI (Most Rev. C. B.), Tradition of the Syriac Church of Antioch, concerning the Primacy and Prerogatives of S. Peter and of his successors, the Roman Pontiffs. 8vo., 21s.; for 7s. 6d.
Berchmans (Bl. John), New Miracle at Rome, through the intercession of Bl. John Berchmans. 12mo., 2d.
Bernardine (St.) of Siena, Life of. With Portrait. 12mo., 5s.
Bertha; or, the Consequences of a Fault. 8vo., 2s.
Bessy; or, the Fatal Consequence of Telling Lies. 12mo., 1s.; stronger bound, 1s. 6d.; gilt, 2s.

BESTE (J. R. Digby, Esq.), Catholic Hours. 32mo., 2s.; red edges, 2s. 6d.; roan, 3s.; morocco, 6s.
——— Church Hymns. (Latin and English.) 32mo., 6d.
——— Holy Readings. 32mo., 2s., 2s. 6d.; roan, 3s.; mor., 6s.
BESTE (Rev. Fr.), Victories of Rome. 8vo., 1s.
Bible. Douay Version. 12mo., 3s.
Bible (Douai). 18mo., 2s. 6d.; Persian, 5s.; calf or morocco, 7s.; gilt, 8s. 6d. 4to., Illustrated, morocco, £5 5s.; superior, £6 6s.
Bible History for the use of Schools. *See* Gilmour (Rev. R.).
Biographical Readings. By A. M. Stewart. 12mo., 4s. 6d.
Blessed Lord. *See* Ribadeneira; Rutter (Rev. H.).
Blessed Virgin, Devotions to. From Ancient Sources. *See* Regina Sæculorum. 12mo., 1s. and 3s.
——— Devout Exercise in honour of. From the Psalter and Prayers of S. Bonaventure, 32mo., 1s.
——— History of. By Orsini. Translated by Provost Husenbeth. Illustrated, 12mo., 3s. 6d.
——— Life of. In verse. By C. E. Tame, Esq. 16mo., 2s.
——— Life of. Proposed as a model to Christian women. 12mo., 1s.
——— in North America, Devotion to. By Rev. X. D. Macleod. 8vo., 5s.
——— Veneration of. By Mrs. Stuart Laidlaw. 16mo., 4d.
——— *See* Our Lady, p. 22; Leaflets, p. 16; May, p. 19.
Blessed Virgin's Root in Ephraim. *See* Laing (Rev. Dr.).
Blindness, Cure of, through the Intercession of Our Lady and S. Ignatius. 12mo., 2d.
BLOSIUS, Spiritual Works of :—The Rule of the Spiritual Life; The Spiritual Mirror; String of Spiritual Jewels. Edited by Rev. Fr. Bowden. 12mo., 3s. 6d.; red edges, 4s.
Blue Scapular, Origin of. 18mo., 1d.
BLYTH (Rev. Fr.), Devout Paraphrase on the Seven Penitential Psalms. To which is added "Necessity of Purifying the Soul," by St. Francis de Sales. 18mo., 1s.; stronger bound, 1s. 6d.; red edges, 2s.
BONA (Cardinal), Easy Way to God. Translated by Father Collins. 12mo., 3s.
BONAVENTURE (S.), Devout Exercise in honour of Our Lady. 32mo., 1s.
——— Life of St. Francis of Assisi. 12mo., 3s. 6d.
Boniface (S.), Life of. By Mrs. Hope. 12mo., 6s.
Book of the Blessed Ones. By Miss Cusack. 12mo., 4s. 6d.
BORROMEO (S. Charles), Rules for a Christian Life. 18mo., 2d.
BOUDON (Mgr.), Book of Perpetual Adoration. Translated by Rev. Dr. Redman. 12mo., 3s.; red edges, 3s. 6d.
BOURKE (Rev. Ulick J.), Easy Lessons : or, Self-Instruction in Irish. 12mo., 3s. 6d.
BOWDEN (Rev. Fr. John), Spiritual Works of Louis of Blois. 12mo., 3s. 6d.; red edges, 4s.

BOWDEN (Mrs.), Lives of the First Religious of the Visitation of Holy Mary. 2 vols., 12mo., 10s.
BOWLES (Emily), Eagle and Dove. Translated from the French of Mdlle. Zénaïde Fleuriot. 12mo., 2s. 6d. and 5s.
BRADBURY (Rev. Fr.), Journey of Sophia and Eulalie to the Palace of True Happiness. 12mo., 1s. 6d.; extra cloth, 3s. 6d.
BRICKLEY'S Standard Table Book. 32mo., ½d.
BRIDGES (Miss), Sir Thomas Maxwell and his Ward. 12mo., 1s. and 2s.
Bridget (S.), Life of, and other Saints of Ireland. 12mo., 1s.
Broken Chain. A Tale. 18mo., 6d.
BROWNE (E. G. K., Esq.), Monastic Legends. 8vo., 6d.
——— Trials of Faith; or the Sufferings of Converts to Catholicity. 18mo., 1s.
BROWNLOW (Rev. W. R. B.), Church of England and its Defenders. 8vo., 1st letter, 6d.; 2nd letter, 1s.
——— "Vitis Mystica"; or, the True Vine: a Treatise on the Passion of our Lord. 18mo., 4s.; red edges, 4s. 6d.
BURDER (Abbot), Confidence in the Mercy of God. By Mgr. Languet. 12mo., 3s.
——— The Consoler; or, Pious Readings addressed to the Sick and all who are afflicted: By Père Lambilotte. 12mo., 4s. 6d.; red ed., 5s.
——— Souls in Purgatory. 32mo., 3d.
——— Novena for the Souls in Purgatory. 32mo., 3d.
Burial of the Dead. For Children and Adults. (Latin and English.) Clear type edition, 32mo., 6d.; roan, 1s. 6d.
Burke (Edmund), Life of. *See* Robertson (Professor).
BURKE (S.H., M.A.), Men and Women of the English Reformation. 12mo., 2 vols., 10s.; Vol. II., 5s.
BURKE (Father), and others, Catholic Sermons. 12mo., 2s.
BUTLER (Alban), Lives of the Saints. 2 vols., 8vo., 28s.; gilt, 34s.; 4 vols., 8vo., 32s.; gilt, 48s.; leather, 64s.
——— One Hundred Pious Reflections. 18mo., 1s.; stronger bound, 2s.
BUTLER (Dr.), Catechisms. 32mo., 1st, ½d.; 18mo., 2nd, 1d.; 3rd, 1½d.
CALIXTE—Life of the Ven. Anna Maria Taigi. Translated by A. V. Smith Sligo. 8vo., 5s.
Callista. Dramatised by Dr. Husenbeth. 12mo., 2s.
Captain Rougemont; or, the Miraculous Conversion. 8vo., 2s.
Cassilda; or, the Moorish Princess of Toledo. 8vo., 2s.
Catechisms—The Catechism of Christian Doctrine. Good large type on superfine paper. 32mo., 1d., or in cloth, 2d.
——— The Catechism of Christian Doctrine. Illustrated with passages from the Holy Scriptures. By the Rev. J. B. Bagshawe. 12mo., 2s. 6d.
——— The Catechism made Easy. By Rev. H. Gibson. 12mo., Vol. I. (out of print); Vol. II, 4s.; Vol. III., 4s.
——— Lessons on Christian Doctrine. 18mo.. 1½d.

Catechisms—General Catechism of the Christian Doctrine. By the Right Rev. Bishop Poirier. 18mo., 9d.
——————— By Dr. Butler. 32mo., 1st, ½d.; 18mo., 2nd, 1d.; 3rd, 1½d.
——————— By Dr. Doyle. 18mo., 1½d.
——————— Fleury's Historical. Complete Edition. 18mo., 1½d.
——————— Frassinetti's Dogmatic. 12mo., 3s.
——————— of the Council. 12mo., 2d.
Catherine Hamilton. By M. F. S. 12mo., 2s. 6d.; gilt, 3s.
Catherine Grown Older. By M. F. S. 12mo., 2s. 6d.; gilt, 3s.
Catholic Calendar. Yearly. 12mo., 6d.
Catholic Hours. *See* Beste (J. R. Digby).
Catholic Piety. *See* Prayer Books, page 30.
Catholic Sick and Benefit Club. *See* Richardson (Rev. R.).
CHALLONER (Bishop), Grounds of Catholic Doctrine. Large type edition. 18mo., 4d.
——————— Memoirs of Missionary Priests. 8vo., 6s.
——————— Think Well on't. 18mo., 2d.; cloth, 6d.
Chances of War. An Irish Tale. By A. Whitelock. 8vo., 5s.
CHARDON (Abbe), Memoirs of a Guardian Angel. 12mo., 4s.
Chats about the Rosary. *See* Aunt Margaret's Little Neighbours.
CHAUGY (Mother Frances Magdalen de), Lives of the First Religious of the Visitation. With Two Photographic Portraits. 2 vols., 12mo., 10s.
Child (The). *See* Dupanloup (Mgr.).
Children of Mary in the World, Association of. 32mo., 1d.
Choir, Catholic, Manual. By C. B. Lyons. 12mo., 1s.
Christian Armed. *See* Passionist Fathers.
CHRISTIAN BROTHERS' Reading Books.
Christian Doctrine, Lessons on. 18mo., 1½d.
Christian, Duties of a. By Ven. de la Salle. 12mo., 2s.
Christian Politeness. By the same Author. 18mo., 1s.
Christian Teacher. By the same Author. 18mo., 1s. 8d.
Christmas Offering. 32mo., 1s. a 100; or 7s. 6d. for 1000.
Christmas (The First) for our dear Little Ones. 15 Illustrations. 4to., 5s.
Chronological Sketches. *See* Murray Lane (H.).
Church Defence. *See* Marshall (T. W. M.).
Church History. By Alzog. 8vo., 3 vols. each 20s.
——————— By Darras. 4 vols., 8vo., 48s.
——————— Compendium. By Noethen. 12mo., 8s.
——————— for Schools. By Noethen. 12mo., 5s. 6d.
Church of England and its Defenders. *See* Brownlow (Rev.).
Cistercian Legends of the XIII. Century. *See* Collins (Fr.).
Cistercian Order: its Mission and Spirit. *See* Collins (Fr.).
Civilization and the See of Rome. *See* Montagu (Lord).
Clare (Sister Mary Cherubini) of S. Francis, Life of. Preface by Lady Herbert. With Portrait. 12mo., 3s. 6d.
Cloister Legends; or, Convents and Monasteries in the Olden Time. 12mo., 4s.

COGERY (A.), Third French Course, with Vocabulary. 12mo., 2s.
COLLINS (Rev. Fr.), Cistercian Legends of the XIII. Century. 12mo., 3s.
—————— Cistercian Order: its Mission and Spirit. 12mo., 3s. 6d.
—————— Easy Way to God. Translated from the Latin of Cardinal Bona. 12mo., 3s.
—————— Spiritual Conferences on the Mysteries of Faith and the Interior Life. 12mo., 5s.
COLOMBIERE (Father Claude de la), The Sufferings of Our Lord. Sermons preached in the Chapel Royal, St. James', in the year 1677. Preface by Fr. Doyotte, S.J. 18mo., 1s.; stronger bound, 1s. 6d.; red edges, 2s.
Colombini (B. Giovanni), Life of. By Belcari. Translated from the editions of 1541 and 1832. With Portrait. 12mo., 3s. 6d.
Columbkille, or Columba (S.), Life and Prophecies of. By St. Adamnan. 12mo., 3s. 6d.
Comedy of Convocation in the English Church. Edited by Archdeacon Chasuble. 8vo., 2s. 6d. *See* page 19.
COMERFORD (Rev. P.), Handbook of the Confraternity of the Sacred Heart. 18mo., 3d.
—————— Month of May for all the Faithful; or, a Practical Life of the Blessed Virgin. 32mo., 1s.
—————— Pleadings of the Sacred Heart. 18mo., 1s.; gilt, 2s.; with the Handbook of the Confraternity, 1s. 6d.
COMPTON (Herbert), Semi-Tropical Trifles. 12mo., boards, 1s.; extra cloth, 2s. 6d.
Conferences. *See* Collins, Lacordaire, Mermillod, Ravignan.
Confession, Auricular. By Rev. Dr. Melia. 18mo., 1s. 6d.
Confession and Holy Communion: Young Catholic's Guide. By Dr. Kenny. 32mo., 4d.; cloth, 6d.; red edges, 9d.; French morocco, 1s. 6d.; calf or morocco, 2s. 6d.
Confidence in God. By Cardinal Manning. 16mo., 1s.
Confidence in the Mercy of God. By Mgr. Languet. Translated by Abbot Burder. 12mo., 3s.
Confirmation, Instructions for the Sacrament of. A very complete book. 18mo., 6d.
CONSCIENCE (Hendrick), The Amulet. 12mo., 4s.
—————— Count Hugo, of Graenhove. 12mo., 4s.
—————— The Fisherman's Daughter. 12mo., 4s.
—————— Happiness of being Rich. 12mo., 4s.
—————— Ludovic and Gertrude. 12mo., 4s.
—————— The Village Innkeeper. 12mo., 4s.
—————— Young Doctor. 12mo., 4s.
Consoler (The). Translated by Abbot Burder. 12mo., 4s. 6d. and 5s.
Consoling Thoughts. *See* Francis of Sales (S.).
Contemplations on the most Holy Sacrament of the Altar. 18mo., 1s. and 2s.; red edges, 2s. 6d.
Continental Fish Cook. By M. J. N. de Frederic. 18mo., 1s.

Convent Martyr; or, "Callista." By the Rev. Dr. Newman. Dramatised by Rev. Dr. Husenbeth. 12mo., 2s.
Convent Prize Book. By Mme. Agnew. 12mo., 2s. 6d. and 3s. 6d.
Conversion of the Teutonic Race. By Mrs. Hope. 2 vols. 12mo., 10s.
Convocation, Comedy of. By the Author of "The Oxford Undergraduate of Twenty Years Ago." 8vo. 2s. 6d.
Convocation in Crown and Council. See Manning (Cardinal).
CORTES (John Donoso), Essays on Catholicism, Liberalism, and Socialism. Translated from the Spanish by Rev. W. Macdonald. 12mo., 6s.
Count Hugo of Graenhove. By Conscience. 12mo., 4s.
Crests, The Book of Family. Comprising nearly every bearing and its blazonry, Surnames of Bearers, Dictionary of Mottoes, British and Foreign Orders of Knighthood, Glossary of Terms, and upwards of 4,000 Engravings, Illustrative of Peers, Baronets, and nearly every Family bearing Arms in England, Wales, Scotland, Ireland, and the Colonies, &c. 2 vols., 12mo., 24s.
Crown of Jesus. See Prayer Books, page 31.
Crucifixion, The. A large picture for School walls, 2s.
CULPEPPER. An entirely new edition of Brook's Family Herbal 12mo., 3s. 6d.; coloured plates, 5s. 6d.
CUSACK (M. F.):—Sister Mary Francis Clare.
    Book of the Blessed Ones. 12mo., 4s. 6d.
    Devotions for Public and Private Use at the Way of the Cross. Illustrated. 32mo., 1s.; red edges, 1s. 6d.
    Father Mathew, Life of. 12mo., 2s. 6d.
    Ireland, Illustrated History of. 8vo., 12s.
    Ireland, Patriot's History of. 18mo., 2s.
    Jesus and Jerusalem; or, the Way Home. 12mo., 4s. 6d.
    Joseph (S.), Life of. 32mo., 6d.; cloth, 1s.
    Mary O'Hagan, Abbess and Foundress of the Convent of Poor Clares, Kenmare. 8vo., 6s.
    Memorare Mass. 32mo., 2d.
    Ned Rusheen. 12mo., 6s.
    Nun's Advice to her Girls. 12mo., 2s. 6d.
    O'Connell; his Life and Times. 2 vols. 8vo., 18s.
    Patrick (S.), Life of. 8vo., 6s., gilt, 10s.; 32mo., 6d.; cloth, 1s. Illustrated by Doyle (large edition), 4to., 20s.
    Patrick's (S.) Manual. 18mo., 3s. 6d.
    Pilgrim's Way to Heaven. 12mo., 4s. 6d.
    Stations of the Cross, for Public and Private Use. Illustrated. 16mo., 1s.; red edges, 1s. 6d.
    The Liberator; his Public Speeches and Letters. 2 vols. 8vo., 18s.
    Woman's Work in Modern Society. 8vo., 4s. 6d.
Daily Exercises. See Prayer Books, page 30.
DALTON (Canon), Sermon on Death of Provost Husenbeth. 8vo., 6d.

DARRAS (Abbe), General History of the Catholic Church. 4 vols., 8vo., 48s.
Daughter (A) of S. Dominick; (Bells of the Sanctuary). By Grace Ramsay. 12mo., 1s. and 1s. 6d.; better bound, 2s.
DEAN (Rev. J. Joy), Devotion to Sacred Heart. 12mo., 3s.
DECHAMPS (Mgr.), The Life of Pleasure. 18mo., 1s. 6d.
Defence of the Roman Church. *See* Gueranger.
DEHAM (Rev. F.) Sacred Heart of Jesus, offered to the Piety of the Young engaged in Study. 32mo., 6d.
Diary of a Confessor of the Faith. 12mo., 1s.
Directorium Asceticum. By Scaramelli. 4 vols., 12mo., 24s.
DIXON (Fr., O.P.) Albert the Great: his Life and Scholastic Labours. From original documents. By Dr. Joachim Sighart. With Photographic Portrait. 8vo.
——— Life of St. Vincent Ferrer. From the French of Rev. Fr. Pradel. With a Photograph. 12mo., 5s.
Dove of the Tabernacle. By Rev. T. H. Kinane. 18mo., 1s. 6d.
DOYLE (Canon, O.S.B.), Life of Gregory Lopez, the Hermit. With a Photographic Portrait. 12mo., 3s. 6d.
DOYLE (Dr.), Catechism. 18mo., 1½d.
DOYOTTE (Rev. Fr., S.J.), Elevations to the Heart of Jesus. 12mo., 3s.
——— Sufferings of Our Lord. *See* Columbiere (Fr.) [2s.
DRAMAS—Convent Martyr; or, "Callista" dramatised. 12mo.,
——— Ernscliff Hall (Girls, 3 Acts). 12mo., 6d.
——— Expiation (Boys, 3 Acts). 12mo., 2s.
——— Filiola (Girls, 4 Acts). 12mo., 6d.
——— He would be a Lord (Boys, 3 Acts), a Comedy. 12mo., 2s.
——— Major John Andre [Historical] (Boys, 5 Acts), 2s.
——— Reverse of the Medal (Girls, 4 Acts). 12mo., 6d.
——— Shandy Maguire (Boys, 2 Acts), a Farce. 12mo., 2s.
——— St. Louis in Chains (Boys, 5 Acts). 12mo., 2s.
——— St. William of York (Boys, 2 Acts). 12mo., 6d.
——— The Duchess Transformed. By W. H. A. (Girls, 1 Act). A Comedy. 12mo., 6d.
——— *See* Shakespeare.
Duchess (The), Transformed. A Comedy. By W. H. A. (Girls, 1 Act). 12mo., 6d.
DUMESNIL (Abbe), Recollections of the Reign of Terror. 12mo., 2s. 6d.
DUPANLOUP (Mgr.), Contemporary Prophecies. 8vo., 1s.
——— The Child. Translated by Kate Anderson. 12mo., 3s. 6d.
Dusseldorf Gallery. 357 Engravings. Large 4to. Half-morocco, gilt, £5 5s. nett.
——— 134 Engravings. Large 8vo. Half-morocco, gilt, 42s.
Dusseldorf Society for the Distribution of Good Religious Pictures. Subscription, 8s. 6d. a year. *Catalogue* 3d.
Duties of a Christian. By Ven. de la Salle. 12mo., 2s.
Eagle and Dove. *See* Bowles (Emily).

E. A. M. Countess Adelstan. 12mo., 1s. and 2s. 6d.
——— Paul Seigneret. 12mo., 6d., 1s., 1s. 6d., 2s.
——— Regina Sæculorum. 12mo., 1s. and 3s.
——— Rosalie. 12mo., 1s., 1s. 6d., 2s.
Early English Literature. *See* Tame (C.E.).
Easy Way to God. By Cardinal Bona. 12mo., 3s.
Ebba ; or, the Supernatural Power of the Blessed Sacrament. *This book is in French.* 12mo., 1s. 6d.; cloth, 2s. 6d.
Edmund (S.) of Canterbury, Life of. From the French of Rev. Fr. Massée, S.J. By George White. 18mo., 1s. & 1s. 6d.
Electricity and Magnetism ; an Enquiry into the Nature and Results of. By Amyclanus. Illustrated. 12mo., 6s. 6d.
England (History of). A Catechism. By E. Chapman. 18mo., 1s.
English Religion (The). By Arthur Marshall. 8vo., 1s.
Epistles and Gospels. Good clear type edition, 32mo., 6d.; roan, 1s. 6d.; larger edition, 18mo., French morocco, 2s.
———, Explanation of. By Rev. F. Goffine. Illustrated, 8vo., 7s.
Epistles of S. Paul, Exposition of. *See* MacEvilly (Rt. Rev. Dr.).
Ernscliff Hall. A Drama in Three Acts, for Girls. 12mo., 6d.
Essays on Catholicism. *See* Cortes.
Eucharistic Year ; Preparation and Thanksgiving for Holy Communion. 18mo., 4s.
Eucharist (The) and the Christian Life. *See* La Bouillerie.
Europe, Modern, History of. With Preface by Bishop Weathers. 12mo., 5s.; roan, 5s. 6d.; cloth gilt, 6s.
Expiation (The). A Drama in Three Acts, for Boys. 12mo., 2s.
Extemporaneous Speaking. By Rev. T. J. Potter. 12mo., 5s.
Extracts from the Fathers and other Writers of the Church. 12mo., 4s. 6d.
Fairy Tales for Little Children. By Madeleine Howley Meehan. 12mo., 6d.; stronger bound, 1s. and 1s. 6d.; gilt, 2s.
Faith of Our Fathers. *See* Gibbons (Rt. Rev. Dr.).
Fall, Redemption, and Exaltation of Man. 12mo., 1s.
Familiar Instructions on Christian Truths. By a Priest. 12mo. 1. Detraction 4d. 2. Dignity of the Priesthood, 3d 3. Hearing the Word of God, 3d.
Farleyes of Farleye. By Rev. T. J. Potter. 12mo., 2s. 6d.
Father Mathew (Life of). By M. F. Cusack. 12mo., 2s. 6d.
FAVRE (Abbe), Heaven Opened by the Practice of Frequent Confession and Communion. 12mo., 2s.; stronger bound, 3s. 6d.; red edges, 4s.
Feasts (The) of Camelot, with the tales that were told there. By Mrs. T. K. Hervey. 12mo., 3s. 6d.
Festival Tales. By J. F. Waller, Esq. 12mo., 5s.
Filiola. A Drama in Four Acts, for Girls. 12md., 6d.
First Apostles of Europe. *See* Hope (Mrs.).
First Communion and Confirmation Memorial. Beautifully printed in gold and colours, folio, 1s. each, or 9s. a dozen, nett.
First Religious of the Visitation of Holy Mary, Lives of.

Fisherman's Daughter. By Conscience. 12mo., 4s.
FLEET (Charles), Tales and Sketches. 8vo., 2s.; stronger bound, 2s. 6d.; gilt, 3s. 6d.
FLEURIOT (Mlle. Zenaide), Eagle and Dove. Translated by Emily Bowles. 12mo., 2s. 6d. and 5s.
FLEURY'S Historical Catechism. Large edition, 12mo., 1½d.
Florence O'Neill. *See* Stewart (Agnes M.).
Flowers of Christian Wisdom. *See* Henry (Lucien).
Fluffy. A Tale for Boys. By M. F. S. 12mo., 3s. 6d.
Following of Christ. *See* A'Kempis.
Foreign Books. *See* R. W.'s Catalogue of Foreign Books.
Francis of Assisi (S.) Life of. By S. Bonaventure. Translated by Miss Lockhart. 12mo., 3s. 6d.
FRANCIS OF SALES (S.), Consoling Thoughts. 18mo., 2s.
———— The Mystical Flora; or, the Christian Life under the Emblem of Saints. 4to., 8s.
———— Necessity of Purifying the Soul. *See* Blyth (Rev. Fr.).
———— Sweetness of Holy Living. 18mo., 1s.; levant, 3s.
Franciscan Annals and Monthly Bulletin of the Third Order of St. Francis. 8vo., 6d.
FRANCO (Rev. S.) Devotions to the Sacred Heart. 12mo., 4s.; cheap edition, 2s.
Frank O'Meara; *see* Artist of Collingwood.
FRASSINETTI—Dogmatic Catechism. 12mo., 3s.
FREDERIC (M. J. N. de), Continental Fish Cook; or, a Few Hints on Maigre Dinners. 18mo., 1s., soiled covers, 6d.
Freemasons, Irish and English, and their Foreign Brothers. 4to., 2s.
From Sunrise to Sunset. By L. B. 12mo., 3s. 6d.
Garden of the Soul. *See* page 32.
Garden (Little) of the Soul. *See* page 30.
GAYRARD (Mme. Paul) Harmony of the Passion of Our Lord. Compiled from the four Gospels, in Latin and French. 18mo., 1s. 6d.
General Questions in History, &c. *See* Stewart (A. M.)
German (S.), Life of. 12mo., 3s. 6d.
GIBBONS (Rt. Rev. James, D.D.), The Faith of Our Fathers; Being a Plain Exposition and Vindication of the Church Founded by our Lord Jesus Christ. 12mo., 4s. Paper covers, 2s. nett.
GIBSON (Rev. H.), Catechism made Easy. 12mo., Vol. I. (out of print); Vol. II., 4s.; Vol. III., 4s.
GILMOUR (Rev. R.), Bible History for the Use of Schools. Illustrated. 12mo., 2s.
God our Father. By a Father of the Society of Jesus. 12mo., 4s.
GOFFINE (Rev. F.), Explanation of the Epistles and Gospels. Illustrated. 8vo., 7s.
Gold and Alloy in the Devout Life. *See* Monsabré.
Good Thoughts for Priests and People. *See* Noethen.
Gospels, An Exposition of. *See* MacEvilly (Most Rev. Dr.).

GRACE RAMSAY. A Daughter of S. Dominick (Bells of the Sanctuary, No. 4). 12mo., 1s.; stronger bound, 1s. 6d. and 2s.
GRACIAN (Fr. Baltasar), Sanctuary Meditations for Priests and Frequent Communicants. Translated from the Spanish by Mariana Monteiro. 12mo., 4s.
GRANT (Bishop), Pastoral on St. Joseph. 32mo., 4d.; cloth, 6d.
Gregorian, or Plain Chant and Modern Music. By the Professor of Music, All Hallows College, Dublin. 8vo., 2s. 6d.
Gregory Lopez, the Hermit, Life of. By Canon Doyle, O.S.B. With a Photographic Portrait. 12mo., 3s. 6d.
Grounds of the Catholic Doctrine. By Bishop Challoner. Large type edition, 18mo., 4d.
Guardian Angel, Memoirs of a. By Abbé Chardon. 12mo., 4s.
GUERANGER (Dom), Defence of the Roman Church against F. Gratry. Translated by Canon Woods. 8vo., 1s. 6d.
Guide to Sacred Eloquence. *See* Passionist Fathers.
HALL (E.), Munster Firesides; or, the Barrys of Beigh. 12mo., 3s. 6d.
Happiness of Being Rich. By Conscience. 12mo., 4s.
Happiness of Heaven. By a Father of the Society of Jesus. 12mo. 4s.
Harmony of Anglicanism. By T. W. Marshall. 8vo., 2s. 6d.
HAY (Bishop), Sincere Christian. 18mo., 2s. 6d.
——— Devout Christian. 18mo., 2s. 6d.
He would be a Lord. A Comedy in 3 Acts. (Boys). 12mo., 2s.
Heaven Opened by the Practice of frequent Confession and Holy Communion. By the Abbé Favre. 12mo., 2s.; stronger bound, 3s. 6d.; red edges, 4s.
HEDLEY (Bishop), Five Sermons—Light of the Holy Spirit in the World. 12mo., 1s.; cloth, 1s. 6d. Separately:— Revelation, Mystery, Dogma and Creeds, Infallibility, 1d. each.
HEIGHAM (John), A Devout Exposition of the Holy Mass. Edited by Austin John Rowley, Priest. 12mo., 4s.
Henri V. (Comte de Chambord). *See* Walsh (W. H.).
HENRY (Lucien), Flowers of Christian Wisdom. 18mo., 2s.; red edges, 2s. 6d.
Herbal, Brook's Family. 12mo., 3s. 6d.; coloured plates, 5s. 6d.
HERBERT (Wallace), My Dream and Verses Miscellaneous. With a frontispiece. 12mo., 5s.
——— The Angels and the Sacraments. 16mo., 1s.
HERGENRÖTHER (Dr.), Anti-Janus. Translated by Professor Robertson. 12mo., 6s.
HERVEY (Eleanora Louisa), My Godmother's Stories from many Lands. 12mo., 3s. 6d.
——— Our Legends and Lives. 12mo., 6s.
——— Rest, on the Cross. 12mo., 3s. 6d.
——— The Feasts of Camelot, with the Tales that were told there. 12mo., 3s. 6d.
HILL (Rev. Fr.), Elements of Philosophy, comprising Logic

Holy Childhood. A book of simple Prayers and Instructions for very little children. 32mo., 1s.; gilt, 1s. 6d.
Holy Communion. By Hubert Lebon. 12mo., 4s.
Holy Family, Confraternity of. *See* Manning (Card.).
Holy Places: their Sanctity and Authenticity. *See* Philpin.
Holy Readings. *See* Beste (J. R. Digby Esq.).
Homely Discourse: Mary Magdalen. 12mo., 6d.
HOPE (Mrs.), The First Apostles of Europe. Originally published under the title of "The Conversion of the Teutonic Race." 2 vols., 12mo., 10s.
Horace. Literally translated by Smart. 18mo., 2s.
HUGUET (Pere), The Power of S. Joseph. Meditations and Devotions. Translated by Clara Mulholland. 18mo., 1s. 6d.
HUMPHREY (Rev. W., S.J.), The Panegyrics of Fr. Segneri, S.J. Translated from the orignal Italian. With a Preface by the Rev. W. Humphrey, S.J. 12mo., 5s.
HUSENBETH (Rev. Dr.), Convent Martyr. 12mo., 2s.
———— History of the Blessed Virgin. Translated from Orsini. Illustrated. 12mo., 3s. 6d.
———— Life and Sufferings of Our Lord. By Rev. H. Rutter. Illustrated. 12mo., 5s.
———— Life of Mgr. Weedall. 8vo., 1s.
———— Little Office of the Immaculate Conception. In Latin and English. 32mo., 4d.; cloth, 6d.; roan, 1s.; calf or morocco, 2s. 6d.
———— Our Blessed Lady of Lourdes. 18mo., 6d.; with the Novena, 1s.; cloth, 1s. 6d. Novena, separately, 4d.; Litany, 1d.
———— Roman Question. 8vo., 6d.
Husenbeth (Provost), Sermon on his Death. By Very Rev. Canon Dalton. 8vo. 6d.
HUTCH (Rev. W., D.D.), Nano Nangle, her Life and her Labours. 12mo., 7s. 6d.
Hymn Book. 136 Hymns, 32mo., 1d.; cloth, 2d.
Iceland (Three Sketches of Life in). By Carl Andersen. 12mo.
IGNATIUS (S.), Spiritual Exercises. By Fr. Bellecio, S.J. Translated by Dr. Hutch. 18mo., 2s.
Ignatius (S.), Cure of Blindness through the Intercession of Our Lady and S. Ignatius. 12mo., 2d.
Illustrated Manual of Prayers. 32mo., 3d.; cloth, 4d.
Imitation of Christ. *See* A'Kempis.
Immaculate Conception, Definition of. 12mo., 6d.
———— Little Office of. *See* Husenbeth (Rev. Dr.).
———— Little Office of, in Latin and English. Translation approved by the Bp. of Clifton. 32mo., 3d.
Indulgences. *See* Maurel (Rev. F. A.).
Infallibility of the Pope. By the Author of "The Oxford Undergraduate of Twenty Years Ago." 8vo., 1s.
In Suffragiis Sanctorum. Commem. S. Josephi; Commem. S. Georgii. Set of 5 for 4d.

Insurrection of '98. By Rev. P. F. Kavanagh. 12mo., 2s. 6d.
IOTA. The Adventures of a Protestant in Search of a Religion : being the Story of a late Student of Divinity at Bunyan Baptist College; a Nonconformist Minister, who seceded to the Catholic Church. 12mo., 3s. 6d. ; cheap edition, 2s.
Ireland (History of). By Miss Cusack. 18mo., 2s. A larger edition, illustrated by Doyle, 8vo., 11s.
Ireland (History of). By T. Young. 18mo., 2s. 6d.
Ireland Ninety Years ago. 12mo., 1s.
Irish Board Reading Books.
Irish Intermediate Education. 12mo., 2s.
Irish Monthly. 8vo. 4 Vols., 7s. 6d. each.
Irish, Self-Instruction in. By Rev. Ulick J. Bourke. 12mo., 3s. 6d.
Italian Revolution (The History of). The History of the Barricades (1796-1849). By Keyes O'Clery, M.P. 8vo., 7s. 6d.
JACOB (W. J., Esq.), Personal Recollections of Rome. 8vo., 6d.
JENKINS (Rev. O. L.) Student's Handbook of British and American Literature. 12mo., 8s.
Jesuits (The), and other Essays. *See* Nevin (Willis, Esq.)
Jesus and Jerusalem ; or, the Way Home. *See* Cusack (Miss).
John of God (S.), Life of. With Photographic Portrait. 12mo., 5s.
Joseph (S.), Life of. By Miss Cusack. 32mo., 6d.; cloth, 1s.
——— Novena of Meditations in Honour of St. Joseph. 18mo., 1s. 6d.
——— Novena to, with a Pastoral by the late Bishop Grant. 32mo., 4d.; cloth, 6d.
——— Power of. *See* Huguet.
——— *See* Leaflets.
Journey of Sophia and Eulalie to the Palace of True Happiness. From the French by Rev. Fr. Bradbury. 12mo., 1s. 6d.; better bound, 3s. 6d.
KAVANAGH (Rev. P. F.), Insurrection of '98. 12mo., 1s. 6d.
Keighley Hall, and other Tales. By E. King. 18mo., 6d.; cloth, 1s.; stronger bound, 1s. 6d.; gilt, 2s.
KENNY (Dr.), New Year's Gift to our Heavenly Father. 32mo., 4d.
——— Young Catholic's Guide to Confession and Holy Communion. 32mo., 4d.; cloth, 6d.; red edges, 9d.; roan, 1s. 6d.; calf or morocco, 2s. 6d.
KERNEY (M. T.), Compendium of History. 12mo., 5s.
Key of Heaven. *See* Prayers, page 31.
KINANE (Rev. T. H.), Dove of the Tabernacle. 18mo., 1s. 6d.
KING (Elizabeth), Keighley Hall, and other Tales. 18mo., 6d.; cloth, 1s.; stronger bound, 1s. 6d.; gilt, 2s.
——— The Silver Teapot. 18mo., 4d.
Knight of the Faith. *See* Laing (Rev. Dr.).

LA BOUILLERIE (Mgr. de), **The Eucharist and the Christian Life.** Translated by L. C. 12mo., 3s. 6d.

LACORDAIRE'S Conferences. 12mo., God, 6s.; God and Man, 6s.; Jesus Christ, 6s.; Life, 3s. 6d.

Lady Mildred's Housekeeper, A Few Words from. 12mo., 2d.

LAIDLAW (Mrs. Stuart), **Letters to my God-child.** No. 4. On the Veneration of the Blessed Virgin. 16mo., 4d.

LAING (Rev. Dr.), **Blessed Virgin's Root traced in the Tribe of Ephraim.** 8vo., 10s. 6d.

———— **Descriptive Guide to the Mass.** 12mo., 1s. and 1s. 6d.

———— **Knight of the Faith.** 12mo., 4s.

    Absurd Protestant Opinions concerning *Intention*, and Spelling Book of Christian Philosophy. 4d.
    Catholic, not Roman Catholic. 4d.
    Challenge to the Churches of England, Scotland, and all Protestant Denominations. 1d.
    Favourite Fallacy about Private Judgment and Inquiry. 1d.
    Protestantism against the Natural Moral Law. 1d.
    What is Christianity? 6d.
    Whence does the Monarch get his right to Rule? 2s. 6d.

LAMBILOTTE (Pere), **The Consoler.** Translated by Abbot Burder. 12mo., 4s. 6d.; red edges, 5s.

LANGUET (Mgr.), **Confidence in the Mercy of God.** Translated by Abbot Burder. 12mo., 3s.

Last of the Catholic O'Malleys. By M. Taunton. 18mo., 1s. 6d.; stronger bound, 2s.

Leaflets. 1d. each, or 1s. 2d. per 100 post free.
    Act of Consecration to the Sacred Heart. 6s. per 100.
    Act of Reparation to the Sacred Heart.
    Archconfraternity of the Agonising Heart of Jesus and the Compassionate Heart of Mary: Prayers for the Dying.
    Archconfraternity of Our Lady of Angels.
    Ditto, Rules.
    Christmas Offering (or 7s. 6d. a 1000).
    Devotions to S. Joseph.
    Explanation of the Medal or Cross of St. Benedict. 6s. per 100.
    Gospel according to St. John, *in Latin*. 1s. 6d. per 100.
    Indulgenced Prayers for Souls in Purgatory.
    Indulgenced Prayers for the Rosary of the Dead. 6s. per 100.
    Indulgenced Prayer before a Crucifix. 6s. per 100.
    Indulgences attached to Medals, Crosses, Statues, &c., by the Blessing of His Holiness and of those privileged to give his Blessing.
    Intentions for Indulgences.
    Litany of Our Lady of Angels.
    Litany of S. Joseph.

Picture of Crucifixion, "I thirst" (or 7s. 6d. a 1000).
Prayer for One's Confessor.
Prayer to S. Philip Neri. 6s. per 100.
Prayers, to be said three days before and three days after Holy Communion. 6s. per 100.
Union of our Life with the Passion of our Lord by a daily Offering.
Visit to the Blessed Sacrament. 2s. 6d. per 100.

League of the Cross. By Fr. Richardson. 32mo., 1d.
LEBON (Hubert), Holy Communion—It is my Life! 12mo., 4s.
Legends of the Saints. By M. F. S. 16mo., 3s. 6d.
Lenten Thoughts. By Bishop Amherst. 18mo., 2s.; red edges, 2s. 6d.
Letters to my God-child. Letter IV. On the Veneration of the Blessed Virgin. By Mrs. Stuart Laidlaw. 16mo., 4d.
Letter to George Augustus Simcox. 8vo., 6d.
Life in the Cloister. By Miss Stewart. 12mo., 3s. 6d.
Life of Pleasure. By Mgr. Dechamps. 12mo., 1s. 6d.
Light of the Holy Spirit in the World. Five Sermons, by Bishop Hedley. 12mo., 1s.; cloth, 1s. 6d.
LIGUORI (S.), Fourteen Stations of the Cross. 18mo., 1d.
——— **Officium Parvum.** Latin and English. With Novena. 12mo., 1s.; cloth, 2s.; red edges, 3s.
——— **Selva;** or, a Collection of Matter for Sermons. 12mo., 5s.
——— **Way of Salvation.** 32mo., 1s.
Lily of S. Joseph: A little manual of Prayers and Hymns for Mass. 64mo., 2d.; cloth, 3d., 4d., and 6d.; gilt, 8d.; roan, 1s.; French morocco, 1s. 6d.; calf or morocco, 2s.; gilt, 2s. 6d.
Limerick Veteran; or, the Foster Sisters. *See* Stewart (Agnes M.).
Literature, Philosophy of, An Essay contributing to a. By B. A. M. 12mo., 6s.
Literature, Student's Handbook. *See* Jenkins (Rev. O. L.).
Little Hunchback. By Countess Ségur. 12mo., 3s.
Little Prayer Book. 32mo., 3d.
Lives of the First Religious of the Visitation of Holy Mary. By Mother Frances Magdalen de Chaugy. With 2 Photographs. 2 vols., 12mo., 10s.
Lost Children of Mount St. Bernard. 18mo., 6d.
Louis (St.), in Chains. Drama, Five Acts (Boys). 12mo., 2s.
Lourdes, Our Blessed Lady of. By Rev. Dr. Husenbeth. 18mo., 6d.; with the Novena, 1s.; cloth, 1s. 6d.
——— **Novena of,** for the use of the Sick. 4d.
——— Litany of, 1d. each.

MACEVILLY (Bishop), Exposition of the Epistles of St. Paul and of the Catholic Epistles. 2 vols., large 8vo. 18s.
——— Exposition of the Gospels. Large 8vo., Vol. I., 12s. 6d.
MACLEOD (Rev. X. D.), Devotion to Our Lady in North America. 8vo., 5s.
Major John Andre. An Historical Drama for Boys. Five Acts. 12mo., 2s.
MANNING (Cardinal), Church, Spirit and the Word. 8vo., 6d.
——— Confidence in God. 16mo., 1s.
——— Confraternity of the Holy Family. 8vo., 3d.
——— Convocation in Crown and Council. 8vo., 6d.
——— Glory of S. Vincent de Paul. 12mo., 1s.
——— Temporal Sovereignty of the Popes. 12mo., 1s.
MANNOCK (Patrick), Origin and Progress of Religious Orders, and Happiness of a Religious State. Translated from the Latin of Rev. F. Platus. 12mo., 2s. 6d.
Manual of Catholic Devotions. *See* Prayers, page 31.
Manual of Devotions in honour of Our Lady of Sorrows. Compiled by the Clergy at St. Patrick's, Soho. 18mo., 1s. 6d.
Manual of the Cross and Passion. *See* Passionist Fathers.
Manual of the Seven Dolours. *See* Passionist Fathers.
Manual of the Sisters of Charity. 18mo., 6s.
Margarethe Verflassen. Translated from the German by Mrs. Smith Sligo. 12mo., 1s. and 3s.; gilt, 3s. 6d.
Margaret Roper. By A. M. Stewart. 12mo., 6s.; extra, 7s.
MARQUIGNY (Pere), Life and Letters of Countess Adelstan. 12mo., 1s. and 2s. 6d.
MARSHALL (A. J. B., Esq.), Comedy of Convocation in the English Church. 8vo., 2s. 6d. *
——— English Religion. 8vo., 1s.
——— Infallibility of the Pope. 8vo., 1s. *
——— Oxford Undergraduate of Twenty Years Ago. 8vo., 2s. 6d.; cloth, 3s. 6ds *
——— Reply to the Bishop of Ripon's Attack on the Catholic Church. 8vo., 6d. *
MARSHALL (T. W. M., Esq.), Harmony of Anglicanism—Church Defence. 8vo., 2s. 6d. *
MARSHALL (Rev. W.), The Doctrine of Purgatory. 12mo., 1s.
MARTIN (Rev. E. R.), Rule of the Pope-King. 8vo., 6d.
Mary, A Remembrance of. 18mo., 2s.; roan, 3s.; calf, 4s. 6d.
Mary Christina of Savoy (Venerable). 18mo., 6d.
Mary, The Path of. 12mo., 6d. and 1s.
Mass, Descriptive Guide to. By Rev. Dr. Laing. 12mo., 1s., or stronger bound, 1s. 6d.
Mass, Devotions for. Very *Large type*, 18mo., 2d.
Mass, Life of our Lord in the. *See* Bagshawe (Bishop).
. *The* 5 (*) *in one Volume*, 8vo., 6s.

Mass, Memorare. By Miss Cusack. 32mo., 2d.
Mass (The) a Devout Method. *See* Tronson.
Mass, A Devout Exposition of. *See* Rowley (Rev. A. J.).
Mathew (Father), Life of. By Miss Cusack. 12mo., 2s. 6d.
MAUREL (Rev. F. A.), Christian Instructed in the Nature and Use of Indulgences. 12mo., 3s.
Maxims of the Kingdom of Heaven. 12mo., 5s.; red edges, 5s. 6d.; calf or mor., 10s. 6d. Old Testament, 1s. 6d.; Gospels, 1s.
May, Month of, for all the Faithful. By Rev. P. Comerford. 32mo., 1s. [18mo., 2s.
May, Month of, for Interior Souls. By M. A. Macdaniel.
May, Month of, principally for the use of Religious Communities. 18mo., 1s. 6d.
May Readings for the Feasts of Our Lady. By Rev. A. P. Bethell. 18mo., 1s.; stronger bound, 1s. 6d.
M'CORRY (Rev. Dr.), Monks of Iona and the Duke of Argyll. 8vo., 3s. 6d.
——— **Rome, Past, Present, Future.** 8vo., 6d.
MEEHAN (M. H.), Fairy Tales for Little Children. 12mo., 1s.; stronger bound, 1s. 6d.; gilt, 2s.
MELIA (Rev. Dr.), Auricular Confession. 18mo., 1s. 6d.
Men and Women of the English Reformation from the days of Wolsey to the death of Cranmer. By S. H. Burke, M.A. 12mo., 2 Vols., 10s.; Vol. II., 5s.
MERMILLOD (Mgr.), The Supernatural Life. Translated from the French, with a Preface by Lady Herbert. 12mo., 5s.
M. F. S., Catherine Hamilton. 12mo., 2s. 6d.; gilt, 3s.
——— **Catherine Grown Older.** 12mo., 2s. 6d.; gilt, 3s.
——— **Fluffy.** A Tale for Boys. 12mo., 3s. 6d.
——— **Legends of the Saints.** 16mo., 3s. 6d.
——— **Stories of Holy Lives.** 12mo., 3s. 6d.
——— **Stories of Martyr Priests.** 12mo., 3s. 6d.
——— **Stories of the Saints.** 12mo., 3s. 6d.; gilt, 4s. 6d.
——————— Second Series. 12mo., 3s. 6d.; gilt, 4s. 6d.
——— **Story of the Life of S. Paul.** 12mo., 2s. 6d.
——— **The Three Wishes.** A Tale. 12mo., 2s. 6d.
——— **Tom's Crucifix, and other Tales.** 12mo., 3s.
Message from the Mother Heart of Mary. 18mo., 4d. and 6d.
MILES (G. H.), Truce of God. A Tale. 12mo., 4s.
MILNER (Bishop), Devotion to the Sacred Heart of Jesus. 32mo., 3d.; cloth, 6d.; gilt, 1s.
Miniature Prayer Book. *See* Prayers, page 31.
Miracles. A New Miracle at Rome, through the intercession of B. John Berchmans. 12mo., 2d.
——— **Cure of Blindness,** through the intercession of Our Lady and S. Ignatius. 12mo., 2d.
Mirror of Faith: your likeness in it. *See* Passionist Fathers.

Monastic Legends. By E. G. K. Browne. 8vo., 6d.
MONK (Rev. T. V.), Daily Exercises. *See* Prayers, page 30.
Monks of Iona and the Duke of Argyll. *See* M'Corry.
MONSABRE (Rev. Pere), Gold and Alloy. 12mo., 2s. 6d.
MONTAGU (Lord Robert), Civilization and the See of Rome. 8vo., 6d.
Montalembert (Count de). By George White. 12mo., 6d.
Mr. Vernon. A Novel. 8vo., 3 vols., 8s.; or in 1 vol., 7s. 6d.
MULHOLLAND (Rosa), Prince and Saviour: The Story of Jesus. 12mo., Coloured Illustrations, 2s. 6d.; 32mo., 6d.
Multiplication Table, on a sheet. 3s. per 100.
Munster Firesides. By E. Hall. 12mo., 3s. 6d.
MURRAY-LANE (Chevalier H.), Chronological Sketch of the Kings of England and the Kings of France. 12mo., 2s. 6d.; or in 2 vols., 1s. 6d. each.
MUSIC: Ave Maria, for Four Voices. By W. Schulthes. 1s. 3d.
   Cæcilian Society. *See* Separate List.
   Catholic Hymnal (English Words). For one, two, or four voices, with accompaniment. By Leopold de Prins. 4to., 2s.; bound, 3s.
   Cor Jesu, Salus in Te sperantium. By W. Schulthes, 2s.; with Harp Accompaniment, 2s. 6d.; abridged, 3d.
   Evening Hymn at the Oratory. By Rev. J. Nary. 3d.
   Hymns. By F. Faber. Large size. 9d. each. Pilgrims of the Night—O Paradise—True Shepherd—Sweet Saviour—Souls of Men—I come to Thee—O God, whose Thoughts—Jesus, my Lord—O come to the Merciful—How gently flow—Our Heavenly Father.
   Litanies (36) and Benediction Service. By W. Schulthes. 6s.
   Litanies (6). By E. Leslie. 6d.
   Litanies (18). By Rev. J. McCarthy. 1s. 3d.
   Mass of the Holy Child Jesus. By W. Schulthes. 3s. The vocal part only, 4d.; or 3s. per doz. Cloth, 6d.; or 4s. 6d. per doz.
   Ne projicias me a facie Tua. Motett for Four Voices. By W. Schulthes. 1s. 3d.
   Oratory Hymns. By W. Schulthes. 2 vols., 8s.
   Recordare. Oratorio Jeremiæ Prophetæ. By the same. 1s.
   Regina Cœli. Motett for Four Voices. By W. Schulthes. 3s. Vocal Arrangement, 1s.
   Twelve Latin Hymns. By W. Schulthes. 1s. 6d.
   Veni Domine. Motett for Four Voices. By W. Schulthes. 2s. Vocal Arrangement, 6d.
   Vespers and Benediction Service. Composed and harmonized by Leopold de Prins. 4to., 3s. 6d.
   *** *All the above (music) prices are nett.*
My Conversion and Vocation. By Rev. Father Schouvaloff, Barnabite. Translated from the French, with an Appendix, by Rev. C. Tondini. 12mo., 5s.

My Dream; and Verses Miscellaneous. *See* Herbert.
My Godmother's Stories from many Lands. By Mrs. T. K. Hervey. 12mo., 3s. 6d.
Mystical Flora of St. Francis de Sales. 4to., 8s.
NARY (Rev. J.) Evening Hymn at the Oratory. Music, 3d.
Nano Nangle; her Life, her Labours, &c. *See* Hutch.
Necessity of Enquiry as to Religion. *See* Pye (Henry John).
Ned Rusheen. By Miss Cusack. 12mo., 6s.
NEVIN (Willis, Esq.), The Jesuits, and other Essays. 12mo., 1s.; cloth, 2s. 6d.
NEWMAN (Rev. Dr.), Historical Sketches, 3 vols., 18s.; Miracles, 6s.; Discussions and Arguments, 6s.; Miscellanies, 6s.; Critical and Historical Essays, 2 vols., 12s.; Callista, 5s. 6d.; Arians, 6s.; Idea of a University, 7s.; Tracts, Theological and Ecclesiastical, 8s.; Loss and Gain, 5s. 6d.; Certain Difficulties felt by Anglicans, second series, 5s. 6d.
——— Characteristics from the Writings of. By W. S. Lilly. 12mo., 6s.
New Model for Youth; or, Life of Richard Aloysius Pennefather. By one of his Masters. 12mo., 3s. 6d.
New Testament (Rheims), with Annotations, References, and Index. 12mo., 2s. 6d. Illustrated, large 4to., 7s. 6d.
New Year's Gift to Our Heavenly Father. 32mo., 4d.
Nicholas; or, the Reward of a Good Action. 18mo., 6d.
NICHOLS (T. L.), Forty Years of American Life. 12mo., 5s. [18mo., 6d.
Nina and Pippo, the Lost Children of Mt. St. Bernard.
NOETHEN'S (Rev. T.), Good Thoughts for Priests and People; or, Short Meditations for every Day in the Year. 12mo., 8s.
——— Compendium of the History of the Catholic Church. 12mo., 8s.
Noethen's History of the Catholic Church. 12mo., 5s. 6d.
Novena to Our Blessed Lady of Lourdes for the use of the Sick. 18mo., 4d.
Novena of Meditations in honour of St. Joseph, according to the method of St. Ignatius, preceded by a new method of hearing Mass according to the intentions of the Souls in Purgatory. 18mo., 1s. 6d.
Nun's Advice to her Girls. By Miss Cusack. 12mo., 2s. 6d.
Occasional Prayers for Festivals. *See* Prayers, page 31.
O'CLERY (Keyes, M.P., K.S.G.), The History of the Italian Revolution. First Period—The Revolution of the Barricades (1796-1849). 8vo., 7s. 6d.
O'Connell: his Life and Times. *See* Cusack (M. F.).
O'Connell; his Speeches and Letters. *See* Cusack (M. F.).
O'Hagan (Mary), Abbess and Foundress of the Convent of the Poor Clares. By Miss Cusack. 8vo., 6s.
O'MAHONY (D.P.M.), Rome semper eadem. 8vo., 1s. 6d.

Oratorian Lives of the Saints. With Portrait, 12mo., 5s. a vol
   I. S. Bernardine of Siena, Minor Observatine.
   II. S. Philip Benizi, Fifth General of the Servites.
   III. S. Veronica Giuliani, and B. Battista Varani.
   IV. S. John of God. By Canon Cianfogni.
Our Lady (Devotion to) in North America. *See* Macleod.
Our Lady's Lament. *See* Tame (C.E.).
Our Lady's Month. By Rev. A. P. Bethell. 18mo., 1s. and 1s. 6d.
Our Legends and Lives. By E. L. Hervey. 12mo., 6d.
Our Lord's Life, Passion, Death, and Resurrection. Translated from Ribadeneira. 12mo., 1s.
———— By Rev. H. Rutter. Illustrated. 12mo., 5s.
OXENHAM (H. N.), Dr. Pusey's Eirenicon considered in relation to Catholic Unity. 8vo., 6d.
———— **Poems.** 12mo., 3s. 6d.
Oxford Undergraduate of Twenty Years Ago. By a Bachelor of Arts. 8vo., 2s. 6d.; cloth, 3s. 6d.
OZANAM (A. F.), Protestantism and Liberty. Translated from the French by Wilfrid C. Robinson. 8vo., 1s.
Pale (The) and the Septs. A Romance of the Sixteenth Century. By Emelobie de Celtis. 2 vols., 12mo., 16s.
Panegyrics of Fr. Segneri, S.J. Translated from the original Italian. With a Preface, by Rev. W. Humphrey, S.J. 12mo., 5s.
Paradise of God; or the Virtues of the Sacred Heart. By Author of "God our Father," "Happiness of Heaven." 12mo., 4s.
Paray le Monial, and Bl. Margaret Mary. 18mo., 6d.
Passion of Our Lord, Harmony of. *See* Gayrard.
PASSIONIST FATHERS:—
    Christian Armed. 32mo., 1s. 6d.
    Guide to Sacred Eloquence. 18mo., 2s.
    Life of S. Paul of the Cross. 18mo., 3s.
    Manual of the Cross and Passion. 32mo., 3s.
    Manual of the Seven Dolours. 32mo., 1s. 6d.
    Mirror of Faith. 12mo., 3s.
    School of Jesus Crucified. 18mo., 5s.
Pastor and People. By Rev. T. J. Potter. 12mo., 5s.
Path of Mary. By One of Her Loving Children. 12mo., 6d. and 1s.
Path to Paradise. *See* Prayers, page 31.
Patrick (S.); the Apostle of Ireland. Who he was—where he came from—what he taught. 8vo., 1s.
Patrick (S.), Life of. 12mo., 1s.
Patrick's (S.) Manual. By Miss Cusack. 18mo., 3s. 6d.
Patron Saints. By E. A. Starr. Illustrated. 12mo., 10s.
Paul of the Cross (S.), Life of. *See* Passionist Fathers.
Penitential Psalms. *See* Blyth (Rev. F.).
PENS, Washbourne's Free and Easy. Fine, or Middle, or Broad Points, 1s. per gross.
People's Martyr. A Legend of Canterbury. 12mo., 4s.
Percy Grange. By Rev. T. J. Potter. 12mo., 3s.

Perpetual Adoration, Book of. Translated from the French of Mgr. Boudon; edited by Rev. Dr. Redman. 12mo., 3s. and 3s. 6d.
Peter (S.), his Name and his Office. *See* Allies (T. W.), Esq.
Peter, Years of. By an ex-Papal Zouave. 12mo., 1d.
Philip Benizi (S.), Life of. *See* Oratorian Lives of the Saints.
Philosophy, Elements of. By Rev. W. H. Hill. 8vo., 6s.
PHILPIN (Rev. F.), Holy Places; their sanctity and authenticity. With three Maps. 12mo., 2s. 6d. and 6s.
Photographs (10) illustrating the History of the Miraculous Hosts, called the Blessed Sacrament of the Miracle. 2s. 6d. the set.
Pilgrim's Way to Heaven. By Miss Cusack. 12mo., 4s. 6d.
Pius IX. 32mo., 6d.; 4to., 1d.
Pius IX., his early Life to the Return from Gaeta. By Rev. T. B. Snow, O.S.B. 12mo., 6d.
Plain Chant. *See* Gregorian.
——— The Cecilian Society Music kept in stock.
PLATUS (Rev. F.), Origin and Progress of Religious Orders, and Happiness of a Religious State. 12mo., 2s. 6d.
PLAYS. *See* Dramas, page 10.
POIRIER (Bishop), A General Catechism of the Christian Doctrine. 18mo., 9d.
POOR CLARES OF KENMARE. *See* Cusack (Miss).
Pope-King, Rule of. By Rev. E. R. Martin. 8vo., 6d.
Pope of Rome. *See* Tondini (Rev. C.).
POTTER (Rev. T. J.), Extemporaneous Speaking. Sacred Eloquence. 12mo., 5s.
——— Farleyes of Farleye. 12mo., 2s. 6d.
——— Pastor and People. 12mo., 5s.
——— Percy Grange. 12mo., 3s.
——— Rupert Aubrey. 12mo., 3s.
——— Sir Humphrey's Trial. 16mo., 2s. 6d.
POWELL (J., Esq.), Two Years in the Pontifical Zouaves. Illustrated. 8vo., 3s. 6d.
PRADEL (Fr., O. P.), Life of St. Vincent Ferrer. Translated by Rev. Fr. Dixon. With a Photograph. 12mo., 5s.
PRAYER BOOKS. *See* page 30.
Prince and Saviour. *See* Mulholland (Rosa).
PRINS (Leopold de). *See* Music.
Pro-Cathedral, Kensington. Tinted View of the Interior, 11 × 15 inches, 1s.; Proofs, on larger paper, 2s.
Prophecies, Contemporary. By Mgr. Dupanloup. 8vo., 1s.
Protestantism and Liberty. *See* Robinson (W. C.).
Protestant Principles examined by the Written Word. 18mo., 1s.
Prussian Spy. A Novel. By V. Valmont. 12mo., 4s.
Psalmist, Catholic. By C. B. Lyons. 12mo., 4s.
Purgatory, A Novena in favour of the Souls in. 32mo., 3d.
Purgatory, The Doctrine of. By Rev. W. Marshall. 12mo., 1s.

Purgatory, Souls in. By Abbot Burder. 32mo., 3d.
Pusey's (Dr.) Eirenicon considered. *See* Oxenham (H. N.).
PYE (Henry John, M.A.), Necessity of Enquiry as to Religion. 32mo., 4d.; cloth, 6d.
RAM (Mrs. Abel), The Spiritual Life. Conferences, by Père Ravignan. 12mo., 5s.
RAMIÈRE (Rev. H.), Apostleship of Prayer. 12mo., 6s.
RAVIGNAN (Pere), The Spiritual Life, Conferences. Translated by Mrs. Abel Ram. 12mo., 5s.
Ravignan (Pere), Life of. 12mo., 9s.
RAWES (Rev F.), Homeward. 8vo., 2s.
———— Sursum. 12mo., 1s.
Reading Lessons. By the Marist Brothers. Book 2. 18mo., 7d.
Recollections of the Reign of Terror. *See* Dumesnil (Abbé).
REDMAN (Rev. Dr.), Book of Perpetual Adoration. By Mgr. Boudon. 12mo., 3s.; red edges, 3s. 6d.
12mo., 1s.
REDMOND (Rev. Dr.), Eight Short Sermon Essays.
Reflections, One Hundred Pious. *See* Butler.
Regina Sæculorum; or, Mary Venerated in all Ages. Devotions to the Blessed Virgin from Ancient Sources. 12mo., 1s. and 3s.
Religious Orders. *See* Platus (Rev. F.).
Rest, on the Cross. By Eleanora Louisa Hervey. 12mo., 3s. 6d.
Reverse of the Medal. A Drama for Girls. 12mo., 6d.
RIBADENEIRA—Life, Passion, Death and Resurrection of our Lord. 12mo., 1s.
RICHARDSON (Rev. Fr.), Catholic Sick and Benefit Club; or, the Guild of our Lady; and St. Joseph's Catholic Burial Society. 32mo., 4d.
———— Catholic Total Abstinence League of the Cross. 32mo., 1d.
———— Holy War. Rules, ½d.; Crosses, 2d.
———— Little by Little; or, the Penny Bank. 32mo., 1d.
———— S. Joseph's Catholic Burial Society. 2d.
———— The Crusade; or, Catholic Association for the Suppression of Drunkenness. 32mo., 1d.
Ritus Servandus in Expositione et Benedictione S.S. 4to., cloth, 5s. 6d.
Road to Heaven. A Game. By Miss M. A. Macdaniel. 3s. 6d.
ROBERTSON (Professor), Lectures on the Life, Writings, and Times of Edmund Burke. 12mo., 3s. 6d.
———— Anti-Janus. By Hergenröther. 12mo., 6s.
———— Lectures on Modern History and Biography. 12mo., 6s.
ROBINSON (Wilfrid C.), Protestantism and Liberty. Translated from the French of Professor Ozanam. 8vo., 1s.
Roman Question, The. By Rev. Dr. Husenbeth. 8vo., 6d.
———— and her Captors: Letters collected and edited by Count Henri d'Ideville, and Translated by F. R. Wegg-Prosser. 12mo., 4s.

Rome, Past, Present, and Future. By Dr. M'Corry. 8vo., 6d
——— Personal Recollections of. By W. J. Jacob, 8vo., 6d.
——— semper eadem. By D. P. M. O'Mahony. 8vo., 1s. 6d.
———, The Victories of. By Rev. F. Beste. 8vo., 1s.
Rosalie; or, the Memoir of a French Child, told by herself. 12mo., 1s.; stronger bound, 1s. 6d.; gilt, 2s.
Rosary, Fifteen Mysteries of, and Fourteen Stations of the Cross. In One Volume, 32 Illustrations. 16mo., 1s. 6d.
Rosary for the Souls in Purgatory, with Indulgenced Prayer. 6d. and 9d. Medals separately, 1d. each, or 9s. gross. Prayers separately, 1d. each, 9d. a dozen, or 6s. for 100.
Rosary, Chats about the. *See* Aunt Margaret's Little Neighbours.
ROWLEY (Rev. Austin John), A Devout Exposition of the Holy Mass. Composed by John Heigham. 12mo., 4s.
Rupert Aubrey. By Rev. T. J. Potter. 12mo., 3s.
RUTTER (Rev. H.) Life and Sufferings of Our Lord, with Introduction by Rev. Dr. Husenbeth. Illustrated. 12mo., 5s.
Sacred Heart, Act of Consecration to. 1d.; or 6s. per 100.
———————, Act of Reparation to. 1s. 2d. per 100.
———————, Devotions to. By Rev. S. Franco. 12mo., 4s.; cheap edition, 2s.
———————, Devotions to. By Bishop Milner. 32mo., 3d.; cloth, 6d.; gilt, 1s.
———————, Devotions to. Translated by Rev. J. Joy Dean. 12mo., 3s.
———————, Elevations to the. By Rev. Fr. Doyotte, S.J. 12mo., 3s.
———————, Handbook of the Confraternity, for the use of Members. 18mo., 3d.
———————, Little Treasury of. 32mo., 2s.; French morocco, 2s. 6d.; calf, 5s.; morocco, 6s.
———————, Manual of Devotions to the, from the writings of Blessed Margaret Mary. 32mo., 3d.
——————— offered to the Piety of the Young engaged in Study. By Rev. F. Deham. 32mo., 6d.
——————— *See* Paradise of God.
——————— Pleadings of. By Rev. M. Comerford. 18mo., 1s.; gilt edges, 2s.; with Handbook of the Confraternity, 1s. 6d.
———————, Treasury of. 18mo., 3s. 6d.; roan, 4s. 6d.
Saints, Lives of. By Alban Butler. 4 vols., 8vo., 32s.; gilt, 48s.; and leather, gilt, 64s.; or the 4 vols. in 2, 28s.; gilt, 34s.
——————— for every day in the Year. Beautifully printed, within borders from ancient sources, on thick toned paper. 4to., gilt, 16s.
——————— Patron. By E. A. Starr. Illustrated. 12mo., 10s.
Sanctuary Meditations for Priests and Frequent Communicants. Translated from the Spanish of Fr. Baltasar Gracian, by Mariana Monteiro. 12mo., 4s.
SCARAMELLI—Directorium Asceticum; or, Guide to the

SCHMID (Canon), Tales. Illustrated. 12mo., 3s. 6d. Separately:—The Canary Bird, The Dove, The Inundation, The Rose Tree, The Water Jug, The Wooden Cross. 6d. each; gilt, 1s.
SCHOOL BOOKS. Supplied according to order.
School of Jesus Crucified. By the Passionist Fathers. 18mo., 5s.
SCHOUVALOFF (Rev. Father, Barnabite), My Conversion and Vocation. Translated from the French, with an Appendix, by Fr. C. Tondini. 12mo., 5s.
SCHULTHES (William). See Music.
Scraps from my Scrapbook. See Arnold (M. J.).
SEGNERI (Fr., S.J.), Panegyrics. Translated from the original Italian. With a Preface, by Rev. W. Humphrey, of the same Society. 12mo., 5s.
SEGUR (Mgr.), Books for Little Children. Translated. 32mo., 3d. each. Confession, Holy Communion, Child Jesus, Piety, Prayer, Temptation and Sin. In one volume, cloth, 2s.
———— Practical Counsels for Holy Communion. 18mo., 9d.
SEGUR (Countess de), The Little Hunchback. 12mo., 3s.
Seigneret (Paul), Life of. 12mo., 6d., 1s., and 1s. 6d.; gilt, 2s.
Selva; a Collection of Matter for Sermons. By St. Liguori. 12mo., 5s.
Semi-Tropical Trifles. By H. Compton. 12mo., 1s.; cloth, 2s. 6d.
Sermon Essays. By Rev. Dr. Redmond. 12mo., 1s.
Sermons. By Dr. Husenbeth. 8vo., 6d. each. 1. Lady Bedingfield. 2. Hon. Mary Stafford Jerningham. 3. Right Hon. George Lord Stafford. 4. Hon. Edwin Stafford Jerningham.
———— By Father Burke, O.P., and others. 12mo., 2s.
———— The Light of the Holy Spirit in the World. By Bishop Hedley. 1s.; cloth, 1s. 6d.
———— One Hundred Short. By Rev. Fr. Thomas. 8vo., 12s.
Serving Boy's Manual, and Book of Public Devotions. Containing all those prayers and devotions for Sundays and Holydays, usually divided in their recitation between the Priest and the Congregation. Compiled from approved sources, and adapted to Churches, served either by the Secular or Regular Clergy. 32mo., embossed, 1s.; French morocco, 2s.; calf, 4s.; with Epistles and Gospels, 6d. extra.
Seven Sacraments Explained and Defended. 18mo., 1s. 6d.
SHAKESPEARE. Expurgated edition. By Rosa Baughan. 8vo., 6s. The Comedies only, 3s. 6d.
Shandy Maguire. 2 Acts. A Farce for Boys. 12mo., 2s.
Siege of Limerick (Florence O'Neill). See Stewart (Agnes M.).
SIGHART (Dr.) Albert the Great. See Albert.
Silver Teapot. By Elizabeth King. 18mo., 4d.
Simple Tales—Waiting for Father, &c., &c. 16mo., 2s. 6d.
Sir Ælfric and other Tales. See Bampfield (Rev. G.).
Sir Humphrey's Trial. By Rev. T. J. Potter. 16mo., 2s. 6d.
Sir Thomas Maxwell and his Ward. By Miss Bridges. 12mo, 1s. and 2s.
Sir Thomas More. See Stewart (A. M.).

SMITH-SLIGO (A. V., Esq.), Life of the Ven. Anna Maria Taigi. Translated from the French of Calixte. 8vo., 2s. 6d. and 5s. [3s. 6d.
————— (Mrs.) Margarethe Verflassen. 12mo., 1s., 3s., and
SNOW (Rev. T. B.), Pius IX., His early Life to the Return from Gaeta. 12mo., 6d.
Soul (The), United to Jesus. 32mo., 1s. 6d.
SPALDING'S (Abp.) Works. 5 vols., 52s. 6d.; or separately: Evidences of Catholicity, 10s. 6d.; Miscellanea, 2 vols., 21s.; Protestant Reformation, 2 vols., 21s.
Spalding (Archbishop), Life of. 8vo., 10s. 6d.
————— Sermon at the Month's Mind. 8vo., 1s.
Spiritual Conferences on the Mysteries of Faith and the Interior Life. By Father Collins. 12mo., 5s.
Spiritual Life. Conferences by Père Ravignan. Translated by Mrs. Abel Ram. 12mo., 5s.
Spiritual Works of Louis of Blois. Edited by Rev. F. John Bowden. 12mo., 3s. 6d.; red edges, 4s.
STARR (Eliza Allen), Patron Saints. Illustrated. 12mo., 10s.
Stations of the Cross, Devotions for Public and Private Use at the. By Miss Cusack. Illustrated. 16mo., 1s. and 1s. 6d.
Stations of the Cross. By S. Liguori. 18mo., 1d.
Stephen Langton, Life of. 12mo., 2s. 6d.
STEWART (A. M.), Alone in the World. 12mo., 4s. 6d.
————— St. Angela's Manual. *See* Angela (S.)
————— Biographical Readings. 12mo., 4s. 6d.
————— Florence O'Neill, the Rose of St. Germains; or, the Days of the Siege of Limerick. 12mo., 5s.; extra, 6s.
————— General Questions in History, Chronology, Geography, the Arts, &c. 12mo., 4s. 6d.
————— Life and Letters of Sir Thomas More. Illustrated, 10s. 6d.; gilt, 11s. 6d.
————— Life of S. Angela Merici. 12mo., 4s. 6d.
————— Life in the Cloister. 12mo., 3s. 6d. [extra, 6s.
————— Limerick Veteran; or, the Foster Sisters. 12mo., 5s.;
————— Margaret Roper. 12mo., 6s.; extra, 7s.
Stories for my Children—The Angels and the Sacraments. 16mo., 1s.
Stories of Holy Lives. By M. F. S. 12mo., 3s. 6d.
Stories of Martyr Priests. By M. F. S. 12mo., 3s. 6d.
Stories of the Saints. By M. F. S. 12mo., 1st Series, 3s. 6d.; gilt, 4s. 6d. 2nd Series, 3s. 6d.; gilt, 4s. 6d.
Stormsworth, with other Poems and Plays. By the author of "Thy Gods, O Israel." 12mo., 3s. 6d.
Story of Marie and other Tales. 12mo., 2s.; gilt, 3s.; or separately:—The Story of Marie, 2d.; Nelly Blane, and a Contrast, 2d.; A Conversion and a Death-bed, 2d.; Herbert Montagu, 2d.; Jane Murphy, the Dying Gipsy, and the Nameless Grave, 2d.; The Beggars, and True and False Riches, 2d.; Pat and his Friend. 2d.

Story of the Life of St. Paul. By M. F. S., author of "Stories of the Saints." 12mo., 2s. 6d.

Sufferings of our Lord. Sermons preached by Father Claude de la Colombière, S.J., in the Chapel Royal, St. James's, in the year 1677. 18mo., 1s.; stronger bound, 1s. 6d.; red edges, 2s.

Supernatural Life, The. By Mgr. Mermillod. Translated from the French, with a Preface by Lady Herbert. 12mo., 5s.

Supremacy of the Roman See. By C. E. Tame, Esq. 8vo., 6d.

Sure Way to Heaven. A Little Manual for Confession and Holy Communion. 32mo., 6d.; Persian, 2s. 6d.; calf or morocco, 3s. 6d.

Sweetness of Holy Living; or, Honey culled from the Flower Garden of S. Francis of Sales. 18mo., 1s.; French morocco, 3s.

Taigi (Anna Maria), Life of. Translated from the French of Calixte by A. V. Smith-Sligo, Esq. 8vo., 2s. 6d. and 5s.

Tales and Sketches. *See* Fleet.

TAME (C. E., Esq.), Early English Literature. 16mo., 2s. a vol. I. Our Lady's Lament, and the Lamentation of S. Mary Magdalene. II. Life of Our Lady, in verse.

———— **Supremacy of the Roman See.** 8vo., 6d.

TANDY (Rev. Dr.), Terry O'Flinn. 12mo., 1s.; stronger bound, 1s. 6d.; gilt, 2s.

TAUNTON (M.), Last of the Catholic O'Malleys. 18mo., 1s. 6d.; stronger bound, 2s.

———— **One Hundred Pious Reflections,** from Alban Butler's Lives of the Saints. 18mo., 1s.; stronger bound, 2s.

Temperance Books. *See* Richardson (Rev. Fr.).

———— Cards (Illuminated), 3d. each. [3d. each.

———— Medals—Immaculate Conception, St. Patrick, St. Joseph.

Terry O'Flinn. By Rev. Dr. Tandy. 12mo., 1s.; stronger bound, 1s. 6d.; gilt, 2s.

Testimony; or, the Necessity of Enquiry as to Religion. By John Henry Pye, M.A. 32mo., 4d.; cloth, 6d.

THOMAS (H. J.), One Hundred Short Sermons. 8vo., 12s.

Three Wishes. A Tale. By M. F. S. 12mo., 2s. 6d.

Threshold of the Catholic Church. *See* Bagshawe.

Tom's Crucifix, and other Tales. By M. F. S. 12mo., 3s.

TONDINI (Rev. Cæsarius), My Conversion and Vocation. By Rev. Fr. Schouvaloff. 12mo., 5s.

———— **The Pope of Rome and the Popes of the Oriental Orthodox Church.** An essay on Monarchy in the Church, with special reference to Russia, from original documents, Russian and Greek. Second Edition. 12mo., 3s. 6d.

———— **Some Documents concerning of the Association Prayers in Honour of Mary Immaculate, for the Return of the Greek-Russian Church to Catholic Unity.** 12mo., 3d.

Trials of Faith. *See* Browne (E. G. K.).

TRONSON (Abbe), The Mass: a devout Method of assisting at it. 32mo., 4d.

Truce of God. A Tale of the XI. Century. *See* Miles (G. H.).
Two Colonels. By Father Thomas. 12mo., 6s.
Ursuline Manual. *See* Prayers, page 32.
VALMONT (V.), The Prussian Spy. A Novel. 12mo., 4s.
Veronica Giuliani (S.), Life of, and B. Battista Varani. With a Photographic Portrait. 12mo., 5s.
Village Innkeeper. By Conscience. 12mo., 4s.
Village Lily. A Tale. 12mo., 1s.; gilt, 1s. 6d.
Vincent Ferrer (S.), of the Order of Friar Preachers; his Life, Spiritual Teaching, and Practical Devotion. By Rev. Fr. Andrew Pradel, O.P. Translated from the French by the Rev. Fr. T. A. Dixon, O.P., with a Photograph. 12mo., 5s.
VINCENT OF LIRINS (S.). A Translation of the Commonitory of S. Vincent of Lirins. 12mo., 1s. 3d.
Vincent of Paul (S.), Glory of. *See* Manning (Archbishop).
VIRGIL. Literally translated by Davidson. 12mo., 2s. 6d.
"Vitis Mystica"; or, the True Vine. *See* Brownlow.
WALLER (J. F., Esq.), Festival Tales. 12mo., 5s.
WALSH (W. H., Esq.), Henry V. 8vo., 6d.
Way of Salvation. By S. Liguori. 32mo., 1s.
Weedall (Mgr.), Life of. By Rev. Dr. Husenbeth. 8vo., 1s.
WEGG-PROSSER (F. R.), Rome and her Captors. 12mo., 4s.
What is Christianity? By Rev. F. H. Laing, D.D. 12mo., 6d.
Whence the Monarch's Right to Rule? *See* Laing (Rev. D.).
WHITE (George), Cardinal Wiseman. 12mo., 1s. and 1s. 6d.
———— Comte de Montalembert. 12mo., 6d.
———— Life of S. Edmund of Canterbury. 1s. and 1s. 6d.
———— Map of London, Showing the Churches. 6d.
WHITELOCK (A.), The Chances of War. An Irish Tale. 8vo., 5s.
William (St.), of York. A Drama in Two Acts. (Boys.) 12mo., 6d.
WILLIAMS (Canon), Anglican Orders. 12mo., 3s. 6d.
Wiseman (Cardinal), Life and Obsequies. 12mo., 1s. and 1s. 6d.
———— Recollections of. By M. J. Arnold. 12mo., 2s. 6d.
Woman's Work in Modern Society. *See* Cusack (M. F.)
WOODS (Canon), Defence of the Roman Church against F. Gratry. Translated from the French of Gueranger. 8vo., 1s. 6d.
WYATT-EDGELL (Alfred), Stormsworth, with other Poems and Plays. 12mo., 2s. 6d.
———— Thy Gods! O Israel. 12mo., 2s.
Young Catholic's Guide to Confession and Holy Communion. By Dr. Kenny. 32mo., 4d.; cloth, 6d.; red edges, 9d.; French morocco, 1s. 6d.; calf or morocco, 2s. 6d.
Young Doctor. By Conscience. 12mo., 4s.
YOUNG (T., Esq.), History of Ireland. 18mo., 2s. 6d.
Zouaves, Pontifical, Two Years in. By Joseph Powell, Z.P. Illustrated. 8vo., 3s. 6d.

PRAYER BOOKS.

Garden, Little, of the Soul. Edited by the Rev. R. G. Davis. *With Imprimatur of the Archbishop of Westminster.* This book, as its name imports, contains a selection from the "Garden of the Soul" of the Prayers and Devotions of most general use. Whilst it will serve as a *Pocket Prayer Book* for all, it is, by its low price, *par excellence*, the Prayer Book for children and for the very poor. In it are to be found the old familiar Devotions of the "Garden of the Soul," as well as many important additions, such as the Devotions to the Sacred Heart, to Saint Joseph, to the Guardian Angels, and others. The omissions are mainly the Forms of administering the Sacraments, and Devotions that are not of very general use. It is printed in a clear type, on a good paper, both especially selected, for the purpose of obviating the disagreeableness of small type and inferior paper. Tenth thousand.

32mo., price, cloth, 6d.; with rims, 1s. Embossed, red edges, 9d.; with rims and clasp, 1s. 3d.; Strong roan, 1s.; with rims and classs 1s. 6d. French morocco, 1s. 6d.; with rims and clasp, 2s. French morocco extra gilt, 2s.; with rims and clasp, 2s. 6d. Calf or morocco, 3s.; with rims and clasp, 4s. Calf or morocco, extra gilt, 4s.; with rims and clasp, 5s. Morocco antique, 7s. 6d., 10s. 6d., 12s., 16s. Velvet, rims and clasp, 5s., 8s. 6d., and 10s. 6d. Russia, 5s.; with clasp, &c., 8s.; Russia antique, 17s. 6d. Ivory, with rims and clasp, 10s. 6d., 13s., 15s., 17s. 6d. Imitation ivory, with rims and clasp, 3s. With oxydized silver or gilt mountings, in morocco case, 25s.

Catholic Hours: a Manual of Prayer, including Mass and Vespers. By J. R. Digby Beste, Esq. 32mo., cloth, 2s.; red edges, 2s. 6d.; roan, 3s.; morocco, 6s.

Catholic Piety; or, Key of Heaven, with Epistles and Gospels. Large 32mo., roan, 1s. 6d. and 2s.; French morocco, with rims and clasp, 2s. 6d.; extra gilt, 3s.; with rims and clasp, 3s. 6d.; velvet, 3s. 6d. and 10s.

Catholic Piety; or, Key of Heaven. 32mo., 6d.; rims and clasp, 1s.; French morocco, 1s.; velvet, with rims and clasp, 2s. 6d.; with Epistles and Gospels, roan, 1s.; French morocco, 1s. 6d.; with rims and clasp, 2s.; extra gilt, 2s.; Persian, 2s. 6d.; imitation ivory, 3s.; morocco, 3s. 6d.; velvet, rims and clasp, 3s. 6d.

Crown of Jesus. 18mo., Persian calf, 6s. Calf or Morocco, 7s. 6d. and 8s. 6d.; with rims and clasp, 10s. 6d. Calf or morocco, extra gilt, 10s. 6d.; with rims and clasp, 12s. 6d; with turn-over edges,

Eucharistic Year: Preparation and Thanksgiving for Holy Communion. 18mo., 4s.
Holy Childhood. Simple Prayers for very little children. 32mo., 1s.; gilt, 1s. 6d.
Illustrated Manual of Prayers. 32mo., 3d.; cloth, 4d.
Key of Heaven. *Very large type.* 18mo., 1s.; leather, 2s. 6d.; extra gilt, 3s.
Lily of St. Joseph, The; a little Manual of Prayers and Hymns for Mass. 64mo., price 2d.; cloth, 3d., 4d., 6d., or 8d.; roan, 1s.; French morocco, 1s. 6d.; calf or morocco, 2s.; gilt, 2s. 6d.
Little Prayer Book, The, for Ordinary Catholic Devotions. 32mo., cloth, 3d.
Manual of Catholic Devotions. Small, for the waistcoat pocket. 64mo., 6d.; with Epistles and Gospels, cloth, rims, 1s.; roan, 1s.; with tuck, 1s. 6d.; calf or morocco, 2s. 6d. Imitation Ivory, 2s.
Manual of the Sisters of Charity. 18mo., 6s.
Memorare Mass. By the Poor Clares of Kenmare. 32mo., 2d.
Miniature Prayer Book, 48mo., 6d.; cape, 1s. calf, 2s. 6d.; imitation ivory, rims and clasp, 3s.; morocco, rims and clasp, 4s. 6d.; with tuck, 4s. 6d.; velvet, with rims and clasp, 4s. 6d.; ivory, with clasp, 7s. 6d.; russia, with clasp, 10s. 6d.
Missal (Complete). 18mo., Persian, 8s. 6d.; calf or morocco, 10s. 6d.; with rims and clasp, 13s. 6d.; calf or mor., extra gilt, 12s. 6d., with rims and clasp, 15s. 6d.; morocco, with turn-over edges, 13s. 6d.; morocco antique, 15s.; velvet, 20s.; Russia, 20s.; ivory, with rims and clasp, 31s. 6d. and 35s.
——— A very beautiful edition, handsomely bound in morocco, gilt mountings, silk linings, edges red on gold, in a morocco case. Illustrated, £5. [clasp, 8s.
Missal and Vesper Book, in one vol. 32mo., morocco, 6s.; with
Occasional Prayers for Festivals. By Rev. T. Barge. 32mo., 4d. and 6d.; gilt, 1s.
Path to Paradise. 32 full-page Illustrations. 32mo., cloth, 3d. With 50 Illustrations, cloth, 4d. Superior edition, 6d. and 1s.
Serving Boy's Manual and Book of Catholic Devotions, containing all those Prayers and Devotions for Sundays and Holidays, usually divided in their recitation between the Priest and the Congregation. Compiled from approved sources, and adapted to Churches served either by the Secular or the Regular Clergy. 32mo., Embossed, 1s.; with Epistles and Gospels, 1s. 6d.; French morocco, 2s., with Epistles and Gospels, 2s. 6d.; calf, 4s., with Epistles and Gospels, 4s. 6d.
Soul united to Jesus in the Adorable Sacrament. 32mo., 1s. 6d.
S. Patrick's Manual. Compiled by Sister Mary Frances Clare. 18mo., 3s. 6d.
Sure Way to Heaven. 32mo., cloth, 6d.: Persian, 2s. 6d.; calf

Garden of the Soul. (WASHBOURNE'S EDITION.) Edited by the Rev. R. G. Davis. *With Imprimatur of the Archbishop of Westminster.* Thirteenth Thousand. This Edition retains all the Devotions that have made the GARDEN OF THE SOUL, now for many generations, the well-known Prayer-book for English Catholics. During many years various Devotions have been introduced, and, in the form of appendices, have been added to other editions. These have now been incorporated into the body of the work, and, together with the Devotions to the Sacred Heart, to Saint Joseph, to the Guardian Angels, the Itinerarium, and other important additions, render this edition pre-eminently the Manual of Prayer, for both public and private use. The version of the Psalms has been carefully revised, and strictly conformed to the Douay translation of the Bible, published with the approbation of the LATE CARDINAL WISEMAN. The Forms of administering the Sacraments have been carefully translated, *as also the rubrical directions*, from the Ordo Administrandi Sacramenta. To enable all present, either at baptisms or other public administrations of the Sacraments, to pay due attention to the sacred rites, the Forms are inserted without any curtailment, both in Latin and English. The Devotions at Mass have been carefully revised, and enriched by copious adaptations from the prayers of the Missal. The preparation for the Sacraments of Penance and the Holy Eucharist have been the objects of especial care, to adapt them to the wants of those whose religious instruction may be deficient. Great attention has been paid to the quality of the paper and to the size of type used in the printing, to obviate that weariness so distressing to the eyes, caused by the use of books printed in small close type and on inferior paper.

32mo. Embossed, 1s.; with rims and clasp, 1s. 6d.; with Epistles and Gospels, 1s. 6d.; with rims and clasp, 2s. French morocco, 2s.; with rims and clasp, 2s. 6d.; with E. and G., 2s. 6d.; with rims and clasp, 3s. French morocco extra gilt, 2s. 6d.; with rims and clasp, 3s.; with E. and G., 3s.; with rims and clasp, 3s. 6d. French morocco, antique, with monogram and clasp, 10s., with E. and G., 10s. 6d. Calf, or morocco 4s.; with rims and clasp, 5s. 6d.; with E. and G., 4s. 6d., with rims and clasp, 6s. Calf or morocco extra gilt, 5s.; with rims and clasp, 6s. 6d.; with E. and G., 5s. 6d.; with rims and clasp, 7s. Velvet, with rims and clasp, 7s. 6d., 10s. 6d., and 13s.; with E. and G., 8s., 11s., and 13s. 6d. Russia, antique, with clasp, 10s., 12s. 6d.; with E. and G., 10s. 6d., 13s., with corners and clasps, 20s.; with E. and G., 20s. 6d. Ivory 14s., 16s., 20s., and 22s. 6d.; with E. and G., 14s. 6d.; 16s. 6d., 20s. 6d., and 23s. Morocco antique, with 2 patent clasps, 12s.; with E. and G., 12s. 6d.; with corners and clasps, 18s.; with E. and G., 18s 6d.

The Epistles and Gospels, in cloth, 6d.; roan, 1s. 6d.

' This is one of the best editions we have seen of one of the best of all our Prayer Books. It is well printed in clear, large type, on good paper."—*Catholic Opinion* "A very complete arrangement of this which is emphatically the Prayer Book of every Catholic household. It is as cheap as it is good, and we heartily recommend it."—*Universe.* "Two striking features are the admirable order displayed through-

www.ingramcontent.com/pod-product-compliance
Lightning Source LLC
Chambersburg PA
CBHW030808230426
43667CB00008B/1124